THE GIANTS AND THEIR CITY

The GIANTS *and* THEIR CITY

Major League Baseball
in San Francisco, 1976–1992

Lincoln A. Mitchell

The Kent State University Press
Kent, Ohio

© 2021 by The Kent State University Press, Kent, Ohio 44242
All rights reserved
Library of Congress Catalog Number 2021005738
ISBN 978-1-60635-420-9
Manufactured in the United States of America

Library of Congress Cataloging-in-Publication Data
Names: Mitchell, Lincoln Abraham, author.
Title: The Giants and their city : Major League Baseball in San Francisco,
    1976-1992 / Lincoln A. Mitchell.
Description: Kent, Ohio : The Kent State University Press, [2021] |
    Includes bibliographical references and index.
Identifiers: LCCN 2021005738 | ISBN 9781606354209 (paperback) |
    ISBN 9781631014482 (pdf) | ISBN 9781631014475 (epub)
Subjects: LCSH: San Francisco Giants (Baseball team)--History. | Baseball
    teams--California--San Francisco--History.
Classification: LCC GV875.S34 M58 2021 | DDC 796.357/640979461--dc23
LC record available at https://lccn.loc.gov/2021005738

25 24 23 22 21   5 4 3 2

CONTENTS

ACKNOWLEDGMENTS

The COVID-19 pandemic made the summer of 2020 a strange time to finish writing a book about baseball in San Francisco. The baseball season did not begin until mid-July, and games were played in ballparks with no fans in attendance. For older Giants fans, the empty ballparks did not feel entirely unprecedented as some of us still remember the mid-1970s. Nonetheless, although we can hope that MLB returns to a full schedule with fans in the stands, as I write this, we do not yet know if that will happen in 2021. Similarly, most of this book was written in 2019, when San Francisco's economy was booming and the city was crowded and congested. The pandemic changed that as well.

The absence of Giants baseball for most of the 2020 season and my own inability to go to San Francisco from my home in New York was not only an unusual context in which to complete a book about the San Francisco Giants but also a disorienting twist to a journey that began in 1976. That was not only the year that Bob Lurie and George Moscone saved the team from going to Toronto, but it was also the year I became a Giants fan. I have remained a fan of the team to this day. Accordingly, this book reflects my perspective as both a scholar of baseball and San Francisco and also as a fan.

Both of these aspects of my writing were enriched by interviews with several former Giants players, including Dusty Baker, Vida Blue, Will Clark, Dave Dravecky, Atlee Hammaker, Mike Krukow, Duane Kuiper, Gary Lavelle, Kevin Mitchell, John Montefusco, Chris Speier, and Robby Thompson. They were all very generous with their time and helped me get a sense of what the team was like when they were playing. Current and former baseball executives, including Larry Baer, Peter Ueberroth, and Bud Selig, were also very valuable interview subjects. Pat Gallagher offered excellent insight into the history of the Croix de Candlestick, the Crazy Crab, and other Giants marketing gambits. Nobody has been with the Giants longer than Mike Murphy. The great stories he told me made this a better book. Bruce Jenkins has observed and written about the Giants for decades. I am grateful for his insights into these years. Three former San Francisco mayors, Art Agnos, Frank Jordan, and Dianne Feinstein, explained how the challenge of keeping the Giants in San Francisco looked from City Hall. Dean Macris, who served as city planner for Mayors Feinstein and Agnos, provided additional information about the efforts to get a downtown ballpark in the 1980s.

Mario Alioto and Suzanna Mitchell from the San Francisco Giants assisted me in contacting some of the former Giants and also in finding the photographs for this book. Pat Johnson, Dennis Desprois, and the George H. W. Bush Library and Museum generously allowed me to use some of their excellent photographs as well. Susan Wadsworth-Booth and her team at the Kent State University Press were great colleagues with whom to work on *The Giants and Their City*.

Had Bob Lurie not stepped up in 1976 and invested in keeping the team in San Francisco, my life as a baseball fan would have been very different. More than 40 years later, when I approached Bob to discuss the idea of writing this book, he immediately offered to do whatever he could to help me with the project. After that meeting, Bob and Connie Lurie were extremely kind and hospitable and made themselves available for several interviews as well as email exchanges and informal conversations. They also gave me access to their personal Giants archives. Corey Busch encouraged me to write this book, read and gave feedback on early drafts, and helped me set up many of the interviews that contributed to *The Giants and Their City*. I would not have been able to write this book without his help.

From 1976 to 1992, being a Giants fan was alternately an exhilarating, disappointing, fun, and odd experience. However, I did not have to experience all of that alone. Christian Ettinger, Charles A. Fracchia Jr., Charles Karren, John Maschino, Michael Mason, and my late brother Jonathan Mitchell were my companions while shivering away countless evenings, as well as enjoying more than a few sunny days, at Candlestick Park. In addition to those friends, my family has also helped make this book possible. In the late 1970s, my mother used to drop my brother and I off at the bus stop at Clay and Van Ness so we could catch the Ballpark Express to Candlestick Park. Forty years later she continues to be supportive of, and slightly puzzled by, my passion for baseball. My wife, Marta Sanders, shares both of those sentiments. My two sons, Asher and Reuben, have managed to become Giants fans despite never having lived in San Francisco, although for some reason they are more focused on the team in the twenty-first century. Once again, Isis the dog has been my faithful, patient, and usually silent research assistant.

My father, Alan Sapiro, stopped paying attention to baseball in 1963 when Stan Musial retired, but he read almost everything I wrote for most of the last 20 years. His always encouraging and frequently helpful feedback on my work helped me keep pushing forward with my writing. My father died in September 2019, but part of me still wants to send him my latest column, article, or, in this case, book. I cannot do that anymore, but I can, and do, dedicate this book to him.

INTRODUCTION

On October 29, 2014, with two outs in the bottom of the ninth of Game Seven of the World Series, and the tying run on third, Kansas City Royals catcher Salvador Perez hit a 2–2 pitch from San Francisco Giants ace Madison Bumgarner into foul territory near third base. Pablo Sandoval, the Giants' star third baseman, tapped his thigh with his glove, caught the ball, and then collapsed in happiness onto the field. The Giants had won their third championship in five years.

The Giants have been one of baseball's most successful franchises in the twenty-first century. In addition to their extraordinary five year run from 2010 to 2014, the team plays in a beautiful ballpark nestled next to the San Francisco Bay and sells out almost every game—even when the team is losing. They are a beloved institution, and a good civic presence in the city that has been their home since 1958.

For baseball fans with a sense of history, this seems kind of natural. The Giants are one of the oldest and most famous franchises in baseball and trace their roots back to the 1880s in New York. While playing in New York in the early part of the twentieth century, when big-league baseball as we know it was taking shape, the Giants emerged as the game's marquee franchise, before ceding that claim to the Yankees in the late 1920s.

Many of the game's best and most famous players have been Giants. Christy "Matty" Mathewson, the great pitcher of baseball's early years, was one of the first baseball stars who became a national celebrity. Matty's longtime manager, John McGraw, is still considered a groundbreaking and brilliant baseball man. Willie Mays, the greatest player of the postwar era, spent almost his entire career with the Giants in both New York and San Francisco. Other well-known Giants stars, including Frankie Frisch, Mel Ott, Bill Terry, Willie McCovey, and Juan Marichal, have been among the best and most famous players of their eras. More recently, the slugger Barry Bonds, who was the best player of his generation, spent the last 15 years of his career with the Giants, but has also become, in the eyes of some, the face of the Performance-Enhancing Drug (PED) era in Major League Baseball (MLB).

The Giants have also been a very good team for most of their existence. The pennant they won in 2014 was their 20th. Since the beginning of the twentieth century, only the Yankees have played in the World Series more times than the Giants have. Because of their success, the Giants have been part of some of the greatest moments in baseball history, including Bobby Thomson's "shot heard 'round the world" against the Brooklyn Dodgers in 1951, and Willie Mays's great catch against the Indians in the first game of the 1954 World Series. Fred Merkle's failure to touch second base during a crucial game against the Cubs in 1908, while shrouded in mystery and the mists of time, is one of the most remembered, discussed, and debated moments of baseball's early years. Mathewson's three shutouts in the 1905 World Series may still be the greatest postseason pitching performance ever. Carl Hubbell's feat of striking out five consecutive batters, future Hall of Famers Babe Ruth, Lou Gehrig, Jimmie Foxx, Al Simmons, and Joe Cronin, in the 1934 All-Star Game may have been the greatest pitching display in the history of the Midsummer Classic. Willie McCovey's sharp line drive with the tying and winning runs on base to end Game Seven of the 1962 World Series and the earthquake that disrupted the 1989 World Series at Candlestick Park are also important parts of baseball lore and reminders of the centrality of the Giants to baseball over the decades.

Since the Giants, and their archrivals the Brooklyn Dodgers moved to California in 1958, seven new teams have joined the National League (NL), while another NL team, the Braves, moved from Milwaukee to Atlanta, and two other teams, the Brewers and the Astros, switched leagues. Only 10 of the 30 MLB franchises have been playing in their current city longer than the Giants have been in San Francisco. Baseball fans who watched Bumgarner, Sandoval, star catcher Buster Posey, and manager Bruce Bochy, all of whom had been on the Giants for all three championships, celebrate the one-run, Game Seven victory in the 2014 World Series, could have been forgiven for thinking they were watching a team that had long been a stable and successful franchise.

This perception was certainly true by 2014, and even a few years before that, but the foundation for that success was laid in a very different era of Giants baseball, and of San Francisco in general. It was a foundation that at times looked like it might not hold and was frequently very shaky. The years 1976 to 1992 were critical to building that foundation, but they are often overlooked in the history of the Giants, and indeed in the history of the city the team has called home for well over half a century.

This was the period when, on the field, the Giants, while not terrible all the time, were rarely memorable to the larger baseball world. During a period of 25 months in the early seventies, the Giants traded away or released the four future Hall of Famers who had been the faces of their franchise for years, and in the case of Willie Mays, for a generation. As the 1975 season wrapped up, Willie Mays and Juan Marichal were already retired, Gaylord Perry was pitching for the Texas Rangers and continuing to rank among the best pitchers in the game, and Willie McCovey was still hitting home runs, but for a not-very-good San Diego Padres team.

During this 17-year period, the Giants won one pennant and two NL West titles. They also were strong contenders in 1978 and 1982 before finishing in third place both years. They were not always a terrible team of lovable losers during this period, though. Rather, they were a team that sometimes contended, was dreadful in a few other years, and overall was more or less mediocre. This is reflected in their .486 overall winning percentage from 1976 to 1992.[1] Despite that mediocre percentage, the Giants had some very exciting seasons, coming within one win of the NL pennant in 1987, leading the NL West for much of the 1978 season, remaining in contention until the last weekend of the 1982 season, and finally winning a pennant in 1989.

The Giants' performance on the field in these years always took place in the context of their off-the-field struggles around finding a place to play. Although for this entire period the Giants made their home in Candlestick Park, the cavernous stadium in the southeastern corner of the city that had been state of the art when it was constructed for them in 1960, there was never any certainty about what their future would hold in this regard. A year, and rarely a few months, went by without rumors of the team being sold and moved out of town, talk of the need for a new ballpark, discussions about the Giants moving down the peninsula to the south of the city, or even proposals to dome Candlestick Park. This period began in 1976 when the Giants future in the city, for the first time since moving there, was genuinely imperiled, and ended in late 1992 when the process that would eventually lead to the construction of the new ballpark, now Oracle Park, was set in motion in earnest.

This chapter in Giants history is somewhat incongruous. It was the time in the history of an otherwise successful franchise when they struggled the most. The team that for generations featured household names like Mays, Mathewson, Ott, and Terry had, other than a few years of the aging Willie McCovey, no such player during these years. For this reason, it is not surprising that this important time in the history of the team is so frequently forgotten. Oddly, a similar dynamic has occurred with regards to the city where the Giants play. By 1976, the Summer of Love was over, and almost nobody was coming to San Francisco with flowers in their hair anymore. In 1992, the tech revolution that would so dramatically reshape the city's economy, culture, politics, and appearance had not yet arrived. It was still a time when having an email address, or knowing what email was for that matter, marked somebody as preternaturally interested in computers or perhaps simply weird.

The story of the Giants during these years cannot be separated from what was occurring in San Francisco at the time, and despite the Summer of Love being long over and the tech moment not yet upon us, there was a lot going on. Harvey Milk was elected to the Board of Supervisors in November 1977. A year later, Milk and Mayor George Moscone were assassinated. That ushered in the progrowth mayoralty of Dianne Feinstein who facilitated the early days of the gentrification that is now complete in many parts of the city. The late 1970s and early 1980s also saw the beginning of the AIDS epidemic that hit San Francisco harder than any city in America. The Summer of Love may have been history, but a vibrant punk rock scene flourished in its wake. All of this provided the context for the Giants both on and off the field during these years.

The 17 years from 1976 to 1992 were transitional for MLB as well: Free agency began and salaries skyrocketed; baseball front offices were modernized and professionalized; the number of players from Latin America increased; the first major work stoppage occurred; and the modern day closer role was created. In 1976, the highest-paid player in the game was Catfish Hunter, who had left the Oakland A's when his contract was voided on a technicality and signed a lucrative contract with the Yankees. In 1992, the highest-paid player in the game, Bobby Bonilla of the Mets, was making $6.1 million, almost 10 times the $640,000 Hunter earned in 1976.

These years were also the end of an era. By the mid-1990s baseball had switched to three divisions in each league, rather than two, and introduced a wild card for the first time. Interleague play was introduced in 1997, helping to further break down the distinctions between the two leagues that for so long had been part of the game. Free agency and increasing salaries meant more money, and a greater focus on the economic aspects of baseball. For much of baseball history most teams had been owned by very wealthy men who lived in and had strong ties to the city where their team played, but this, too, was beginning to change as more teams were owned by consortiums, partnerships, and holding companies.

From 1976 to 1992, 275 men played for the Giants. Some, like Willie Mc-Covey, Will Clark, Vida Blue, Jack Clark, or Matt Williams, were great players who were part of the team for many years. Others, like Joe Pettini, Skip James, or Bill Bordley, had shorter careers, while some, like Steve Carlton, Dan Quisenberry, Goose Gossage, Al Oliver, and Joe Morgan, were stars who spent their best years in other cities. Seven men took the helm as manager of the Giants, while three served as general managers. The longest-serving in each of these capacities was Roger Craig, who managed the team from late 1985 to 1992, and Al Rosen, who was general manager for essentially that same period. The two were instrumental in the only postseason appearances by the Giants in this era.

There was also a fair amount of stability during this time because only one man owned the team. Bob Lurie bought the team in 1976 and sold the team at the end of 1992. For the 17 years he owned the team, Lurie was a constant presence in the minds of San Francisco baseball fans. I was one of those Giants fans who was just getting interested in baseball as an eight-year-old boy in San Francisco in 1976. I lived in San Francisco during almost the entire time Lurie owned the team, and I remain a Giants fan to this day. For us, it was Lurie to whom we turned in the early days of free agency, hoping that he would open his checkbook and sign a big star, or when we felt a manager or general manager needed to be replaced. At least equally significantly, Lurie was always at the center of the discussions, arguments, and political and financial maneuvering about whether the Giants would remain in San Francisco, if it would be possible to build a new stadium, and how to draw fans to a ballpark, Candlestick, that was hard to get to, underserved by public transportation, and, at night games, cold and windy. Although he never played a game and, for the most part, did not seek the spotlight on baseball-related matters, for the Giants, the years 1976 through 1992 were the Bob Lurie years.

Chapter 1

BIG-LEAGUE BASEBALL COMES TO TORONTO

On the morning of January 10, 1976, baseball fans in Toronto were greeted with some very exciting news. For years Toronto had been a minor-league town, home to a baseball team called the Maple Leafs, but they had moved to Louisville in 1968, leaving Toronto without high-level baseball. Now Toronto was getting a major-league team. The headline on the front page of the *Toronto Star* blared out the big news "Giants Agree to Sale, Toronto Warms up for Baseball." A smaller article on the front page promised fans "$1 for Bleacher Seats."[1] There were numerous other headlines and articles in the paper that day and in the days that followed celebrating the arrival of big league baseball. An inside page included a diagram of how a baseball diamond would fit into Canadian National Exhibition Field, Toronto's best outdoor sports facility. Several articles cautioned that there were still formalities to be ironed out but also reported that "the Giants board of directors had accepted the purchase offer from the Canadian company."[2] The Canadian company to which the article referred was a consortium led by Labatt Breweries.

The Giants team that was coming to Toronto had no major stars. The biggest names on the Giants in 1975 had been Bobby Murcer, a slugging outfielder who had hit .298 with 11 home runs in his first year with the team after coming over from the Yankees in a trade, and John "The Count" Montefusco. The Count was one of the most exciting young players in baseball. He was brash, outspoken, and very media friendly. In 1975, he had been the National League Rookie of the Year while going 15–9 with a 2.88 ERA and 215 strikeouts.

The rest of the team was not as well known, but the Giants had a lot of players who were still under 30 and were coming off of decent years. This group

1

included: infielders Derrel Thomas and Chris Speier, only 25 and already a three-time all-star; outfielders Gary Matthews, Von Joshua, and Gary Thomasson; and pitchers Jim Barr, Ed Halicki, Randy Moffitt, and Gary Lavelle. The team had gone 80–81 in 1975, finishing in third place, 27.5 games behind the Cincinnati Reds, and was not likely to contend in 1976, but with its glut of outfielders and pitchers, it was possible that they were a few smart moves away from being a strong team. That didn't matter much to the people of Toronto who were, for the most part, happy to be getting big league baseball.

Off the field, the Giants had not been doing quite as well. In 1975, they had drawn 522,919 fans. The Giants played six doubleheaders in 1975, so they averaged slightly fewer than 7,000 fans for each of the team's 75 home dates. The Giants' attendance was the lowest in all of baseball in 1975, but they had managed to draw 3,000 more fans than in 1974, when they also had the worst attendance in all of baseball.

The news of the Giants moving to Toronto had a very different impact 2,600 miles to the west and south where the people of San Francisco were not at all happy to see their team go. The Giants had been in San Francisco for fewer than 20 years, having moved from New York City in 1958. Although San Franciscans may have lost interest in the Giants once players like Mays and McCovey were no longer on the team, losing Major League Baseball would have been a big blow to a city that was already reeling from labor disputes, high crime rates, racial and political divisions, a stumbling economy, and the hangover from the 1960s, which in many respects were still going strong in San Francisco in the mid-1970s.

The attendance figures in recent years had been terrible, and the team not much better, but that was only part of the problem facing San Francisco and the Giants. The biggest challenge the Giants confronted was where they played. The Giants' ballpark was located in a remote corner of the southeastern part of the city on a spit of land jutting out into the San Francisco Bay. That spit of land, known as Candlestick Point, gave the enormous ballpark its name. During the first decade the Giants played there, Candlestick Park could hold 44,700 fans. After the 1970 season, the outfield was enclosed with an upper deck in anticipation of the 49ers, San Francisco's football team, beginning to play there in 1971. This increased the capacity of the ballpark to 58,000 for baseball and 62,000 for football.[3] Candlestick Park's remote location may have been a good thing given how unpleasant it could be to watch a baseball game there. Day games were fine, even sunny for the first few innings, but night games at Candlestick Park were a difference experience altogether. The ballpark was cold and windy at night. Fans, the few who still bothered to show up in 1974 and 1975, huddled for warmth in layers of winter clothing. I rarely attended a night game at Candlestick Park without at least two layers under a down jacket, and winter gloves if I could find them.

Candlestick Park was such a dreadful place to see a baseball game that even when the team was good, they had a hard time drawing fans. As recently as 1971, the Giants had a winning and exciting team. The Giants that year had something for everybody. A 40-year-old Willie Mays had his last great year, hitting .271/.425/.482 while stealing 23 bases in only 26 tries.[4] Willie McCovey lost some time to injury but still managed to hit .277/.396/.480. Chris Speier, a 21-year-old rookie shortstop, hit only .235 but showed some promise with the bat and fielded his position with élan. The most exciting hitter on that team was the 25-year-old Bobby Bonds, who was one of the first of many Giants prospects to be tagged with the "next Willie Mays" label. Bonds led the team in home runs, stolen bases and RBIs, while playing an excellent right field next to Mays, who was still in center. Longtime pitching stars Juan Marichal and Gaylord Perry combined for 34 wins to help lead the team to their first NL West crown. Despite this, the Giants drew just over 1.1 million fans, 10th in the 12-team National League.

The Giants' future in San Francisco was further complicated by the presence of another team that was struggling to draw fans on the other side of the Bay. The Oakland A's had also won their division in 1971, and like the Giants had been eliminated in the playoffs. However, while the 1971 Giants were ending a decade of strong baseball and frequent contention, the A's were just beginning their upwards trajectory. They went on to win three consecutive World Series from 1972 to 1974. In 1975, they won their division, but lost the ALCS to the Red Sox. The Bay Area, most believed, was not big enough for two teams and it was the Giants who were most likely to leave. This is what had led Giants owner Horace Stoneham, who had brought the team to San Francisco from New York a generation earlier, and who by 1975 had essentially run out of money, to sell the team to the Toronto-based Labatt Breweries.

Despite the bad teams, dreadful ballpark, and paltry attendance figures, the Giants were San Francisco's team. Giants fans did not want them to leave for a faraway city in Canada. Even San Franciscans who had never shivered away an evening at Candlestick Park knew that losing the Giants would make our city look bad on the national stage and would be a big blow to our reputation. Despite the terrible economic shape the Giants were in during the late Horace Stoneham years, somehow the news still seemed hard to believe.

Many San Franciscans shared the view of longtime *San Francisco Chronicle* journalist Bruce Jenkins, who remembered that "an *Examiner* headline simply said 'Giants Moving to Toronto.' That's pretty definitive. I couldn't believe it. It seemed so preposterous that this would happen. . . . The fact is that Horace Stoneham did make that proclamation."[5]

The timing for San Francisco was not great either. The day before the deal to sell the Giants to the Labatt-led consortium was announced, San Francisco's 37th mayor was inaugurated. The previous year, Democrat George Moscone had narrowly won an election that had divided the city. In the runoff, Moscone had crafted a coalition of African Americans, gays and lesbians, Latinos, and progressive neighborhood activists from all backgrounds. His opponent, Republican John Barbagelata, had campaigned, and almost won, on a platform that married socially conservative backlash politics to more conventional probusiness and real estate interests.

The campaign between Barbagelata and Moscone had been extremely divisive as Moscone sought to not only bring a left of center approach to city politics but to empower groups that had been long-excluded from governance in San Francisco. Barbagelata and his supporters believed that the city had gone off track in recent years and wanted to return to a more conservative, law-and-order-based approach to city politics. The two candidates, despite both being middle-aged, Italian American Catholics, represented very different sides of a city that was being rapidly, and in the eyes of some, too rapidly, transformed. However, during that tumultuous 1975 mayoral campaign, the possible departure of the Giants had not been an issue. According to Corey Busch, who worked for Moscone from 1971 to 1975 when the future mayor was majority leader of the state senate and then served as press secretary to Moscone once he became mayor, "It [the Giants possibly moving] did come up. . . . George [Moscone] would give the standard answer 'over my dead body. I'll do everything I can to keep them here.' . . . It never came up in any of the debates. It was not a front of mind issue with the public yet."[6]

Moscone, who had an ambitious agenda that included remaking all of the city's commissions and city government to reflect the demographics of San Francisco, reforming the police, limiting growth and development, and empowering the city's neighborhoods, was just beginning his term when he was faced with the first crisis of his mayoralty—the all-but-certain departure of the Giants. Moscone, who had been a member of the San Francisco Board of Supervisors and the majority leader of the California State Senate, was a smart enough politician to know that mayors who get elected narrowly and then lose their city's big league baseball team during their first week in office don't get reelected. Corey Busch, who worked for Moscone in City Hall through 1978 and began working for the Giants and Bob Lurie in 1979, told me that the Giants leaving San Francisco was not just a political problem for Moscone. "It presented Moscone with an immediate crisis. . . . He really felt with all that had been going on in San Francisco in recent years . . . that for the city to lose its baseball team less than twenty years after it got the team would have been a significant blow to San Francisco."[7]

The new mayor's concern about losing the Giants was also genuine. Moscone had been born and raised in San Francisco and had given up a position as the leader of the Democratic majority in the California State Senate, that made him one of the most powerful politicians in the state, to become mayor of a city that was in crisis. Only somebody who truly loved and cared about San Francisco, as Moscone did, would make a decision like that. Nor were sports an abstraction for Moscone. He was a sports fan and had been an all-city high school basketball player in the late 1940s while attending Saint Ignatius College Prep, the city's elite Jesuit high school. The first mentions of George Moscone in the San Francisco media were not for campaigns, politics, or neighborhood activism, but for his exploits on the basketball court while a high school student in the 1940s.

Moscone inherited this problem from his predecessor, Joseph Alioto, in the ninth inning with one or two outs. Because of the immediacy of the crisis, the first thing Moscone had to do was buy some time. The Labatt consortium was trying to finalize the deal as quickly as possible, so Moscone needed to slow down that process. The second part of the challenge was to find an alternative buyer, one who would pledge to keep the Giants in San Francisco. Neither was going to be easy, but both were doable if the new mayor worked quickly and used all of his considerable charm, political skills, and relationships in his hometown.

Many National League teams would have been very happy to see the Giants move. A more successful Giants franchise in Toronto would have been good for the National League. Additionally, many players would have been delighted not to play in Candlestick Park ever again. However, there was one National League owner who wanted the Giants to stay in San Francisco. Walter O'Malley had brought the Dodgers to Los Angeles from Brooklyn and had helped persuade Stoneham to come to San Francisco. O'Malley valued the rivalry between the two teams and knew that more California-based teams made travel and scheduling issues much easier for his team. O'Malley was the most powerful owner in the National League, so San Francisco had an ally, albeit in some respects, an unlikely one.

The possibility of the Giants leaving San Francisco following the 1975 season was not a surprise to baseball insiders. Stoneham had made his intentions to sell the team known. Moreover, the National League was sufficiently concerned about Stoneham's finances that by late 1975 the league had taken over the operation of the team and appointed H. B. "Spec" Richardson, a veteran baseball executive, to run the team. This situation sparked some interest among San Francisco–based potential buyers.

The most prominent of these was Bob Lurie, who had been on the board of the National Exhibition Company, the firm that officially owned the Giants. The 46-year-old Lurie was the only child of Louis Lurie, who had built a massive fortune in real estate primarily in San Francisco, but also in Chicago. In 1975, Louis Lurie was dead and Bob Lurie was busy running the family business, but he had always liked sports, particularly baseball, so he resigned from the board of the National Exhibition Company in mid-1975 to make it easier to pursue a way to buy the Giants and keep them in San Francisco. As the scion of a well-respected San Francisco family that had long been deeply involved in the city's philanthropic and civic life, Lurie was the ideal person to buy the team. It seemed somebody with such deep roots in the city could be trusted to keep the team there. Moreover, because most of Lurie's wealth came from real estate in San Francisco, he would not be able to easily sever ties with the city. Indeed, anything that made San Francisco a more attractive city, such as having a good big league ballclub, would be good for Lurie's real estate holdings as well. While Lurie's interest was a good sign, it was only a start, particularly because Lurie had indicated a desire to find partners who could help with the initial purchase. The price of the team was $8 million, but Lurie was only offering to invest half of that, meaning that he needed a partner or partners who could come up with the other $4 million.

Although Lurie had expressed interest in buying the team, converting that interest into a purchase and navigating the legal challenges that were certain to come from Toronto and Labatt was not going to be easy. Additionally, the Stoneham family, who had owned the team since 1919, was anxious to sell the team and had no interest in seeing the process drag on. Unlike Moscone and Lurie, Horace Stoneham had no deep loyalty to San Francisco. Stoneham had been the owner of the team since 1936, when his father Charles Stoneham had died, but Stoneham had spent most of the first 50 years of his life on the East

Coast. He had already moved the Giants once when the franchise could no longer thrive financially in northern Manhattan, so for him having the Giants go to Toronto so that he could sell the franchise at a good profit was hardly an existential crisis.

Mayor Moscone had a different perspective but did not have a lot of time. Opening Day was only about three months away and even though the Giants had played the previous season in San Francisco, doing nothing was only going to accelerate their departure. The first thing Moscone did was to ask for an injunction to prevent the Giants from seeking the National League's approval of the sale. The relatively flimsy legal point on which the city of San Francisco based this argument was that the Giants had a lease to play in Candlestick Park through 1994. Leases are broken very frequently. While there may be financial penalties for breaking a lease, it is very unusual to get an injunction stopping a tenant from doing that.

On February 3, the request for that injunction was heard in California Superior Court. The judge who was to determine the future of the Giants had not yet finished his second year on the bench. Judge John E. Benson had been appointed by Governor Ronald Reagan in March of 1974, the last of Reagan's eight years in the governor's mansion. Benson, although coming from a different ideological perspective than Moscone, shared some similarities with the mayor. Both were Navy veterans in their late 40s. Moscone was 46: Benson was 47. Benson had grown up in San Francisco and graduated from college and law school at the University of San Francisco, which, like Saint Ignatius, was a Jesuit school. Despite his last name, Benson, like Moscone, was Italian American and active in Catholic and Italian American civic life in San Francisco. Moscone had been born in San Francisco and loved his city, but Benson had moved there to go to school as a young man and decided to build his life there, so he was predisposed to try to do the right thing for his adopted city.[8]

Upon hearing the case, Judge Benson decided to allow the temporary restraining order, but the comments he made with the decision indicated that temporary was the key word:

> The team has lost $6,396,000 over the last eight years. They have lost $3.5 million for the years 1974–75. All their cash reserves are exhausted. They have used all the money acquired . . . when they played in the Polo Grounds as the New York Giants. They have borrowed $1 million from the Bank of America. As of December 1975 their liabilities exceeded their assets by $2 million. If

the Giants stay in San Francisco, they have no more money to operate next month, let alone for the 1976 season. If the court requires the Giants to remain in San Francisco for 1976 and they go bankrupt, what happens then.[9]

While pursuing the restraining order, the Moscone administration had simultaneously sought to find a partner for Lurie. Fortunately, Bob Short, who had previously owned the second iteration of the Washington Senators beginning in late 1968 before moving them to Texas in 1972, had shown some interest in the Giants.[10] Short had sold the Rangers in 1974 after several losing seasons but wanted to get back into the game. Unlike Lurie, Short was not a native San Franciscan, but he had agreed to keep the team in the city.

In Toronto, the response to this decision was concern but by no means panic. Donald J. McDougall, the president of Labatt, responded philosophically, "all we can do is continue to keep our cool."[11] Columnist Milt Dunnell, writing in the *Toronto Star*, did not quite manage to do that, writing somewhat cryptically, "the San Francisco Giants proved, beyond reasonable doubt, that they are prime candidates for the soup lice. . . . Yet, Judge John Benson hesitates to let the impoverished Giants depart to the hospitality of snowbound Toronto." Dunnell managed to calm down enough to spend part of the column discussing whether the Toronto Giants should retain Wes Westrum as manager.[12]

The Lurie and Short partnership formed after Moscone had tried to find various other combinations of ownership groups. The other National League owners were very happy to have Bob Lurie purchase the team but did not feel the same way about Short. His tenure owning the Senators/Rangers from 1969 to 1974 had not been successful on or off the field. During those years, Short had also frustrated or angered many of his fellow owners who were, therefore, not anxious to bring him back into the game. During his relatively brief time as owner of the Rangers, Short must have found a powerful way to alienate his fellow owners because the National League owners refused the sale of the team to Short, alone, after the wealthy businessman had contacted Moscone in January offering to buy the Giants and keep them in San Francisco.

When Moscone went back to the National League with the proposed Lurie-Short partnership, the National League was again hesitant but finally agreed with some conditions. They would approve the deal "only if Lurie, of San Francisco, would either have a larger share than 50 per cent [*sic*] or if not, that Short must agree to place his voting trust in Lurie."[13] This arrangement worked for Lurie and would have satisfied Moscone because Lurie was well known in San Francisco, but, as expected, Short was not happy with this proposed arrangement. Within a day or two of the National League staking out this position, Short was beginning to indicate he might back out of the deal while the two prospective partners tried to sort out their complicated relationship.

It didn't help that Short was in the hospital in Minnesota with a broken elbow and pelvis. Despite his painful condition and what amounted to a personal rebuke from the National League owners, Short remained optimistic, but firm, telling *San Francisco Chronicle* columnist Wells Twombly: "This thing about Bob Lurie being the majority partner hurt me. Why deny that? I didn't go into this deal to become Bob's employee any more than he went into it to become my employee. . . . He's got an ego and so do I. But we're compatible. That doesn't mean there won't be problems, but I think we can work them out. I like the guy. He likes me."[14] It was not hard to see that even when Short was trying to put a nice face on the situation, there was already real tension between the two prospective partners.

During February and March, both cities, Toronto and San Francisco, watched in relative helplessness as the fate of the Giants appeared to be in the hands of the courts in California as they determined whether or not to hold up the sale to Labatt, National League owners who had to give final approval to any sale, and Mayor Moscone, whose search for an ownership team was growing increasingly desperate. Giants players were caught in the middle of this as they did not know where they would be playing in the quickly approaching 1976 season.

Bobby Murcer spoke for many of the players on the Giants in early February when he said: "This is kind of a key week. And besides, it's already February. Something has to break in the players' disputes and the Giants situation very quickly. I want to go to work."[15] Murcer was not an ordinary ballplayer. He had been an all-star for the fifth straight year in 1975. His .298/.396/.432 slash line had made him one of the best hitters on the Giants. Murcer had been making $100,000 or more every year since 1973, making him one of the best-paid Giants of that era. For a player like Murcer, wanting to know where his team would play was a reasonable and natural desire, but the uncertainty was not a source of financial concern.

For other players who had to think about where their family would live during the season and how to pay for any family expenses associated with the team's potential move to Toronto, the situation was different. Salary information from that era is difficult to determine, but Murcer was the highest-paid player on the 1975 Giants, with many of his teammates making well under half of his salary. For those players, a move meant unexpected expenses and, for those with families, stress related to that. It didn't help that Toronto was in Canada.

Chris Speier, the Giants' star shortstop in 1975, a Bay Area native, and the father of young children, reflected in a 2019 interview that "immediately it was panic in regards to oh shoot family, young family, kids moving completely not just to a different city but out of the country." Speier further explained the stress the potential move was causing him: "The whole financial structure back then was we were able to make ends meet and things like that but then you're thinking of how can I or can I be able to maintain two homes or do I rent something and be away from my family all the way in Toronto and they're all the way back there in California? . . . We thought for sure it was happening."[16]

On March 1, the day by which the National League had insisted the deal be finalized, Lurie and Short had still not worked out the terms of their partnership, but the league gave them a brief extension to smooth over their differences, while not moving from their position that Lurie be the voice of the Giants in matters relating to the National League. Over the next days and hours events moved very quickly for Bob Lurie, George Moscone, the Giants, and the cities of San Francisco and Toronto.

It became increasingly apparent that Lurie and Short were not going to reach an agreement that honored the wishes of the National League while satisfying Short. Within a few hours of the extension being granted, Short walked away from the deal. He didn't actually walk because of his broken pelvis, but he nonetheless took his money and metaphorically went home. This left the Giants one step closer to Toronto, but the people of that city barely had to time to celebrate before another abrupt change occurred.

For Lurie, Moscone, and all of San Francisco, the fear of the Giants leaving was becoming more real with every passing day, so Lurie tried to buy some time to find a partner. Lurie described a call with the National League owners on March 1 when he sought to extend the league's deadline: "I say 'I would like 48 hours to review this.' . . . After a short period of time they say 'five hours.'"[17] Even Walter O'Malley could not help Lurie get more than an afternoon to try to save the future of the Giants in San Francisco.

Five hours is not a lot of time. It would cause stress for many of us if we had to find a dog walker, a babysitter, a friend to help move, or somebody from whom we could borrow $100 in only five hours. Lurie's task was a lot more daunting than that. The man who hoped to buy the Giants did the only thing he could do but came up empty: "That afternoon, went back to the office and started calling people that had said they'd had an interest in doing it and . . .

everybody was out to a four hour lunch. Nobody answered the phone."[18] The inability of Lurie, a wealthy, respected, and well-connected San Franciscan, to find a partner in the city remains baffling but demonstrates the economic condition at the time. Looking back more than 40 years later, the journalist Bruce Jenkins concurred, reflecting "That did strike me as strange. Nobody was really stepping up. . . . Where are the local people?"[19]

While Lurie was trying to find a partner, the Mayor continued to look for a last-minute savior for the franchise, recognizing that, as Busch noted in a 2019 discussion with me and Bob Lurie, "we [the Moscone administration] were thinking if we lose this, we're screwed."[20] Busch then described the odd phone call that came into the mayor's office that afternoon:

> I walked in to my office and my secretary handed me one of those little pink slips that said 'while you were out' and it said 're: Giants.' . . . I was getting calls from kids in the Richmond District saying 'I'll give you all my money in my piggy bank. Please don't let my Giants go.' . . . It's Bud Herseth calling from Arizona, so I called him. . . . He asked me what was the deal. I told him. . . . I ran down to the mayor's office and told him about it. George called him right away and I stood right there and midway through the conversation with him he goes 'call Lurie.' . . . Within a couple of hours you [Lurie] called back and you had a deal.[21]

Corey Busch recalled that Herseth initially thought that there was real estate in Casa Grande, Arizona that would be included in the purchase. When he learned this was not the case, Lurie feared the deal would fall through, but ultimately Herseth decided to become a partner in the Giants.[22]

The above-the-masthead headline in the next day's *Chronicle* Sporting Green section did not even mention Short. Instead, it blared "Beef King Saves Lurie, Giants."[23] At the last possible moment, Bud Herseth, who had made his fortune in cattle, reached out to the mayor's office offering to take Short's place as Lurie's partner. Moreover, he professed a commitment to keeping the team in San Francisco and agreed to let Lurie have a slight majority and therefore become the voting partner. This extraordinary development at almost the last possible moment, just about a month before Opening Day, proved to be the formula that persuaded the National League and kept the Giants in San Francisco. Mayor Moscone, grateful that the Giants would not be leaving and recognizing the drama of the situation alluded to the most famous home run in Giants history and told the press "Bobby Thomson lives."[24]

Lurie and Herseth were, from the beginning, an odd partnership. Jenkins described Herseth as "a country guy talking about shooting rattlesnakes and here's Bob Lurie this San Francisco sophisticate. It couldn't have been more different," adding, "Bud Herseth, people don't realize what a heroic figure he is in Giants lore."[25]

Had the Giants moved to Toronto in 1976, baseball history would have been different in ways that are unknowable, but so would the history of San Francisco itself. The Giants brief time in San Francisco would have been a footnote to baseball history notable only for Willie Mays, one exciting but losing World Series, and a team that finished in second place a lot. San Francisco might have successfully acquired an expansion team, but it is also possible that a city known increasingly for urban problems, radical politics, and, in the 1980s, for being at the center of the AIDS epidemic, would have struggled to win a franchise, at least for a while. The absence of a big-league team might have meant little, but some would have probably seen it as evidence that the city had not regained its midcentury status as an important American city. Today, the Giants are a significant part of the fabric of the city, but that city would have looked and felt very different if the events of 1976 had played out differently.

THE TEAM

The team that Herseth and Lurie had bought and kept in San Francisco was almost the definition of mediocre, having finished in third place, but well out of contention, in a six team division in 1975. During an off-season when the team was largely rudderless with no clear sense of what the future held, it was very difficult for the Giants to make any moves to improve the team. However, once Lurie and Herseth got control of the Giants they had to make several important personnel decisions. Horace Stoneham had been acting as his own general manager for several years, before the National League had appointed Spec Richardson, so the Giants needed somebody to fill that role. Additionally, they had to decide whether or not they wanted to bring back Wes Westrum, who had taken over as manager midway through the 1974 season.

With Stoneham gone, Westrum was one of the team's last remaining ties to New York. Westrum had spent his entire 11-year career with the New York Giants, but his last year as a player was 1957, the team's final year in New York. Westrum had been a good ballplayer on those Giants teams and had been the starting catcher on pennant-winning Giants teams in 1951 and 1954. After his final season, Westrum was a Giants coach during their first two years in San Francisco. Despite his ties to the franchise, Westrum was fired by Stoneham in one of the latter's last moves before selling the team. The new owners could have rehired Westrum but decided not to.

Lurie then decided to keep Richardson on as general manager. Having a veteran baseball man—Richardson had previously served as general manager of the Houston Astros—in that position, given a new ownership team with no prior baseball experience, made some sense. Whether or not Richardson, who was best-known for a multiplayer trade in 1971 that sent Joe Morgan to the Reds for Lee May, was the best person for that job was a different question. Although Lurie had been a sports enthusiast who had played tennis in college, he had spent his professional life in real estate and business, not baseball, and recognized that he needed somebody with experience running the team.

Almost immediately after the purchase was finalized, Lurie and Herseth made their choice for manager, hiring former Giants player and manager Bill Rigney for the position. Rigney had emerged as Lurie's favorite for the job as early as January, so his hiring was no surprise. Lurie explained his decision to hire Rigney to me by saying simply that he "was a friend and was knowledgeable around baseball."[26]

Rigney had deep ties both to the Bay Area and the Giants. He had been born and raised across the bay from San Francisco in Alameda County. Rigney had played for the New York Giants from 1946 through 1953. Like his former teammate Wes Westrum, Rigney had spent his entire big-league career with the Giants. Shortly after his playing career ended, he was hired to manage the only team for which he had ever played. He held that job from 1956 to 1960, making him the team's last manager in New York and its first in San Francisco. Rigney had also managed the Angels from 1961 to 1969 and the Minnesota Twins from 1970 to 1972. Rigney was a well-liked baseball man, but he was also a figure from the increasingly distant Giants past.

Although Rigney was in his fourth decade in big league baseball by 1976, he had almost a quarter century remaining in the game. After his second time around as the Giants' skipper, he became a scout for the Angels, and for the last 20 years of his life, with the A's. Choosing Rigney was not an inspired choice. It was a conservative placeholder move, but Rigney was well known and well liked in San Francisco and seemed to be able to offer some badly needed stability to the team.

As the season approached, the Giants looked a lot like the team that had finished in third place in 1975. During the off-season, the most significant move they made was swapping left-handed pitcher Pete Falcone, who had gone 12–11 with a 4.17 ERA as a 21-year-old rookie in 1975, to the Cardinals for third baseman Ken Reitz. Reitz was an excellent defender who had won the Gold Glove for his position in 1975, but he was coming off a season when he had hit .269/.298/.340. The trade was hardly a blockbuster, but on balance it was not a good one for the Giants. Falcone had a strong 1976 season for St. Louis, going 12–16 with a 3.23 ERA before turning into a journeyman and staying in the game through 1984. Reitz was a solid defender at third for the Giants but hit an anemic .267/.293/.333. After the season, he was sent back to the Cardinals for pitcher Lynn McGlothen.

Going into the season, the Giants had two clear strengths. First, in shortstop Chris Speier and the outfield of Gary Matthews, Von Joshua, and Bobby Murcer, they had a nucleus of four position players who would all be 30 years old or younger during the 1976 season and who were among the best in the league at their positions. All four could hit and contribute with the glove as well. Their second strength was a good core of starting pitchers. John Montefusco, who was reigning Rookie of the Year, as well as Ed Halicki and Jim Barr, were all good right-handed pitchers and considerably younger than 30 during the 1976 season.

There were some weaknesses as well. Since Pete Falcone has been traded away, the only left-handed starting pitcher was Mike Caldwell, who had been unimpressive in 1975, going 7–13 with a 4.79 ERA. The rest of the lineup, Dave Rader and Marc Hill behind the plate, Willie Montañez at first, Derrel Thomas at second, and the recently acquired Ken Reitz at third, was at best solid but nothing more. It looked like the kind of team that could finish third again, maybe even win a few more games, but barring something extraordinary was not going to come close to the Reds or Dodgers.

As spring training began and the saga of where the Giants would play in 1976 wound down, there was not a lot to report about the team. The Giants team that begin spring training in 1976 looked a lot like the team that had been together at the end of 1975. The new manager wasn't really new at all, so reporters needed stories. On March 26, *San Francisco Examiner* reporter Glenn Schwarz found one, reporting that the "Giants discover their first spring nugget." That nugget was Jack Clark, who Schwarz described as "the rage of San Francisco Giants training camp . . . a rookie bursting with confidence and ability." Schwarz quoted Clark immodestly comparing himself to Bobby Murcer, the man who Clark hoped to displace as the Giants every day right fielder: "I know I can play in this league. In fact I think I can do more things than Bobby Murcer. . . . I know Bobby's one of the best in the game, but there are always better players coming up, right?"[27]

Clark's confidence was not unfounded. In 1975, as a 19-year-old with the Giants' AA affiliate, the Lafayette Drillers, Clark hit .303/.385/.513 with 23 home runs and nine stolen bases in nine attempts. In a brief stint with the big-league team in 1975, Clark had four hits and a walk in 19 plate appearances, respectable numbers for a 19-year-old who had graduated from high school only two years and a few months earlier. Clark did not make the big-league team out of spring training in 1976, but the impression he made on the Giants and their more astute fans was not soon forgotten.

The Giants first game was scheduled for April 9 at home against the Dodgers. However, even something as simple as opening day against the Dodgers was not so easy for the Giants in 1976. After spending his first weeks in office trying to keep the Giants from leaving, George Moscone was recognized for the role he had played keeping the team in town.[28] However, the fate of the city's baseball team was just one of the challenges the mayor confronted during his first months in office.

On March 30, the Board of Supervisors, the city's legislature, had voted to reduce fringe benefits and wages of craft workers, so the craft workers went on strike. The craft workers included most city employee unions, such as bus drivers, maintenance workers, mechanics, gardeners, and others who labored to maintain, clean, and keep city buildings and facilities in good condition. One of the buildings where these city employees worked was Candlestick Park, so the players' union, the Major League Baseball Players Association (MLBPA), began to raise concerns about asking players to cross a picket line to play.

The craft strike had put Mayor Moscone in a difficult situation. As a candidate the previous year he had enjoyed strong support from organized labor, particularly in the runoff against the conservative Republican John Barbagelata. Additionally, as a state senator for nine years before becoming mayor, and indeed throughout his entire political career, Moscone had earned a reputation as being strongly prolabor. However, like most progressive mayors, Moscone was caught between his prolabor sympathies and the budget realities of governing a city like San Francisco.

The mood at the time in San Francisco, despite being a city with a history of strong support for labor, was not sympathetic to the demands of the unions. This was in part due to a strike by the city's police in 1975. Moscone's predecessor, Joe Alioto, a more conservative and law-and-order-oriented politician than Moscone, had quickly acceded to the union's demands. While this may have prevented an increase in chaos and crime in San Francisco, it strengthened conservative forces advocating a tough position on labor, while simultaneously raising expectations from other city unions that they would be treated equally well. Had Moscone done what Alioto did and simply given in to the union's demands, his antilabor critics, including Supervisors John Barbagelata and Quentin Kopp, would have attacked him as being controlled by labor and undermined the mayor's support with the public just as his term was starting.

As the season approached, pickets were present outside of Candlestick Park, forcing both players and fans to cross the picket line for the game. The picket would be almost entirely symbolic because almost everybody who worked at the ballpark was an employee of the team, not the city. "Moscone pointed out that on a given day at Candlestick, only six city workers are involved—four operating engineers, one gardener and one groundkeeper." However, if there were pickets at the ballpark, other union workers, such as vendors and janitors, would not cross the picket line, making it very tough for the game to be played.[29]

Lurie was understandably not amenable to postponing or moving the game. Lurie had spent the entire off-season working to keep the Giants in San Francisco, so the game meant a lot to him and to many San Franciscans. It was also important for many in the city that the game be played in San Francisco. Accordingly, the game occurred as scheduled. Several players were concerned about this, but once the teams decided to play, they had little choice. Mike Marshall, the star reliever for the Dodgers, even met with Lurie to discuss his concerns before the game, before deciding to play. Moscone did not attend the game because he would not cross the picket line, but he threw out the first pitch at a game a few days later.

The Dodger lineup the Giants were preparing to face was loaded. The heart of their order featured three formidable right-handed sluggers, Dusty Baker, Steve Garvey, and Ron Cey. Their leadoff hitter and left-fielder that day was a 27-year-old left-handed hitter who had played his first game with the Dodgers in 1969 and would play until 1990. Before he was done, he would amass more than 2,700 hits, but he would always be remembered for a ground ball that went through his legs while playing first base for the Red Sox in the sixth game of the 1986 World Series. In 1976, Bill Buckner was simply a solid hitter adept at getting on base and setting the table for the Dodgers' potent middle of the order. The Dodgers' starting pitcher against the Giants, Don Sutton, was the ace of the staff. Sutton was one of the top pitchers in the National League and would eventually end up in the Hall of Fame.

The Giants' Opening Day starter was their ace, John "the Count" Monte-fusco. In addition to being one of the best young pitchers in the game, The Count was very popular with the fans and the only player on the team, other than Murcer, who had any real star power. As a 25-year-old rookie in 1975, he had gone 15–9 with a 2.88 ERA. Montefusco's path to the big leagues had not been easy, and at one point he "ended up taking a job as a clerk with a large telecommunications company and spent his summers playing semipro ball at the New Jersey shore,"[30] before signing his first professional contract as a 22-year-old, undrafted free agent. However, once The Count made it to the big leagues, his humor, confidence, and brashness, as well as his work on the mound, enamored him to Giants fans. It didn't hurt that Montefusco was particularly effective against the Dodgers in his rookie year. In five starts against Los Angeles, Montefusco was 3–2 with a 1.67 ERA, striking out 34 batters in 37²/₃ innings and pitching one shutout.

Chris Speier played with Montefusco from late in the 1974 season, when Montefusco was promoted from the minors to the big-league team, until early 1977 when Speier was traded to the Expos for Tim Foli. Speier remembered Montefusco fondly: "You gotta love him . . . most of the time he backed up what he said. . . . He had some good stuff, good numbers with us. He had that swagger about him. For us and the team, he was the one guy who people gravitated to because of his bravado."[31] Bruce Jenkins described The Count similarly, saying that the Giants onetime top pitcher was "kind of a hoot. . . . A little bit of a meteor flying across the sky. . . . He said a lot of wacky things, but he was a pretty badass pitcher for a while there."[32]

One of the first moves Bob Lurie made after taking over the team was to re-sign his budding ace, who he described to me as a "fun, nice guy . . . who could be considered a little bit obnoxious,"[33] to a one-year contract for $60,000. That was a very big contract for the time, which Montefusco pointed out at the press conference, announcing that the signing was "the highest ever paid for a second year pitcher in Major League history." The Count made this claim with no evidence to support it, but it went largely unchallenged. He then made another comment that at first just seemed like Montefusco's typical bravado; the Count made a public challenge to Andy Messersmith, who he assumed would be the Dodgers starter for the first game of the season, to "a duel on opening day. I'll beat him and shut him out." However, Montefusco had preceded that comment by attacking Messersmith's decision to challenge the reserve clause, which bound players to their teams, and blaming the right-handed pitcher for "all this delay in getting spring training started."[34]

Messersmith's bold decision to play out his option and, therefore, automatically be paid his 1974 salary in 1975, led more or less directly to the advent of free agency, causing thousands of ballplayers to see huge increases in their earning power. Montefusco himself was a beneficiary of that when he signed a three-year, $2.3 million contract with the Padres prior to the 1982 season. At the time of Montefusco's boast, Messersmith was not a Dodger anymore, but a free agent looking for a team. A few weeks after Montefusco's press conference, after the season had already started, Messersmith signed a three year $1 million contract with the Atlanta Braves.[35]

Montefusco made good on that promise of a shutout for two thirds of an inning, but after retiring leadoff hitter Bill Buckner, and the number two hitter Ted Sizemore on flyballs, Dusty Baker, the third batter of the game, hit a home run. The Giants got that run back in the bottom of the first on a home run from their number three batter, right fielder Bobby Murcer, off of Don Sutton. After that initial home run, Montefusco pitched well. leaving the game with one out in the eighth inning after giving up only one more run. By that time, the Giants were leading 4–2.

The Giants top lefty reliever, Gary Lavelle, shut down the Dodgers the rest of the way to secure the win for the Giants. With two outs and a man on first in the ninth, Mike Marshall, who had sloughed off his concerns about picket lines enough to pitch two perfect innings of relief, was due up, but Dodger manager Walter Alston decided to pinch-hit for him with one of the Dodgers' own top prospects. The prospect in question was a 23-year-old outfielder named Glenn Burke. Burke's big-league debut was not memorable, as he hit a ground ball to Chris Speier who flipped it to Derrel Thomas, who was covering second for the last out of the game.

Burke's big-league career was relatively brief. He never hit much and had a hard time breaking into a crowded Dodger outfield. Midway through the 1978 season, he was traded to the A's and was out of baseball by 1980. Burke is now recognized as an important figure in baseball history as he was the first out gay big leaguer. He was never quite out during his career, although his sexual orientation was essentially an open secret, but after retiring he came out and wrote a book about his experiences called *Out at Home*. Burke died of AIDS-related illnesses in 1995.

The Dodgers and Giants had a day off following Opening Day but met two days later for the second game of their season. The Giants won again, this time with a four-run, come-from-behind rally in the eighth inning, capping off a 6–4 victory. Two wins against the Dodgers was a great start to the season and to a new period in the Giants' history, but that was more or less the highlight of the team's season. The Giants then traveled to Houston, where they were swept by the Astros, and by April 27 they were below .500 and would remain there for the rest of the season.

The season ended with the Giants in fourth place, 28 games behind the Reds. San Francisco still had a team, but other than that there was little to be excited about on the field during the 1976 season. The Giants scored the 10th most runs in the league, while giving up the ninth most. There were some bright spots. Gary Matthews (.279/.359/.443) and Bobby Murcer (.269/.362/.433) were the only productive players in an otherwise unimpressive offense. The Count had another solid season, going 16–14 with a 2.84 ERA. Jim Barr, a 28-year-old right-handed pitcher in his fifth full season with the ball club, went 15–12 with a 2.89 ERA. A pair of 27-year-old relievers had strong seasons. The righty Randy Moffitt went 6–6 with a 2.27 ERA and 14 saves in 103 innings. Moffitt had a couple more solid seasons with the Giants before injuries derailed his career. On balance, Moffitt was a fine relief pitcher, but the real athlete in his family was his sister, the legendary tennis great Billie Jean King. Lefty Gary Lavelle was 10–6 with a 2.69 ERA and 12 saves in 110$\frac{1}{3}$ innings. Lavelle would go on to be one of the best and most overlooked lefty relievers in baseball for close to a decade. Although Murcer and Matthews were established stars, the outfield began to look a little crowded when, after a great year with the AAA Phoenix Giants, spring phenom Jack Clark got into 26 games late in the season for the Giants. The 20-year-old was a little overmatched, but it was nonetheless clear that he would soon be a good big-league hitter. Clark, like Matthews and Murcer, was a good defender but lacked the speed to play center field.

Those first two games against the Dodgers were highlights of the Giants season for another reason as well. For the brief season-opening series against the Dodgers, the Giants drew 62,920 fans. That was more than 10 percent of the attendance they drew for the entire season. If Giants fans were grateful to still have their team in San Francisco, they did not show it by flocking to Candlestick Park. Ultimately, Bob Lurie and George Moscone's machinations to keep the team in town could not overshadow the reality that they were still a mediocre team playing in a terrible ballpark.

Overall, the 1976 season felt like a step backwards for the Giants. Key players from 1975, like catcher Dave Rader, shortstop Chris Speier, and center fielder Von Joshua failed to build upon their good 1975 seasons. By midseason, Joshua had lost the center field job to Larry Herndon. Other than Montefusco and Barr, the starting pitching was generally unremarkable.

Bill Rigney, the Giants manager, had managed as recently as 1972 for the Twins and was only 58 years old during the season, but he seemed old and from another era. Other than three years during World War II when he served in the US Navy, Rigney had been in organized baseball since 1938, and the changes in the game were beginning to catch up with him. On the field, Rigney did not do a particularly bad job as those 1976 Giants did not have the talent to compete with the stronger teams in the division, but Rigney was one of many old-school baseball people who saw changes coming in the game that would forever alter the relationship between players and management and dramatically increase salaries, and was unable to adapt. Rigney's inability to make the transition to the rapidly changing world of big-league baseball in the 1970s led him to stop managing at that level. Lurie explained how "Rigney was great except the free agent market got to him. He just couldn't believe . . . the players didn't play for the love of the game."[36] Rigney was a true baseball lifer who continued to scout and coach into his 80s, but after 1976 he would never again manage.

In an effort to shake things up and try something new, the Giants made a trade on June 13, 1976 when they were in last place with a record of 23–38. They sent first baseman Willie Montañez and three minor leaguers to the Braves for middle infielder Marty Perez and first and third baseman Darrell Evans. Over the next year and a half, the trade looked like a winner for Atlanta. Montañez hit .321 over the remainder of the 1976 season and was an all-star in 1977 when he hit .287 with 20 home runs. Evans for his part hit .222 over the rest of 1976 and only .254 in 1977.

Many Giants fans were not happy with the trade, but they were wrong. The trade was one of the best the Giants had made in years. Fans of a team that had been fleeced out of George Foster by the Reds and given Gaylord Perry to Cleveland for a washed-up Sam McDowell were understandably suspicious of any move the team made, but the Evans trade turned out to be a great one. First, after a respectable half season playing a lot of shortstop and second base, Perez was shipped to the Yankees for Terry Whitfield, who for a few years was a decent hitting outfielder who played solid defense and won over fans with his hustle and cheerful demeanor.

The key to the trade was Darrell Evans, who remained with the team through 1983. During his almost seven and a half years as a Giant, Evans hit .255/.358/422 with 142 home runs while playing solid defense at third and first and even spending some time in left field when the team asked him to do that. Evans was one of the best players on those Giants teams but was never seen by most fans as anything more than a solid big leaguer.

From the perspective of today, when advanced analytics have demonstrated the value of plate discipline, Evans looks even better. In the late 1970s and early 1980s, Evans's .255 batting average during his stint with the Giants was the statistic that defined him. Today it would be his .358 on-base percentage, a much more impressive figure, that would be more important. Indeed, from 1977 to 1983, the only National League players who drew more walks than Evans were Hall of Famers Mike Schmidt and Joe Morgan, as well as Keith Hernandez, one of the best players of the era for whom a very good Hall of Fame argument can be made. Evans's 563 walks helped him have the 12th highest on-base percentage among National League batters with more than 2,500 plate appearances over those seven years. Evans also ranks 16th for Wins Above Replacement (WAR)[37] in the National League during the time he was with the Giants. His 21.1 WAR was second only to Jack Clark's 27.5 WAR among Giants from 1977 through 1983. Evans was, on balance, an extremely good player, whose skill set was not appreciated in the era when meaningless statistics like game-winning RBIs passed as sophisticated quantitative analysis. Getting him for Willie Montañez was a great deal.

In his 2001 book *The New Bill James Historical Abstract*, Bill James, a ground-breaking and highly respected baseball analyst, ranked Evans as the 10th greatest third baseman ever, describing him as "the most underrated player in baseball history, absolutely number one on the list. . . . Evans completely failed to convince the American people that he was anything special as a player—yet he was."[38]

Montañez was a good player who, before the trade, was seen as part of the Giants' future. Acquiring Montañez from the Phillies had cost the Giants a top outfield prospect named Garry Maddox. Maddox ended up playing for the Phillies from 1975 to 1986, where he had some good years with the bat while winning eight Gold Glove awards and earning a reputation as the best defensive center fielder of his era. However, with Montañez gone, the Giants first base situation was less stable. Evans could play some first base and held down that position for most of the season after the trade, but his best position was third base, where he was a clear upgrade from Ken Reitz, who had been playing there when the Giants acquired Evans. As a left-handed thrower with a decent bat, but lacking the speed and arm to play the outfield, as long as he was on the team, Montañez, who fielded the position with style and grace, was going to be the starting first baseman. However, since he had been sent to the Braves midway through the 1976 season, the Giants went into the off-season needing a first baseman with some pop.

1977

At first glance, the 1977 season looked a lot like the 1976 season for the Giants. After going 74–88 in 1976, the team improved their record by exactly one game, finishing the 1977 season with a 75–87 record. Despite those similarities, the team was quite different, as several of the players who would define the franchise for the next five years were beginning to play key roles on the Giants. Chris Speier, Gary Matthews, Willie Montañez, and Bobby Murcer, the four best position players on their 1976 Opening Day roster, were gone by early 1977. Over the course of the season, Evans, Bill Madlock, and Jack Clark would replace them and continue to be the heart of the Giants' offense until Madlock was sent to Pittsburgh during the 1979 season. Additionally, a 23-year-old Johnnie LeMaster would, for many, be a less-than-encouraging symbol of the team in this era. LeMaster started 38 games at shortstop, making Tim Foli, who had been acquired in exchange for Speier, appear expendable.

The best hitter on that 1977 team, which could be best described as rebuilding, was not a young, two-time batting champion like Bill Madlock or a top hitting prospect like Jack Clark, but a 39-year-old who had played his first game for the San Francisco Giants when Dwight Eisenhower was in the White House, and had gotten his first hit off of Robin Roberts. Willie McCovey, who was getting older but still had power from the left side of the plate, became a free agent following the 1976 season. Bringing the longtime Giants slugger back to San Francisco looked like it might be a reasonable move, not just for sentimental reasons, but for baseball reasons as well. McCovey rejoined the Giants in January 1977, signing a one-year deal as a free agent.

By 1977, Roberts had been retired for almost a decade and had been inducted into the Hall of Fame the previous summer, but Willie McCovey, spending most of the season as the Giants' starting first baseman and cleanup hitter, slammed 28 home runs and drove in 86 runs, good enough to lead the team in both categories. His .367 on-base percentage and .500 slugging percentage also led the team.

McCovey's power was a welcome addition to a team that scored only 673 runs, 10th in the National League, but McCovey's value to the franchise went well beyond his power numbers. McCovey, who died in October 2018, has always had a special place in the hearts of Giants fans. During his first stint with the team, he was generally overshadowed by Willie Mays, who was the superior player until McCovey briefly surpassed him from 1968 to 70. From 1959 to 1964, McCovey was also fighting for playing time with Orlando Cepeda, another slugging first baseman with Hall of Fame talent. However, McCovey, unlike Mays, had never played for the team in New York, thus San Franciscans more easily saw him as one of ours. McCovey was traded to the Padres after the 1973 season. He spent almost three years there before playing out the 1976 season with the Oakland A's.

Today there are few teams that celebrate, embrace, and market their history as well as the Giants. The Yankees are probably the best at this, but they have also played in the same city for almost 120 years and in the same neighborhood for almost a century. Because of their bifurcated history, having spent roughly equal amounts of time in New York and San Francisco, it is more difficult for the Giants to present their history as continuous and cohesive. Nonetheless, by doing things like bringing the World Series trophy to New York after winning the championship in 2010, retiring the numbers of New York Giant greats like Monte Irvin and Bill Terry, and bringing back more recent stars like Will Clark and Vida Blue to participate in various ceremonies, the Giants have been leaders in this regard in recent years.

The Giants success in that area can be directly dated back to January 6, 1977 when Bob Lurie signed Willie McCovey as a free agent. Although Lurie told me that signing the slugger was "mainly a baseball decision,"[39] it did not seem entirely that way at the time. The Giants were a young team who were looking towards the future. McCovey was not just old; he was coming off a pretty terrible 1976 season during which he hit a combined .204/.283/.336 with only seven home runs and 36 RBIs for the Padres and the A's. Most baseball people saw McCovey as basically finished with what was probably a Hall of Fame career, but not somebody who was ever going to be an impact player again. The evidence of this was the lack of interest other teams showed in him when McCovey became a free agent following the 1976 season.

By bringing McCovey back, Lurie was hoping the aging slugger had a few good years left in him, but also reminding fans of the Giants' history in San Francisco. The signing of McCovey led to a flurry of other player moves in which the Giants moved further away from their mid-70s core. Gary Matthews had already signed with the Braves as a free agent, but in February the Giants sent Bobby Murcer to the Cubs for Bill Madlock. This was another great trade that allowed the Giants to swap Murcer for a better and younger player. Murcer had been made expendable because, by 1977, it was clear that Jack Clark, as he had promised in spring training of 1976, was the better player.

Despite these smart moves and the presence of Willie McCovey, two years into the Bob Lurie era things were not looking great for the Giants. The Giants finished 1977 in fourth place, 23 games behind the Dodgers while drawing only 700,000 fans, worst in the National League and 25th among the 26 Major League teams. Only the A's across the bay had worse attendance numbers. That was a good break for the Giants because it suggested that if one team would leave the Bay Area it might be the A's.

Chapter 2

BOB LURIE'S TEAM AND
BOB LURIE'S CHALLENGES

Two years after Lurie and Moscone worked together to keep the Giants in San Francisco, despite their mediocre performance on the field, the players on the Giants were not the biggest problem facing the franchise. From 1976 to 1992, in fact during almost all of the period from 1960 to 1999, one of the most important and memorable characters around the Giants, which had an enormous impact on their play on the field, relationship to San Francisco, and difficulty succeeding as a franchise, was not a player, manager, or even an owner. It was a huge, multiuse stadium in the southeastern corner of San Francisco. It is impossible to tell the story of the Giants during these years without discussing Candlestick Park. By the time Bob Lurie bought the team in 1976, Candlestick Park had been one of the major reasons the Giants were in such bad financial shape and on the cusp of being sold down the road to Toronto. During the 17 years Lurie owned the team, finding a better place for the Giants to call home was almost as much of a focus for the Giants' management as building a winning team was.

When Mayor Moscone and Bob Lurie led the successful effort to keep the Giants in San Francisco, there was an immediacy that led them to focus narrowly on stalling the final decision to give them time to finalize the ownership team, which eventually led to the Lurie-Herseth partnership. Because of the urgency of that task, at the time little attention was paid to the problem of the ballpark. It was essentially a given that Candlestick was the Giants' home in San Francisco. The problems with the ballpark were evident, but it was not clear whether the bad ballpark or the bad teams were keeping attendance and the overall popularity of the Giants down. Moreover, in 1976 Candlestick Park was not yet 20 years old, and the upper deck in the outfield had not yet been in place for a decade. Given the economic conditions in San Francisco at the time, as evidenced when no local other than Lurie stepped forward with real money to keep the Giants in San Francisco, there was no way the city was going to spend significant amounts of money for a new ballpark for the Giants.

CANDLESTICK PARK

Candlestick was home to the Giants from 1960 through 1999 and to the 49ers, San Francisco's football team, from 1971 to 2013. Thus, for most of the time the Giants called Candlestick Park home, and for all of the years from 1976 through 1992, it was a true multiuse stadium. Today it is very rare for big league baseball teams to share their facility with another sports team. Oracle Park, the park that the Giants have called home since 2000, occasionally hosts non-baseball events but has never been home to the 49ers or any sports franchise other than the Giants. However, for much of the period from about 1960 to 1990, this kind of arrangement was not unusual at all.

During the 1970s, many teams, including the Mets, Braves, Padres, Reds, Astros, Phillies, and Pirates all shared their home with local football teams. There were two major problems with multiuse ballparks. First, during football season the field would get torn up every time a game was played there. During a baseball game, large areas of the field, including most of the outfield, see very little action, so they do not get worn down. Most of the action on a baseball field occurs on the basepaths, which, barring terrible weather, are not too difficult to maintain because they are dirt, not grass.

This problem might not seem too daunting because the overlap of the two seasons is not very long, so a football team would usually only play 2 to 3 home games during the regular baseball season, but after a couple of football games, much of the field cannot be fixed quickly, and the problems would persist throughout the latter part of the season. Will Clark, the great Giants first baseman, recalled how at Candlestick "when the 49ers did start playing, it was a minefield out there. Big dirt clods were missing and all that. The workers would come out and they'd put sand out there and they'd spray paint the sand green, so sometimes you got a baseball and you'd look down and your whole hand was green. . . . We got some unbelievably bad hops. I mean terrible hops."[1]

The other major problem with multiuse stadiums is that a baseball field and football field are sufficiently different in shape that a facility big enough for both does not allow baseball fans to get close to the field. Moreover, for football fans the best seats are on the 50-yard line, but for baseball the best seats are behind home plate. Building a stadium that has good views from both the 50-yard line and home plate is extremely difficult and few stadiums were able to meet this need.

One of the appeals of watching a baseball game in person, if you have good seats, rather than on television is the ability to see the players up close and even to see their faces. This is less of an issue in football because the players are wearing masks anyway. Until 1957, most ballparks, such as Ebbets Field in Brooklyn and the Polo Grounds, which was home to the Giants before they moved to San Francisco, offered this intimacy. Wrigley Field in Chicago and Fenway Park in Boston, which are still in use today, also allow fans to get very close to the action on the field. Many of the newer baseball-only ballparks, like Oracle Park, Camden Yards in Baltimore, or PNC Park in Pittsburgh, do as well. Multiuse stadiums like Candlestick did not.

These problems beset all multiuse stadiums of the era, but Candlestick had an entirely different set of shortcomings that created problems for the team. San Francisco is a city of microclimates. Locals may occasionally over-state the extent to which each neighborhood has a different climate, but it is nonetheless true that the weather can vary substantially from neighborhood to neighborhood. San Franciscans have an intuitive awareness of this. All San Franciscans understand that, for example, the Outer Sunset is almost always foggier and colder than Noe Valley or the Mission, or that the Fillmore is usually warmer than the Richmond District. In general, the western part of the city is cooler than the central part of the city, while the wind is usually strongest either on top of big hills like Twin Peaks or closest to the water.

The climates of different San Francisco neighborhoods are not exactly secrets. Almost all San Franciscans know this, and dress and plan accord-ingly. However, Horace Stoneham was not a San Franciscan and did not immediately reject the idea of a ballpark at Candlestick Point. Candlestick Point is a small peninsula extending out into San Francisco Bay in the south-eastern corner of the city. It is part of a neighborhood known as Hunters Point, or Bayview–Hunters Point. The climate in that neighborhood is not bad. In fact, during the daytime it can be quite pleasant. Hunters Point in the afternoon is a much better place for a ball game than the Sunset, the Rich-mond, or even the Marina District.

Most San Franciscans were aware of this in the late 1950s when the Giants were preparing to move to San Francisco, but they were also aware that at night, the climate at Candlestick Point changes dramatically. By late afternoon, the

wind, sometimes accompanied by fog, blows off the bay, driving the tempera-
ture down rapidly and creating an environment that is not at all amenable to
baseball. As a non–San Franciscan, Horace Stoneham would not have known
this when he visited the location of his future ballpark during the daytime on
his way to a luncheon welcoming him and the Giants to San Francisco. While
Stoneham could be forgiven for this oversight, it is less clear why politicians,
developers, or anyone else who understood San Francisco would have located
a brand-new ballpark in such a dreadful location.

By the time Bob Lurie bought the Giants in 1976, Candlestick had been
the Giants' home for more than 15 years and the legend of the cold and wind
was already formidable. Corey Busch recounted how at the time Lurie bought
the team, there were already concerns about the ballpark: "It was clear that
Candlestick Park was a mistake and it was an inhibitor to economic sustainability or financial sustainability of the team and the team had not really
taken root in the community."[2] When Candlestick was initially designed the
builders and architects were aware of the problem presented by the wind
and cold and sought to address it through an elaborate heating system that
would have warmed up the seats through pumping steam heat through pipes
underneath the floors where seats were located. This was an ambitious idea,
but although the heating system was built, it never worked.

When Candlestick Park was first constructed, the outfield did not have a
second deck. This allowed the wind to enter the ballpark unabated, so before
the 1971 season, at the time the 49ers were moving to Candlestick, the upper
deck was enclosed. This may have reduced the wind, but it also created a
whirlwind effect on windy nights where napkins, hot dog wrappers, occasionally all-star ballots, and the like would blow around the ballpark in dervish-like
circles. The problem was always more acute for baseball, which is meant to
be played in warmer weather, while for the 49ers the weather was never a big
problem at Candlestick. Football players and fans are used to cold weather,
and in San Francisco summer nights can be colder than winter nights.

Players and fans were unified in their disdain for Candlestick. Kevin Mitchell first played in Candlestick Park in 1986 when he was a rookie with the
New York Mets. He described his initial reaction to the Giants' home ballpark:
"The first thing I thought about was how do they play in this ballpark with
all this wind blowing. I could never play here. Never."[3]

Chris Speier played for the Giants from 1971 through early in the 1977 season
and again from late 1987 through 1989 and said that "there is no question in
my mind that Candlestick Park was probably the worst place to play baseball

of any major-league park in the country—or out of the country. Even Montreal in April was warmer or more baseball conducive than Candlestick Park."[4]

Dusty Baker, who has been in baseball for more than 50 years as a player, coach, and manager with several teams, including serving in all three capacities with the Giants, was slightly more charitable in his discussion of Candlestick Park: "It was cold. It was miserable. When it was beautiful, it was beautiful, but it just wasn't beautiful that often." Baker also suggested that the Giants sometimes got an advantage because of their ballpark: "Most of the stars, if they had a west coast trip . . . guys wouldn't take days off in beautiful LA. They wouldn't take days off in San Diego. Because they would try to fatten up their average and it was beautiful, and they would take days off in San Francisco. . . . I couldn't because all my family was there watching."[5]

Bud Selig never played in Candlestick Park, but the longtime Milwaukee Brewers owner and later baseball commissioner described the Giants' erstwhile home in simple and unambiguous language: "It was a horrible ballpark, by the way. . . . My first trip there was in 1964 and I was stunned at that time how bad it was. I was there with the Milwaukee Braves in the middle of summer and you froze to death. It was brutal. . . . It was really wholly inadequate. Bob [Lurie] was absolutely right about that."[6]

Few Giants ever hated Candlestick Park as much as Bobby Murcer. Murcer, who died in 2008, is best known as a Yankee. He played his first games with that franchise in 1965 when he was a 19-year-old, highly touted center field prospect from Oklahoma. This led many in the New York media to call Murcer the next Mickey Mantle (Mantle also hailed from Oklahoma). Murcer never quite lived up to that, but from 1969 to 1974 he was one of the best players in the American League, hitting .285/.357/.464 while being named to four all-star teams. Murcer also ended his career with the Yankees, playing there as a pinch hitter, DH, and occasional outfielder from 1979 to 1983.

Following the 1974 season, the Giants and Yankees made one of the biggest blockbuster trades of the era. The Giants sent Bobby Bonds, a fast and powerful outfielder who was their best player at the time, to the Yankees in exchange for Bobby Murcer—the next Willie Mays for the next Mickey Mantle. Murcer only spent two years with the Giants before being sent to the Cubs for Bill Madlock, but during those two years Murcer was generally miserable playing at Candlestick. Speier described Murcer's view on Candlestick: "It was really funny [Murcer would say] 'I hit three balls today at Candlestick Park that would have been homers at Yankee Stadium this place sucks, get me the hell out of here.' . . . It was miserable for him and most people that came her from different organizations. It was just not a place to play baseball."[7] Long-time Giants clubhouse man Mike Murphy described Murcer's tenure with the Giants as dreadful for the once and future Yankee: "He was great in spring training. . . . Then he got to Candlestick. . . . One day he says 'Murph, I'll pay somebody to blow up this place.' He'd come in between innings . . . and sit in the sauna. He says 'I hate this city. I hate this ballpark. I hate everything.'"[8]

BASEBALL IN THE 1970S

When Bob Lurie took over ownership of the Giants in 1976, much about baseball had changed over the previous 20 years. Expansion had increased the number of teams from 16 to 24—soon to be 26 in 1977. The Giants and Dodgers had led the way to California, but by 1976 the Golden State had five teams. Texas, another huge state where there had been no big-league baseball as late as 1960, had two teams. The American League had adopted the designated hitter rule. The nature of pitching was changing as relief pitchers, particularly the elite relievers like Rollie Fingers of the A's or Sparky Lyle of the Yankees, were becoming an important part of the game. These pitchers were known as firemen in those days because of their ability to come into games in high-pressure situations and prevent the other team from scoring.

By the mid-1970s, baseball had adapted to the changes in the culture and fashion as well. Across the bay from San Francisco, the Oakland A's were the best team around as they won three consecutive World Series from 1972 to 1974. The A's wore various combinations of gold and green uniforms while the team's owner, Charlie O. Finley, encouraged players to grow out their facial hair. The Houston Astros had played the 1975 season in their new uniforms, which featured wide, vertical, red, yellow, and orange stripes across the bottom half of their jerseys.

Some things about baseball, however, looked much as they did in the 1950s. Despite the initial excitement expansion and team movement had brought to cities like Los Angeles, Houston, Atlanta, Kansas City, and not least San Francisco, attendance was still not strong, and many teams struggled financially. For example, in 1975 seven of baseball's 24 teams drew fewer than a million fans while only the Dodgers' and Reds' attendance exceeded two million.[9] In 2019, by contrast, every team but the Miami Marlins drew more than a million fans, while 18 drew more than two million, and five teams drew more than three million fans.[10]

Although the amateur draft had succeeded in ending four decades of Yankees dominance, by the mid-1970s there was still a clear line between baseball's haves and have-nots. Teams like the Cubs, Braves, White Sox, and Angels had not been in contention for years. Some like the Rangers, Brewers, Expos, Padres, and Astros still had never been to the postseason. In the mid-70s, stars were concentrated on teams like: the Reds, whose lineup included Pete Rose, Johnny Bench, Joe Morgan, and Tony Perez; the Dodgers with Steve Garvey, Mike Marshall, Jimmy Wynn, and Don Sutton; and the A's who, from 1969 to 1974, featured Reggie Jackson, Catfish Hunter, Rollie Fingers, and others.

Baseball's owners tended, like Bob Lurie, to be wealthy men with strong ties to the city where their team played. Pirates owner John Galbreath was from the Midwest, although Ohio not Pennsylvania, and had owned the team since the 1940s. Ewing Kauffman had grown up in Kansas City, had owned the Royals since their creation in 1969, and would remain the owner until 1993. Bud Selig, the owner of the Brewers, had very deep roots in Milwaukee. Even the O'Malley family, who brought the Dodgers from Brooklyn, relocated to Los Angeles and become part of the fabric of that city. The man from whom Lurie had bought the Giants, Horace Stoneham, had developed a similar relationship with San Francisco, but one that events of the previous months had demonstrated was not quite as strong. There were some exceptions. For example, George Steinbrenner, the relatively new owner of the Yankees was from Cleveland and spent much of his time in Florida. In almost all cases, teams were run by individuals, many of whom had been in that position for many years.

The relationship between the owners and the players was the same as it had been for decades as well. The reserve clause bound a player to the team that initially signed or drafted him until he was traded or sold to another franchise, at which point he would be similarly bound to the new team. Salaries were low because players had very few ways, other than a one-on-one negotiation during which ownership had almost all the power, to get more money from owners. The only tool the players had was the holdout, but that was only available to the best players. While a holdout from a star player might cause an owner to raise that player's salary, if a journeyman held out, he was usually out of a job.

FREE AGENCY

By 1976, this was beginning to change. Following the 1974 season, Catfish Hunter, the Oakland A's' star who had been the ace pitcher on a team that won three consecutive World Series, was released from his contract due to A's owner Charlie Finley's failure to pay for a life insurance premium as the contract had required him to do. Hunter signed a contract with the Yankees that would pay him $3.2 million over five years. That was an extraordinary amount of money for those days. The size of that contract shocked many in baseball who did not realize how much money there was in the game or how little of it was making its way to the players.

Hunter's contract with the Yankees occurred a year before Andy Messersmith had directly challenged the reserve clause outright and took the Dodgers and MLB to arbitration. When arbiter Peter Seitz sided with Messersmith, he created what came to be known as free agency.[11]

For fans, particularly those unschooled in the business side of baseball, free agency may have seemed to come out of the blue in the months between the 1976 and 1977 seasons, but it had been at least a decade in the making. The man most responsible for this was Marvin Miller, a labor lawyer who was hired by the players in 1966. Miller was instrumental in turning the Major League Baseball Players Association (MLBPA) into a real union capable of making demands on ownership and unafraid to fight for a larger share of the revenue generated by baseball. Miller is one of the perhaps five most important nonplayers in the history of modern Major League Baseball. Branch Rickey, the pioneering executive who created the system of affiliated minor-league teams and later brought Jackie Robinson to the Brooklyn Dodgers, and Judge Kenesaw Mountain Landis, the game's first commissioner who is credited with helping to save baseball in the aftermath of the 1919 Black Sox scandal—and with solidifying the segregated state of big-league baseball that would remain in place until Jackie Robinson—would be in that group, but it is difficult to think of another team or league executive who was more influential and important than Miller.

Miller earned the rancor, even hatred, of many owners who believed he was upsetting long-standing traditions and threatening the character of the game because he wanted players to be compensated fairly. Ironically, Miller's work helped bring a great deal of money into baseball, thus benefitting many of those same owners even more than the players he was representing. The rise in player salaries helped make baseball a much bigger business because in order to pay those salaries owners had to sell more tickets, provide a better product, and generate more television revenue. This required owners to approach their business differently, but the result was a huge influx of money into the game. Nonetheless, because the owners did not like him, Miller, who did so much to change and improve the game, was snubbed by the Hall of Fame for decades. At the time of his death in 2012 at 95 years old, Miller had accepted that he was never going to be recognized with baseball's highest honor and indicated that if he could not get into the Hall of Fame in his life, he did not want to be honored posthumously. In 2019, the Modern Baseball Era Committee of the Hall of Fame voted Miller in despite this request.

Free agency made an enormous impact on MLB almost immediately. Salaries skyrocketed, teams could immediately add impact players without giving anything up other than money, while teams whose owners were unwilling or unable to pay big salaries struggled to contend. In its early years, free agency was clumsier and less free than it has since become. Instead of all eligible free agents being able to negotiate with any team, teams drafted the right to negotiate with players, but no team could draft more than 12 players, while no player could be drafted by more than 12 teams.

In the first free agent draft the Giants selected four players who had spent the 1976 season with the A's: Joe Rudi, Gene Tenace, Rollie Fingers, and Sal Bando.[12] The first year of free agency devastated the A's, who also lost Bert Campaneris, a star shortstop, and Don Baylor, a talented outfielder with speed and power, to free agency that year. Bando was one of the best third basemen in the game during the 1970s. Rudi and Tenace were useful players who could play multiple positions. Both spent some time at first base, but Rudi was also a very good left fielder and Tenace was adept behind the plate. They were both good hitters who would have fit in well on a Giants team that needed more offense. Fingers was one of the best relievers ever and was still in the prime of his career. The Giants also selected Reggie Jackson, another longtime member of the A's, who had spent 1976 with the Orioles, and was considered one of the very best players in the game. Pitchers Wayne Garland and Doyle Alexander and infielders Bobby Grich, Dave Cash, Richie Hebner, Tito Fuentes, and Billy Smith were among the other players the Giants selected. Smith was a young and unproven player, but the others were all valuable players who could have contributed to a team like the Giants right away. The Giants ended up getting none of the major free agents they drafted. Jackson went to the Yankees, Fingers and Tenace to the Padres, Baylor, Rudi, and Grich to the Angels, and others to various teams that were not the Giants.

Betty Cuniberti's article in the *San Francisco Chronicle* discussing the players the Giants were seeking in the reentry draft was accompanied by a photograph not of Fingers, Rudi, or Tenace, the players the Giants had drafted earliest, or of Reggie Jackson, who most agreed was the marquee free agent that year.

Instead the picture was of a man stylishly dressed in a blazer, polka-dot shirt, and plaid cap. Giants fans would have immediately recognized the warm face and smile of Willie McCovey. Nineteen seventy-six had been the worst year of the 38-year-old McCovey's career; he played poorly while splitting his season between the Padres and A's. The caption in the photo read "Candlestick Bound." No team had drafted McCovey, who appeared to be done as a player, thus freeing him to sign with anybody. Cuniberti wrote in the article that "it is well-known that McCovey wishes to return to the Giants."[13]

Although it was difficult to avoid the conclusion that McCovey did not have much gas left in the tank, for a team that was struggling on the field and lacked big name players, bringing back a once-beloved star like Mc-Covey made a lot of sense. About a month after the reentry draft where he was soundly ignored, and days before his 39th birthday, McCovey signed a one-year contract with the Giants for $85,000.

Most analysts would say that the biggest winners in that first year of free agency were the Yankees, who signed Reggie Jackson and Don Gullett, and then won the next two World Series, or the Angels, who signed Rudi, Grich, and Don Baylor and went on to win the AL West in 1979 and 1982, with major contributions from those players, although Rudi had been traded to the Red Sox for Fred Lynn prior to the 1981 season. However, if one were simply measuring dollars well spent, a good argument could be made for the Giants.

In 1977, McCovey won Comeback Player of the Year, helped revive interest in the Giants in San Francisco, and enabled younger fans to connect with the great Giants teams of the past. The initial one-year $85,000 contract was a genuine bargain for the Giants, who got a reenergized slugger at a very steep discount. McCovey made a fraction of the $400,000 Joe Rudi made with his new team in 1977, but had a better year, hitting for a higher batting average, drawing more walks, and hitting 15 more home runs than Rudi. Rudi's Angels teammate Don Baylor, who made just over $250,000 in 1977, slashed .251/.334/.433, thus also falling short of McCovey's production. However, Baylor went on to be named the AL's Most Valuable Player in 1979, while 1977 proved to be McCovey's last good year.

Despite the success they had with McCovey in 1977, the Giants struggled to succeed in the free agent market in its early years. When free agency first started, the best and most expensive players did not simply gravitate to the big market teams, rather they went to teams whose owners were willing to jump into the new system and spend freely. In some cases, these were big market teams. The Yankees have been major players in free agency since its inception. The California Angels were also very active in the first years of free agency, but other big market teams like the Dodgers, Red Sox, and Mets did not fully embrace free agency right away. In the first year of free agency, the San Diego Padres landed Rollie Fingers and Gene Tenace, while their former Oakland teammates Sal Bando and Bert Campaneris signed with the Milwaukee Brewers and Texas Rangers, respectively. The Montreal Expos actually offered Reggie Jackson more money than the Yankees did, but the slugger wanted to play in New York.

Free agency was a new paradigm for baseball. Baseball executives had to take some time to figure out how to operate in this new world. Bob Lurie described how in those early years his "attitude towards free agency was a little cautious . . . it was a learning process . . . you had to get involved and take a look."[14] After signing McCovey in 1977, the Giants sat out the free agent market entirely in 1978, but the next year they were considerably more active. After the 1978 season, they resigned Darrell Evans to a contract that paid him just under $1.5 million over five years. The team made one other major free agent signing between the 1978 and 1979 seasons, inking Bill North to a one-year contract. North had been the speedy leadoff man for the A's when they were winning championships in the early 1970s. He was a valuable player for a disappointing Giants team in 1979, reaching base at a .386 clip while stealing 58 bases. The Giants then resigned him to a three year, $600,000 contract following that year, but after a similarly good year in 1980, North's career wound down quickly.

While the North signing was disappointing, the Evans signing was a great move. There were several bigger name free agents after the 1978 season, most notably Pete Rose. Rose signed a deal for $3.25 million over four years with the Phillies, earning considerably more money than Evans, but for the money spent, Evans was clearly the better player, as Rose only managed 6.4 WAR over the life of his four-year deal, while Evans produced 12 WAR over that same four-year period. The only top free agent of that offseason who performed as well as Evans over the length of his contract was Tommy John, who was 52–26 with a 3.07 ERA while pitching for the Yankees from 1979 to 1981. Evans was a re-signing, so not quite a free agent addition. Nonetheless, in the first three years of free agency, the Giants had not made a big splash. Instead, they made two signings, Evans and McCovey, that drew very little attention outside the Bay Area, but were very wise expenditures of team resources.

In general, the early years of free agency proved to be a puzzle for the Giants. There were some good signings. Milt May, who they acquired following the 1979 season, was an adequate catcher, although never much more than that, during about three and a half seasons for the Giants. The aging Joe Morgan, signed the following offseason, gave the Giants two and a half years of excellent baseball and one very important home run, but there were also bad signings. Rennie Stennett, an oft-injured second baseman who had been a relatively good player as recently as 1977, signed a five-year $3.25 million contract following the 1979 season. That was a huge contract for the time and the biggest up to that point in Giants history. Stennett was released as the 1982 season was about to begin after hitting .242/.282/.295 in only 517 plate appearances during his entire time with the Giants. The Stennett contract is still the gold standard for terrible Giants contracts. When I asked Bob Lurie, almost 40 years after that contract, which free agent signing he most regretted he did not hesitate to say Rennie Stennett. He added that "it just didn't quite work out. . . . It turned out to be something of a disaster . . . [you] just have to forget about it. Can't let it eat at you, but it does eat at you."[15]

Throughout the first decade or so of free agency, the Giants, like many teams, seemed as if they were not quite sure what to make of this new development. Although Bob Lurie was relatively young, only 47 years old by the time the purchase of his team was finalized, his ownership profile was in many respects from a previous generation. By the time Lurie was halfway through his tenure as the Giants owner, many teams had been bought either by extremely wealthy individuals who had recently made their money or by consortiums of businesses and individuals. Lurie was extremely wealthy, but always seemed more of a civic cheerleader and baseball fan than hard-driving businessman. Busch described the transition in ownership styles that began around the time Lurie bought the Giants:

When Bob bought the Giants, the Giants and a lot of clubs in baseball were beginning to transition. . . . All of a sudden people with expertise were being brought in. Teams were no longer looking for baseball people. They needed people who understood financing. They needed people who understood marketing. People who understood publications, and food service and retail and all of that. That was just beginning to happen in baseball overall and that was what was happening with the Giants after Bob bought the club. After he bought the club, the Giants and all of baseball began to morph into what you have today.[16]

Lurie's love for San Francisco, and for baseball, was a major reason why there still was big-league baseball in San Francisco in the 1980s, but it did not help him navigate free agency.

Nonetheless, the Giants made a handful of very good free agent signings during these years. Joe Morgan was instrumental in keeping the team in the pennant race until the last weekend of the 1982 season. A later addition, Brett Butler, signed in the 1987–88 offseason, was an excellent leadoff hitter and defensive center fielder who scored 100 or more runs during each of his three seasons with the Giants, and was an essential part of the pennant-winning 1989 team.

The rest of the Giants' free agent signings were sometimes just terrible, like the Stennett contract, sometimes useful, like acquiring Milt May that same offseason to help with the catching duties, but in general they were puzzling. For example, Bill North gave the Giants a good leadoff hitter in 1979, but they already had an excellent leadoff hitter, and a pretty strong outfield, in 1978. The Giants needed a catcher, a shortstop, and some power that offseason, not another speedy outfielder. Similarly, the three-year, $425,000 contract they gave Jim Wohlford before the 1980 season was kind of pointless as the outfield was already a relative strength, but the team was desperate for pitching.

Many times over the years, the Giants would sign a player, like Manny Trillo before the 1984 season or Kevin Bass after the pennant-winning season in 1989, with much fanfare, as if they were going to be a key contributor in the coming seasons. Many of us who were fans at the time responded to this news not with excitement or disdain, rather we simply asked "Why?" It was never clear to us how the Giants saw this new piece, whoever it was, as so important.

The Giants were not alone in this regard in the late 1970s and early 1980s. Free agency was genuinely new and the idea of bringing in big stars to help revive weak franchises was too appealing for many team owners to resist. This was also a time when a lot less was known about how players aged and, with a few exceptions, lost most of their value after their early 30s. Even some of the biggest stars proved to be of limited value after signing free agent contracts. Joe Rudi, who had been central to three championship A's teams, joined the Angels as a free agent at the age of 30 and was never again a healthy and productive player. His teammate Sal Bando, the captain of those A's team, only had one good season after signing with the Brewers at age 33.

The best Giants free agent signing from outside the organization during the first 15 years of free agency might have been Brett Butler, but the best free agent break was one that got away, longtime Dodger first baseman Steve

Garvey. On November 18, 1982, "standing before an orange and black Giants banner, [Steve] Garvey and his agent Jerry Kapstein, told a press conference the Giants have as good a chance as anyone to sign the former Mr. Dodger first baseman."[17] At the press event, Bob Lurie told the media "I think we need him. He would be a great asset."[18]

Steve Garvey was one of the biggest stars of the era. He had been an all-star every year from 1974 to 1981, had not missed a game since 1975 and was a .301/.337/.459 hitter over his career. 1982 had been a bit of an off year for Garvey as he hit only .281/.301/.418, but he was still viewed as a star player who could be the last piece for a team that, like the Giants, had just missed the playoffs the previous year. However, while Steve Garvey was a very good ballplayer, although one of the most overrated in the history of the game, for Giants fans he was always more than a baseball player.

Steve Garvey was everything we detested about the Dodgers and, at that time, was by far the player most hated by Giants fans. Nobody got booed more loudly or boisterously at Candlestick Park than Garvey. The star first baseman's pretty boy image, clutch hitting, self-righteousness, and right-wing politics made him a natural target for Giants fans in the late 1970s and early 1980s.

The Giants just missed on Steve Garvey, who ended up signing a five-year, $6.6 million contract with the Padres. Garvey gave the Padres a very good season in 1983, bouncing back by hitting .294/.344/.459, but missing about a third of the season due to injury. He was more or less finished after that and was never an impact player again. Even when the Padres won the pennant in 1984, Garvey hit .284 with only 37 extra-base hits. However, he was the MVP of the NLCS that year in large part because of the huge walk-off home run he hit against Hall of Fame Cubs closer Lee Smith in the bottom of the ninth inning of Game Four, with the Padres trailing by one run and two outs away from elimination. Overall, Garvey would have done little to help the Giants through the rough years of the mid-1980s, but more significantly, by 1986, the Giants had a young first baseman who would become the team's best player at that position since Willie McCovey. The thought of an aging Steve Garvey, of all people, keeping a young Will Clark out of the starting lineup is disturbing even now.

While money was always central to free agent pursuits, for the Giants there was another issue as well. As long as the Giants played at Candlestick Park, few players, particularly hitters, would willingly choose to play there. This did not mean the Giants could never sign free agents, just that they had one more obstacle to overcome. Bob Lurie downplayed this, asserting that money considerations were usually more important, but conceded that "obviously it did come up, but . . . unless somebody was so anti-Candlestick . . . the contract x dollars, whatever, that was basically more important." Busch clarified this in his description of the impact of Candlestick Park on free agent negotiations: "All things being equal, we lose all ties."[19]

One tie the Giants lost in this regard was with the California Angels over the services of Rod Carew following the 1978 season. At that point in his career, Carew was a 12-time all-star with a lifetime slash line of .334/.393/.448 and well on his way to a Hall of Fame career with a well-earned reputation as one of the game's greatest hitters. Carew was already 33 years old, and had slowed down a bit, moving from second base to first base in 1976, but he would remain a very productive player through the 1983 season. Carew was not a free agent at that point in his career—his contract with the Twins was set to last through the end of the 1979 season—but he wanted to get out of Minnesota and sign a long-term contract with his new team. The Twins, wary of getting nothing in return for their best player, wanted to trade Carew before he could leave as a free agent.

A trade like that would have been difficult to imagine even in 1975. As long as the reserve clause was in place, teams did not need to worry about losing their best players and getting nothing in return, while players had little ability to force a trade, but within a few years, baseball had changed. The Giants and Twins negotiated a multiplayer trade that would have sent the young, slugging first baseman Mike Ivie, pitching prospect Phil Nastu, and journeyman outfielder Jim Dwyer to Minnesota in exchange for Carew. The trade never happened because Carew did not want to sign an extension with the Giants, asserting that he wanted to remain in the more familiar American League.[20] Carew may have preferred the American League, but Candlestick Park was a major factor as well. When asked if Candlestick Park was an issue in Carew's decision, Lurie responded, "I think so. . . . I think that it did bother him."[21]

In the middle of the 1980s, free agency created a new problem as it was revealed that following the 1985 through 1987 seasons, the had owners worked together to craft an informal agreement to limit how many years and how much money they would offer free agents. This practice is known as collusion and is not legal. During this period, numerous players, including stars like Tim Raines, Jack Clark, and Jack Morris, became free agents but were unable to find suitors who were willing to sign them to lucrative long-term contracts.

A part of the settlement following the 1990 season was to allow several players who had been victimized by free agency to negotiate better deals with new teams. One of these players was Brett Butler, who became a free agent for the second time after this settlement and signed a three-year, $10 million contract with the Dodgers, where he continued to be one of the best leadoff hitters in the game. Al Rosen later commented that he considered failing to re-sign Butler to be one of the biggest mistakes of his career.[22]

THE RAPIDLY CHANGING GAME

In the late 1970s, free agency was the most visible way the game was changing, but the Giants, and baseball in general, were undergoing a period of transformation that could be roughly bookmarked by Andy Messersmith becoming a free agent on one end and the 1994 strike on the other. Bob Lurie's time as the Giants owner overlapped almost entirely with that period. The Giants were one of 26 (for most of those years) teams trying to navigate this changing landscape, but their story is illustrative of the challenges teams faced during this period.

The changes themselves were dramatic and changed how the game was played, managed, and followed by its fans. For baseball fans today, one of the most fun parts of the hot stove league is looking at the best free agents, whether it's Steven Strasburg, Gerrit Cole, Manny Machado, Bryce Harper, or Robinson Cano, or even players from previous generations like Mark Teixeira or Greg Maddux, all the way back to the initial crop that included Rollie Fingers, Reggie Jackson, and Bobby Grich, and thinking how they might fit into their favorite team's lineup or pitching staff. Similarly, any thoughtful fan today must understand contracts in some depth if they want to think through how their team can build a contender or win a World Series. Anybody who has followed baseball during the last 25 years is familiar with terms like salary dump, short-term rental, and team-friendly, long-term contracts for young players. However, in the mid-1970s, not only did this change occur very quickly, it was, for many, completely unexpected.

To understand the speed with which all this occurred it is helpful to compare the 1973–74 offseason with what occurred only three years later. Following the 1973 World Series, when the A's defeated the Mets in a thrilling contest that went the full seven games, there was a flurry of player movement. Several veteran stars changed teams. That was the offseason when the Giants sent Willie Mc-

Covey to the Padres for Mike Caldwell. Horace Stoneham's Giants made only one other significant move any that offseason. They sent aging pitching ace Juan Marichal to Boston in December. The same day as the McCovey trade, the Cubs sent their longtime ace Ferguson Jenkins to the Rangers in exchange for a top prospect, third baseman Bill Madlock. A few months later, the Dodgers sent star outfielder Willie Davis to the Expos for Mike Marshall, hoping that Marshall would shore up their bull pen. There were numerous other trades, many player contracts were sold from one team to another, some players were released, and the only players who signed as free agents were fringe players whose previous team had not offered them a contract. That is how baseball transactions had looked for most of the previous half century. A baseball executive from the 1930s would have been able negotiate the 1973–74 off-season.

A short three years later, the landscape had changed dramatically for everybody. Fans had to accept that the players they understood as part of their team could leave for other teams, with their team having nothing to show for it. However, in those first years of free agency, fans of all teams also could dream of adding a Reggie Jackson, Tommy John, Pete Rose, Rollie Fingers, or Dave Winfield, players who were capable of taking a contending team to the World Series or making a .500 team a contender. Fans could dream of this, but it also became clear that for many fans, including those of the Giants, dreaming was all they could do because, as the 1980s continued, fewer teams were able to sufficiently compete for the top free agents. All of this was a stark reminder, to those that for some reason still needed one, that baseball was a business. Players, like all highly sought-after employees, were now free to seek work for the best pay they could get. Very quickly, fans needed to not only understand baseball statistics, but they also needed some basic financial literacy to understand what their team was doing.

Players, for the first time ever, now had the chance to find out what their real worth was on the open market. This was a great breakthrough for baseball players, but this economic advancement was only available to those players lucky enough to make it to free agency. For players, this changed the incentive structure of the game. Becoming a free agent and signing with the highest bidder, something that could only occur if a player's contract expired and if that player had six full years of big league experience, could be very lucrative, but it also could be risky. A five-year veteran who eschewed the offer of a long term contract in year four, five, or six, and then got hurt—for example, in spring training of his sixth year in the big leagues—would miss the opportunity to make real money. However, if he signed that long-term deal in year four, he might miss out on the bigger money promised by free agency.

For team executives, the fundamental strategy that all strong teams—from the Chicago Cubs who won three consecutive pennants and two World Series from 1906 to 1908, through the 1972 to 1974 A's who had recently completed an even greater streak of dominance—had used was rapidly changing. For years, winning teams were built around a core of homegrown talent which was then supplemented with trades and, occasionally, the purchase of a key player. However, once free agency dawned, that simple formula no longer really applied. Top homegrown talent, like Gary Matthews of the Giants, could simply leave the team when their contract expired, while top-level talent could be added by dipping into that same free agent market.

Most of the owners, naturally, hated free agency. They recognized it as a blow against the absolute power over players that the reserve clause had guaranteed them for decades. The threat of free agency meant that owners who mistreated players, which most owners did for most of baseball history, risked losing those players when they became free agents. It also handed players a lot more leverage before they reached free agency because long term contracts were the best, and in many respects, only, way to keep free agency from costing a team its best players.

In that first year of free agency, the Oakland A's lost so many players, not just because they had so many well-known players who were laboring without long-term contracts, but also because team owner Charlie O. Finley was such a difficult owner to play for. Years of Finley's destructive shenanigans, including his unwillingness to reward rookie pitching sensation Vida Blue a decent contract for his second year, ordering Mike Andrews, whose brother Rob was a Giant from 1977 to 1979, to retire midway through the 1973 World Series after making two costly errors in the 12th inning of Game Two, allowing the facilities in Oakland to fall into disrepair, and generally making life unpleasant for his players, often by publicly humiliating them, meant that most of his top players were anxious to sign with anybody but Oakland once given the chance.

The owners also feared that free agency would make it even more difficult for many teams to contend and turn a profit. Some owners may have been guilty of sleazy and one-sided labor practices, but they were, in many cases, not getting much for their efforts. In the mid to late 1970s, several teams including the Giants, A's, Rangers, Indians, and Padres were struggling to fill their ballparks, put good teams on the field, and remain fiscally solvent. In San Francisco, this led to the short-lived sale of the Giants to Labatt Breweries.

It was not just the Bay Area teams around whom rumors of moves to new cities circulated. Between the 1973 and 1974 seasons, the Padres were thought to be moving to Washington. This came so close to happening that Topps made two sets of baseball cards for the Padres players. One listed the city and team on the front of the card as "San Diego" and "Padres" and the other as "Washington" and "Nat'l Lea." because it was not clear what the team name would be. Washington Padres made no sense and had a terrible ring to it. One of the players for whom cards like that were made was Willie McCovey, who was just starting his three-year sojourn away from San Francisco.

The free agent era changed all this, but in a way that was not at all obvious at first. One of the biggest differences between Major League Baseball today and 40 years ago is that it is a much larger and, at least through the 2019 season, healthier industry now. That did not happen immediately with the dawning of free agency, but the two are related. Free agency raised salaries for players, but it also brought more money into baseball. Ticket prices began to climb, but Major League Baseball also began to more aggressively market licensed products, such as caps, T-shirts, and jerseys. In the late 1970s, it was unusual to see an adult wearing a replica jersey or even a baseball cap outside of the ballpark. For the last several decades, those items have moved beyond being simply ways of displaying one's feelings towards a favorite team and have become items of clothing worn by people who may not have much of an interest in baseball at all. Today, you can see Giants caps, T-shirts, and hooded sweatshirts all over San Francisco and most of the Bay Area, but in the late 1970s and early 1980s, other than at the ballpark, it was relatively unusual to see a Giants cap around town. Attendance rose substantially during these years as well. In 1975, the year before Bob Lurie bought the Giants, the average attendance for a big-league ball game, regardless of who was playing, was 15,403. That number exceeded 20,000 for the first time in 1979. By 1992, it was 26,529.[23] Similarly, it was during this time when MLB began to focus on how to make more money off of television, something they were still figuring out in the late 1970s. In 1975, MLB revenues for television were $154 million, in 2002 dollars. By 1992, it had increased to $465 million in 2002 dollars.[24]

These changes meant that owning a baseball team was a totally different kind of project by the early 1990s compared to the mid-1970s. By 1990, owning a baseball team required a level of professionalization in areas from promotion and public relations to baseball operations and community operations, that was much different than what was needed a decade and a half before that. In the 1970s, there were still many teams that were run by the owner with a relatively small staff. At the time he sold the team, Horace Stoneham was serving as his own general manager. This was a cost-cutting move, but it was not that unusual for a big-league team in the middle of the twentieth century.

Across the bay in Oakland, after losing so many valuable players to free agency in 1977, the A's organization fell into acute disrepair as these changes began to occur. Charlie Finley appeared to lose interest in running the team and refused to make any meaningful investments in the A's. The ballpark became increasingly dilapidated. The front office was understaffed and the team did not bother to find a radio station to broadcast their games, finally settling on KALX, the student-run radio station at nearby UC Berkeley, just before the start of the 1978 season. Finley sold the rights to those games to KALX for one dollar. One of the students who put the deal together was Larry Baer, then an undergraduate at Berkeley, who would go on to play a central role in the post–Bob Lurie Giants.

These kind of low-budget ploys were not unique to the Bay Area, or even to teams thought to be preparing to move. In 1969, the Montreal Expos were a brand-new expansion team and would become the first MLB franchise outside of the United States. Their presence in the league was significant both for Canadian baseball and for MLB. However, despite being awarded a big-league team, Montreal had no facility appropriate for high-level baseball. The Expos ownership finally settled on Jarry Park. Expos historian Jonah Keri described this facility at the time the Expos were preparing for their first season: "Located about three miles northeast of the downtown core, the large municipal park sat in the middle of the Villeray neighborhood surrounded by duplexes and triplexes. . . . [Jarry Park] did contain a true baseball diamond, that field wasn't big enough or in any way suitable for high level minor league play, let alone the big leagues."[25] Keri added, regarding Jarry Park:

> It wasn't just that it seated fewer than 30,000 fans. Its footprint was tiny. There was no upper deck. There was nothing but a low-slung fence circling the exterior of the park from the right field foul pole all the way to dead center. On a summer weekend you could watch Rusty Staub and Bob Bailey, then look across the way and see families everywhere, picnics, kids playing soccer-everything you'd expect from a July Sunday afternoon in Montreal.[26]

By the early 1990s, baseball had changed. Not only were ballparks like Jarry Park, which was replaced by Olympic Stadium in 1977, a thing of the past, but baseball was about to go on a stadium construction binge beginning in the 1990s that would start in Baltimore and Cleveland, but would soon spread as most teams upgraded to newer, baseball-only ballparks that offered better views, better food, a better vibe, and were usually much more expensive than the ballparks that most teams played in during the 1970s. This further underscored the challenges that Candlestick Park had always presented to the Giants.

During this period, teams were beginning to be controlled not by one owner, but by ownership groups. This was largely because the value of teams had increased so much that it was much more difficult for local wealthy individuals to buy teams single-handedly. As ownership structures evolved, so did management structures, as it became more common for people with business backgrounds, rather than simply baseball ones, to take leadership positions with the organization. This was not the same as today when front offices are filled with people with MBAs and statistical training from elite universities, but it was the period when movement in that direction first began to occur.

Lurie bought the team at the tail end of one paradigm but had to adapt to the new one very quickly if he wanted to make the Giants competitive. This was a challenge that many teams including the Giants faced, both on and off the field. Lurie not only had to find a way to use free agency to help build a team, he also had to modernize the management, marketing, and media strategies for the Giants as well. That evolution was a key component of the Giants during the Bob Lurie years.

Chapter 3

CULTS, ASSASSINATIONS, AND BOB LURIE'S FIRST GOOD TEAM

When Bob Lurie and Bud Herseth bought the Giants, the team was several years into a period of persistent mediocrity. The 15 seasons from 1972 to 1986 are still the longest the Giants have ever gone without appearing in the postseason. During those 15 seasons, the Giants only finished above .500 five times. Fans of the Giants in those years had little to get excited about as the team only contended for the division twice. To make matters even worse for Giants fans, during those 15 years the Dodgers won the NL West six times, the pennant four times, and the World Series once, while the Giants never finished higher than third.

Nonetheless, one year stands out as a splendid bright spot during this period. In 1978, the Giants finished in third place, winning 89 games, the highest number of any year during this nadir in franchise history. More importantly, they led their division for 90 days before falling out of first place for good on August 16, and out of contention a few weeks after that. Because of the success of the franchise in the late 1980s, and more strikingly during the 2010 to 2014 run, that 1978 team is not remembered much today—few third-place teams are—but the impact that team had on the Giants history in San Francisco is more substantial than might seem to be the case at first look.

The 1978 Giants were the first successful Giants team since the trade of Willie Mays to the Mets in 1972, and since Bob Lurie's purchase of the team a few years after that. They also generated an excitement that had not been seen in San Francisco in years, drawing more fans to Candlestick than any team since 1960, the first year the ballpark opened. The third-place 1978 team drew more than the division-winning 1971 squad, the 1962 team that won the pennant, or any Giants team during the decades the franchise was based in New York.

As the 1978 season approached, there was little reason for Giants fans to be enthused about the coming season. While Bob Lurie's successful effort to keep the team in San Francisco was still appreciated, attendance was nonetheless down and those who managed to make it out to the 'Stick rarely saw great baseball from the home team. The team had finished in fourth place in both of the seasons since Lurie had purchased the team, winning roughly 46 percent of their games.

During those years, San Franciscans had a lot on their minds other than a mediocre baseball team. The new progressive mayor, George Moscone, was struggling against conservative pushback, and a city legislature where his allies were in the minority, as he sought to remake the city on a more progressive framework. The city had switched from at-large to district-based elections for its legislature, the Board of Supervisors, in 1977. This led to a board that was radically different and more diverse than its predecessors. One of those elected to the new legislature was Harvey Milk, a small businessman and activist from the Castro District who became one of the country's first out, gay elected officials. There was a lot going on in the city with regards to politics, culture, where the Summer of Love era was receding into the background but still influencing the city in many ways, and even religion, where strange sects and cults, like Jim Jones's Peoples Temple, dotted San Francisco. In this context, the Giants were unable to unify the city but were more akin to something odd that was going on in the southeast corner of the city that most San Franciscans ignored most of the time.

Between the end of the 1977 season and the beginning of spring training, the Giants gave their fans little reason to think anything would be different in 1978. During those four months, the Giants only made three transactions, all of which were minor: They purchased outfielder Art Gardner from the Astros; sold shortstop Tim Foli to the Mets, clearing the path for Johnnie LeMaster to be the starter at that position; and signed Mario Guerrero, a light-hitting infielder, as a free agent.

Lurie and Mayor Moscone had worked hard in those first few months of 1976 to ensure the Giants would not leave for Toronto, but by early 1978 many wondered if all that effort had been worth it. Even under new ownership, the Giants were still struggling badly. Moreover, the collapse of the A's, who had one of baseball's best teams from 1970 to 1976, had not meaningfully bolstered the Giants. Through the 1977 season, the A's had played a decade in Oakland. For much of that time, many around baseball speculated that the Bay Area was simply not big enough for two big-league teams; by 1978, that speculation had become an axiom. It was understood that something had to give regarding these two teams, but it was less clear what.

Several different scenarios began to take shape. The A's might move to Denver, leaving the Giants the entire Bay Area market, or the Giants might move to Denver, leaving the A's as the only team in the Bay Area. Florida and Washington, DC, were also mentioned as possible destinations for the Giants. At one point the two Bay Area cities and teams were negotiating for the Giants to play a proportion of their games in the Oakland Coliseum as part of a plan that would eventually see the A's in Denver. In a 2019 interview, Bob Lurie told me he would never have moved the Giants out of San Francisco in the late 1970s. Given both the effort Lurie and Moscone had just made to keep the Giants in San Francisco, and Lurie's deep ties to the city, there is good reason to believe that assertion reflected Lurie's view in the late 1970s. Nonetheless, fans, sportswriters, and others did not feel confident about that at the time.

Throughout the 1970s, the National League West was dominated by the Dodgers and the Reds. As spring training began in 1978, the Dodgers, who had won the National League pennant in 1977, and the Reds, who had won the two before that, were still the class of the division. Those two teams had dominated the NL West for most of the decade. Over the course of the 1970s, the Dodgers and Reds would combine for nine NL West titles, nine second-place finishes in the division, and seven NL pennants. The only team other than the Dodgers or Reds to win the NL West in the 1970s was the Giants in 1971, when the Mays-Marichal-McCovey nucleus, bolstered by veterans like Gaylord Perry and young stars like Bobby Bonds, finished in first place.

THE 1978 SEASON

Going into spring training of 1978, most Giants fans expected the Reds' and Dodgers' dominance to continue and thought a .500 season would be a stretch for their team. However, during spring training the Giants were much more active than they had been in the previous four months, making two trades that would have big impacts in 1978. The first trade the Giants made was an intriguing one, sending infielder Derrel Thomas to the Padres for Mike Ivie. The Giants had originally acquired Thomas from the Padres following the 1974 season. In his three years with the Giants, Thomas had played several different roles. In 1975, he'd been the team's starting second baseman but spent most of 1976 sharing that position with midseason pickup Marty Perez. In 1977, Thomas had managed to play almost every day while splitting his time between the middle infield and the outfield. Because of all the positions he could play, as well as his speed on the base paths, Thomas was a useful player, but he was not much of an offensive force, only hitting .262/.332/.364 over the course of his three years with the Giants. Although a player like that could contribute to a good team, that skill set was less valuable to a team that was struggling to contend. More significantly, towards the end of the 1977 season, Bill Madlock had shifted from third base to second base, precluding a starting role for Thomas there, while the emergence of Larry Herndon in center field meant that Thomas was not going to get much time there either, so he was expendable.

Like Thomas, Mike Ivie had not found the right position for himself, but that was where the similarities ended. Thomas was fast with strong defensive skills but little power at the plate. Ivie was a slow power hitter with little defensive value. Ivie was originally drafted as a catcher, first overall in 1970, but his modest defensive ability at that position limited him to nine big league games behind the plate. He had also played a little third but ended up playing mostly first base, the position where slow sluggers who struggle with the glove usually land. While Ivie's powerful bat from the right side of the plate was a welcome addition to the team, it was not clear where he would play on the Giants either. He was unlikely to push either third baseman Darrell Evans or the great Willie McCovey at first base for playing time. Despite this, the trade seemed like a good one for the Giants who had more speedy outfielders and glove first infielders than they needed and had experienced a hard time scoring runs in 1977.

About two weeks after acquiring Ivie, the Giants made one of their best and most important trades in their time in San Francisco. When spring training of 1978 began, Vida Blue was 28 years old. The lefty had already established himself as one of the very best pitchers in the game. The 121 wins he had accumulated from his breakout 1971 season through 1977 were the ninth most in baseball. His 1,256 strikeouts were seventh in all of baseball for this period. His 26 shutouts were a similarly impressive eighth amongst all pitchers for those years, while only six pitchers had thrown 1,500 or more innings with an ERA lower than Blue's 2.89. Over this period, among left-handed pitchers, Blue had been either the best or second best, behind only Steve Carlton of the Cardinals and Phillies. Bruce Jenkins, who has been watching baseball for well over half a century and as a youth was able to see Sandy Koufax and Don Drysdale pitch at Dodger Stadium, said of Blue: "He and Nolan Ryan were given two of the greatest arms ever bestowed upon a human being. . . . The arm never went bad on him."[1]

Bolstered by the visibility of being a key pitcher on five straight division-winning teams, including three straight World Series winners, with the Oakland A's, Blue was one of the most recognized stars in the game. He was also desperate to get out of Oakland. As 1977 wound down, Blue found himself not preparing for the postseason as had been the case during his first five full seasons with the A's, but on a last-place club. Instead of having teammates like Reggie Jackson, Catfish Hunter, Rollie Fingers, and Bert Campaneris, he was surrounded by less-than-immortals like Wayne Gross, Rob Picciolo, Rick Langford, and Bob Lacey. Blue told me that during his last seasons with the A's "I had been, in my opinion, held hostage by Mr. Finley. . . . It was time I got the heck out of Oakland."[2]

Blue was not stuck with the A's because the team wanted to rebuild around him, but because every time Charlie O. Finley tried to move him to another team, Major League Baseball blocked him. In June of 1976, Finley sold Blue to the Yankees and Rollie Fingers and outfielder Joe Rudi to the Red Sox. However, commissioner Bowie Kuhn voided the deal as not being in the best interest of baseball, presumably because it would have transferred three star players to already strong teams. At the end of the season, Rudi and Fingers left the A's through free agency, signing with the Angels and Padres respectively, but Blue was stuck in Oakland. Despite how bad the 1977 A's were, Blue had a solid year going, 14–19 with a 3.83 ERA. It was not Blue at his best, but he pitched 279.2 innings of league average, or slightly better, baseball. On a contending team, that would have been very valuable.

After the season, Finley again tried to move Blue to another already powerful team—this time to the Cincinnati Reds. The Reds had already strengthened their pitching by adding Tom Seaver midway through the 1977 season, and by adding Blue would have had two top-tier pitchers to go with an offense that was not quite as strong as it had been in 1975–76 but was still one of the best in baseball. In exchange, the A's were to receive first base prospect Dave Revering and $1.75 million. Again, Kuhn reversed the traded, citing the best interests of baseball, and again Blue was back in Oakland.

As spring training of 1978 began, Blue was preparing to play another frustrating season with an A's team that looked not much better than the one from the previous campaign. The Giants had never been part of the Vida

Blue discussions over the previous year or two because they were not seen as a wealthy team who could part with cash to get a pitcher who could make a real difference in the postseason like the Reds and Yankees were, so when news of the trade broke it was a surprise. More surprising was how little the Giants gave up to acquire the star southpaw. Gary Alexander, Dave Heaverlo, Phil Huffman, John Henry Johnson, Gary Thomasson, Alan Wirth, and Mario Guerrero were neither established players nor top prospects. Alexander, a young catcher with some pop in his bat, was probably the best player the Giants sent to Oakland, but the rest of the players were essentially role players who could contribute a little to a big-league team but were never going to be frontline talent. Alexander managed a decent 1978 season with the A's and Indians but never hit much after that and was out of baseball following the 1981 season. The Giants also sent $300,000 to the A's. That was a lot of money for a player in those days, but it was worth it to get Blue.

The Vida Blue trade was finalized in mid-March, but this time Kuhn let the trade stand. The Giants were not a wealthy, or even a particularly good, team so in the view of the commissioner, who was increasingly overwhelmed by the changes associated with free agency, the trade was good for the game. It was certainly good for the Giants. The Giants had landed one of the top pitchers in the game for a bunch of spare parts and $300,000. This trade, along with the addition of Mike Ivie, meant that the Giants, after a slow off-season at first, appeared to be the most improved team in the division.

Blue was immediately slated as the Giants' ace, thus making a relative strength of the team, starting pitching, even stronger. Blue's presence also meant that all the other starting pitchers could labor under less pressure. The Count and Bob Knepper, a young lefty who had impressed in 1977, no longer had to be aces, as Blue would take care of that. The addition of Blue also meant that the Giants top three starting pitchers were as good as those of any team in the league. Similarly, Ed Halicki, the towering righty who stood 6'7" would now be at the back end of the rotation, where he would be much more than adequate. Baseball pundits now had to reevaluate the National League West. Most did not think this trade made the Giants favorites but understood that they could force themselves into the race if everything else fell into place.

The acquisition of Vida Blue was bigger than simply adding a top-notch pitcher: It was a statement as well. Blue was the biggest star the Giants had added in recent memory. Spec Richardson, the general manager who made the trade, had already traded for Bill Madlock and Darrell Evans, but these two players, while very good, were not stars with the cachet of a Vida Blue.

Additionally, the Giants had not done much during the first two years of free agency. The signing of Willie McCovey turned out to be a good move, but McCovey was an aging former star when the Giants reacquired him. The Vida Blue trade was a statement by the Giants indicating that they were no longer going to be pushovers and were going to try to contend in 1978.

Blue himself had been desperate to get out of Oakland and away from Charlie Finley, but once he crossed the bay and changed teams, he had a very different relationship with his team's owner. Bob Lurie spoke very highly of Blue: "Vida Blue—to me just a wonderful excellent guy, very friendly and easy going . . . he was a good part of the team. He'd go out and sell and promote."[3] Blue described the difference between Finley and Lurie as "day and night, night and day," adding, "Lurie was, and still is, a class guy."[4]

Despite the excitement around the Blue trade, as Opening Day approached, it was clear that if the Giants were going to contend, more or less everything had to go right in 1978: Blue had to improve on his 1977 season, which was, by his standards, an off year; the rest of the rotation and the bull pen had to pitch at least as well as they had in 1977; McCovey had to continue to play as well as he did in 1977 despite turning 40 during the off-season; Madlock had to make the shift to second base without any problems and have a good year with the bat; Evans needed to continue his underrated production; and Larry Herndon in center and Terry Whitfield in left needed to build on their promise from 1977. Catcher Marc Hill and shortstop Johnnie LeMaster were not expected to do much. Another major key for the Giants in 1978 would be if Jack Clark could continue to develop as a hitter.

This was a lot to hope for, but the 1978 Giants were a young team, with the entire starting outfield as well as pitcher Bob Knepper 25 years old or younger. Additionally, the rest of the starting rotation, top relievers Randy Moffitt and Gary Lavelle, and infielders Madlock and Ivie, were all under 30. That was a good sign for a team that needed improvement from many of their players to contend.

Amazingly, for the Giants, 1978 was one of those rare years when essentially everything went right. Jack Clark broke through as a star. Bill Madlock became an all-star-caliber second baseman and, after moving to the leadoff spot early in the season, became one of the best in the game in that role as well. Manager Joe Altobelli found a way for Mike Ivie to contribute with his bat with 352 plate appearances. Outfielders Larry Herndon and Terry Whitfield, and even light-hitting shortstop Johnnie LeMaster, improved slightly from 1977 to 1978. Modern analytics show that Clark, Evans, Herndon, Ivie,

LeMaster, Madlock, and Whitfield each had more WAR in 1978 than in 1977. Among position players, only McCovey and Hill accumulated fewer WAR in 1978 than 1977.

Blue ended up having a great 1978 for the Giants, winning 18 games, starting the All-Star Game for the National League and coming in third in the Cy Young Award voting. He, fifth starter Jim Barr, Knepper, who emerged as one of the league's top lefties in 1978, and John Montefusco all had more WAR in 1978 than in 1977. Only Ed Halicki, and relievers Gary Lavelle and Randy Moffitt, regressed in 1978 relative to 1977 according to this measure.

Numbers, particularly ones as anodyne as WAR, only represent a small part of the Giants in 1978. The team was in first place for more than half the season, including almost the entire summer, and started a renaissance of interest in baseball and the Giants in the Bay Area. The more than 1.7 million fans who saw the Giants play at Candlestick that year was not only the most since 1960, but it was well over twice the figure from 1977.

The 1978 team was also significant because other than Willie McCovey, who slumped badly in 1978 and was not a major contributor on the field, this Giants team was young with no connections to the era of Willie Mays. Unlike in 1971, this was not a case of a team managing to squeeze one more postseason appearance out of an aging core, rather it was a team of relative unknowns surprising the baseball world. Only Blue was a nationally known star. Madlock was a respected hitter, and two-time NL batting champion, but he did not enjoy a significant national profile. Other than Blue, the best pitcher on that team was Bob Knepper, who, as a 24-year-old, went 17–11 with a 2.63 ERA. The best hitter, by far, was Jack Clark, who had a breakout season at age 22, hitting .306/.358/.537, including a 26-game hitting streak, the longest of any Giant since the nineteenth century. Both Clark and Knepper were in only their second full year in the big leagues.

The number of young players on the Giants and the degree to which they exceeded expectations during the almost four months they were in first place made the Giants not only a good team, but an exciting and fun one. For most of the season, the pressure was not on the Giants but on the Reds and Dodgers, two teams with star-studded lineups and well-known players who for most of the summer found themselves trailing a Giants team that was getting big hits from the likes of Terry Whitfield and Larry Herndon and great pitching from people like Bob Knepper and Ed Halicki, none of whom were familiar names to baseball fans outside of San Francisco and the Bay Area. Fans who had spent more than 15 years being disappointed by Giants teams that, despite the presence of superstars like Mays, McCovey, Marichal, and later Bobby Bonds, could never win a pennant and hadn't made it back to the World Series since 1962, could look at this team a little differently. These Giants were young, untested, and, for most of the summer, finding a way to stay in first place.

That 1978 season also saw the rivalry with the Dodgers once again mean something on the field. Not since 1971, when the Giants edged out the Dodgers by one game, had these two teams played so many meaningful and memorable games against each other. The Dodgers got the better of the Giants in 11 of the 18 games they played against each other in 1978, but there were still some big Giants victories against Los Angeles that season.

Several of those Giants-Dodgers games from 1978 stand out as some of the most exciting Giants games of the era, but one continues to have a special place in the hearts of older Giants fans. It was still relatively early in the season when the Dodgers came to San Francisco for a Memorial Day weekend series. The two teams split the first two games, setting the stage for a Sunday rubber match. The teams were not scheduled to play each other on the Memorial Day holiday itself.

The Giants began the day with a record of 27–15, the best in the National League, but they were only half a game up on the Reds and two and a half games ahead of the Dodgers. The 56,103 fans who packed Candlestick Park on Sunday, May 28, was at that time the largest ever to see a baseball game in the Bay Area. The season was just about one fourth over, but that day already had the feel of a pennant race. The Dodgers were going with their ace, Don Sutton. The ideal pitching matchup would have pitted Sutton against the new Giants ace, Vida Blue, but Blue had pitched the previous day, giving up only two runs in a seven-inning losing effort. Instead, the Giants' pitcher that day was The Count.

That made for, in some respects, a more exciting matchup because no Giant hated the Dodgers more than John Montefusco. If any player on that Giants team, other than Willie McCovey, who had been around in the early 1960s when the rivalry had been at its most intense ever, personified the Giants-Dodgers rivalry, it was The Count. He made no apologies for hating the Dodgers, attributing that feeling in part to having grown up a Yankees fan in New Jersey. The Dodgers fans and players, in turn, hated Montefusco because of his arrogance as well as his frequent mastery over their team.

Unfortunately, The Count was not at his best that day. He gave up five runs, four earned, on eight hits and four walks in six full innings and part of a seventh. By the time the Giants came to bat in the bottom off the sixth, they were behind 3–0 in a game that, despite occurring in late May, was extremely important for a team that was still hovering between being a real contender and just having a hot spring.

After the first five batters came up in the bottom of the sixth, the feel of the game had begun to shift. Four of those batters had reached base safely, but only one had come in to score. Thus, with one out, the Giants had the bases loaded. Unfortunately, they also had the weakest part of their lineup, backup infielder Vic Harris, who was the shortstop that day, light-hitting, second-string catcher Mike Sadek, and then the pitcher, due up.

One of the keys to the Giants success in 1978 was Joe Altobelli. Altobelli spent parts of three seasons between 1955 and 1961 as an outfielder and first baseman with the Twins and Indians, but never hit enough, as shown by his .210 batting average and five home runs over 290 plate appearances, to have much of a big-league career. After his playing days, Altobelli managed for 11 years in the Orioles' system but was stuck behind future Hall of Fame manager Earl Weaver, who was a fixture in Baltimore. Altobelli finally got his break when the Giants hired him to manage in 1977, but 1978 was the year when the longtime minor-league player and manager had the Midas touch.

The Giants had a chance to get back in the game, but Altobelli, who had turned 46 two days earlier, knew that Harris and Sadek were unlikely to get the runs in. Altobelli decided to go for it and brought in his best bat off the bench even though it was only the sixth inning and his best bat was right-handed and would have the platoon disadvantage against Sutton, who was also a righty. It was precisely the kind of moment for which Mike Ivie, who at that point in the season was hitting around .350 with a couple of home runs as a part time player, was acquired.

Ivie did not disappoint, driving an offering from Sutton over the distant fence in left center field to give the Giants a 5–3 lead. The reaction in the packed Candlestick Park was electric as the fans celebrated the huge grand slam. The Giants held on to win the game 6–5, taking two out of three from the Dodgers in a big early season series. Mike Ivie's grand slam was the most memorable moment in an oddly memorable season. It was also the first truly great moment of the Bob Lurie era, the biggest Giants' hit since 1971, and one of the top highlights of the 16 years the Giants spent between postseason appearances.

Longtime Giants marketing director Pat Gallagher, who was then in his second year with the team in 1978, described the feel of the moment well: "Over 50,000 fans went nuts in the seats. I'll never forget it. I actually had tears running down my cheeks. Broadcaster Lon Simmons just about turned himself inside out with his radio call. I still get goose bumps every time I hear it. I had only known the frustration of losing baseball up until then. All of a sudden, the Giants were on top of the National League West and the excitement and momentum was contagious."[5] Larry Baer, who was a college student and a Giants fan at the time described how "I was completely seduced by the Giants of 1978 with Mike Ivie hitting the grand slam that I'll never forget," and summarized the feel around that team and that moment "and Vida Blue and the Giants kind of were back."[6]

When the Giants hosted the Dodgers in San Francisco on August 3, the season was two thirds over. The Giants record stood at 64–44, the best in the National League and second in all of baseball. However, the Reds and Dodgers were still keeping the pressure on. The standings before that game were the same as they had been the morning of the Ivie grand slam. The Reds were half a game back with the Dodgers only two and a half back. The two teams were set to play each other eight times in a period of only 11 days, four in San Francisco followed by four in Los Angeles the following weekend. The Dodgers could gain ground on the Giants by winning five or more of those games, while if the Giants managed to win six games, they probably could have finished off the Dodgers for the season.

After all eight games had been played, the Dodgers had closed to within one game of the Giants while the Reds had fallen to third place, one and a half games back. The Dodgers' gains came from sweeping a three-game series with the San Diego Padres during the week between the two Giants-Dodgers series. The eight games the two teams played resolved little. A total of more than 400,000 fans poured into Candlestick Park from August 3 to 6 and Dodger Stadium the following weekend. The teams split both series, but other than the first two games in Los Angeles, which the Dodgers won handily, fans saw some great baseball. Two of the games were decided by walkoffs and a third went 11 innings. All told, five of the eight games were decided by one run. Unlike the Mike Ivie game, these eight games occurred in August when, in the pre–wild card era, pennant races already had begun in earnest. Few had expected the Giants to be anywhere near the division lead, let alone in first place by mid-August, but at least for the moment, they were proving to be a very tough team.

Unfortunately, after playing so well against the Dodgers in early August, reality finally caught up with the Giants. Within a week they had fallen two games behind the Dodgers and were never in first place again that year. From

August 14 through the end of the season, the Giants lost more games than they won, while the Dodgers proved themselves a relentless and consistent team, ultimately going on to win the division by 2½ games over the second place Reds and six over the Giants. They then easily handled the Phillies in the NLCS and won the first two games of the World Series before the Yankees won the next four games.

Two of the best players on that 1978 Giants team were Vida Blue and Jack Clark. Blue was only 28 but was already a three-time World Series winner and a recognized star when the Giants acquired him in spring training. Giants fans were already familiar with Blue because he had spent all of his career until then playing across the bay in Oakland. They were aware of his value to the team, but the extent to which he brought new energy, confidence, and a sense of fun to the team could not have been predicted.

Blue's career in Oakland had been a strange one. Following brief trials with the A's in 1969 and 1970, he joined the team full time as a 21-year-old in 1971. He then had one of the greatest seasons ever for a young pitcher. Blue was technically not a rookie in 1971 because of the 80⅔ innings he pitched for the A's in 1969 and 1970, so he could not win the league's Rookie of the Year Award. However, he more than compensated for that by being chosen as the winner of the league's Cy Young and Most Valuable Player Awards. Blue led the league with a 1.82 ERA and eight shutouts while striking out 301 batters on the way to a 24–8 record. The A's won their division that year, but like the Giants lost in the NLCS.

A prolonged contract negotiation in 1972 contributed to Blue having an off year, but the A's won their first of three consecutive World Series. Blue bounced back to be an integral part of the 1973 and 1974 championship teams while establishing himself as one of baseball's premier left-handed pitchers.

The winning teams that Blue played on in Oakland were unlike any baseball had seen before, or since. They wore green and gold uniforms in many different combinations. Many of their players grew their hair long and sported facial hair. When they met the much more conservative looking Reds in the 1972 World Series, the match was described as the hairs versus the squares. The hairs won. Those A's teams had some great characters and egos. Blue, whose swagger and fastball were among the very best in the league, was joined in the starting rotation by recognized ace Catfish Hunter. Hunter was a good old boy from North Carolina who gave up some long home runs but seemed to always come up with a big win when the team needed it most, as reflected in his 7–2 postseason record during his time with the A's. There was no bigger or better-known star on that A's team, or in all of baseball during those years, than their right fielder and best home run hitter, Reggie Jackson. Reggie was one of the most exciting and outspoken stars in the game throughout the 1970s.

Those A's teams were anything but harmonious as they fought a lot with each other and with their owner Charlie O. Finley. Finley was a smart baseball man and ingenious promotor, but he was unable to control his temper, refused to pay people fairly, and had no idea how to run a big-league baseball operation off the field. Beginning with Catfish Hunter's departure via free agency after the 1974 season, and the trade of Reggie Jackson to the Orioles after the following season, the team began to fall apart. By 1977, Blue found himself playing for an owner he did not like, who he still believed never paid him fairly, while all his former teammates were being paid much more to play on much better teams. Naturally, this did not leave him with a reservoir of good feeling for the A's, Finley, or Major League Baseball.

Fortunately, all of that changed when he got to the Giants. Blue embraced being on the Giants as if he had a fresh new start to his career. In addition to his stellar work on the field, he emerged as a team leader. Although he was only 28, Blue had a championship pedigree that no other Giant could approach. Blue was never going to challenge the leadership role of Willie McCovey, who was so respected and beloved in San Francisco by 1978 that Mayor Moscone, who had worked so hard to keep the Giants in town, said that McCovey was a San Francisco institution comparable to the Golden Gate Bridge, but Blue's and McCovey's temperaments were quite different and complimented each other. The star pitcher reflected on having McCovey as a teammate in San Francisco after the two had briefly been teammates with the A's at the end of 1976: "I learned that he [McCovey] was a beloved Giant. When I got traded over here in '78, they put my locker next to his. How cool is that? We lost a good man. . . . He was a great guy. . . . McCovey was a professional guy off the field. Didn't say too much. He was like this gentle giant and people were drawn to him."[7]

Blue, seeking to change things a little bit with his new team, opted to wear his first name on the back of his uniform. This was very unusual in 1978, and even now, but for a player like Vida, who had an unusual first name, it worked. For most of the 1970s, no baseball fan ever had to ask, "Vida who?" Just like there was only one Catfish and one Reggie (although Dodger outfielder Reggie Smith was for a few years about as good as the more famous Reggie), there was only one Vida in baseball. At day games at the 'Stick in 1978, when he wasn't pitching, it was not unusual to see Blue stand up on top of the Giants' dugout to try to get the frequently enormous crowds to cheer for their Giants even more loudly.

Pat Gallagher, who served as director of marketing for the Giants from 1976 through 2008 described Blue's impact in 1978: "Vida . . . pitched for the Giants with a vengeance and also captivated the crowd with his playful attitude and antics in the bull pen when he wasn't on the mound. He whipped up the crowd as a cheerleader. He compared the Giants to 'a little orange skateboard' . . . and the crowds stormed the gates at Candlestick. All of a sudden, Candlestick was the place to be in the summer of 1978."[8] Blue, for his part, said of 1978, "It was a great season, a great time for the city."[9]

Because Blue had been in the Bay Area so long, he seemed to have an understanding of the character of the place, including its irreverence. This led to the description, as noted by Gallagher, of the 1978 Giants to the press as the Little Orange Skateboard. At a time when the NL West was dominated by the Big Red Machine, with the power and hitting efficiency suggested by that name, and the Dodgers, whose manager Tommy Lasorda, seemed to never stop talking about Dodger Blue, the Little Orange Skateboard was the perfect image for the Giants. Skateboards have long been popular and practical, as well as dangerous, in San Francisco because of the city's famous hills. By the late 1970s they were also beginning to be associated with the counterculture, particularly the punk rock scene that was stirring in the city's North Beach neighborhood.

The punk rock scene which had arisen in the aftermath of, and as a reaction to, the Summer of Love and the music and counterculture of the 1960s, contributed to the image of San Francisco by the late 1970s as a strange and even dangerous city. A relatively small number of punks in North Beach, and a huge gay population growing in political power, were helping to solidify San Francisco's stature as being unlike any other American city. For a young person, this gave the city a progressive, avant-garde, and exciting vibe, but for a deeply conservative pastime like baseball, it raised challenges. Gradually the Giants learned how to connect to their unique city, but it took time.

Blue was the first star acquisition of the Bob Lurie era, but Jack Clark was the first real star the farm system had produced since Lurie took over the team. In Lurie's first spring training after he bought the team, Clark was the standout prospect, but he spent most of 1976 in the minor leagues. In 1977, he was already the big-league club's starting right fielder, but he only hit .252/.332/407. Those were very good numbers for a 21-year-old rookie, but they still suggested a player with potential rather than one who was already a significant contributor.

Clark had a terrific season in 1978, emerging as the best hitter on the Giants, a status he retained for the next five years, and one of the best young outfielders in baseball. He hit .306/.358/.537 while leading the team in slugging percentage, OPS[10], runs, hits, doubles, triples, home runs, RBIs, and total bases. He also emerged as the team's most reliable clutch hitter. It was Jack Clark who the fans wanted to see at the plate in any big moment. In 1978, it seemed that more often than not he came through.

All of the other big hitters on that 1978 team, Darrell Evans, Mike Ivie, Bill Madlock, and Willie McCovey had been acquired, or in the case of McCovey reacquired, in recent years. None of them were around when Lurie had bought the team in 1976. Evans, Ivie, and Madlock had cost the team a first baseman who was no longer needed, a utility infielder, and a disgruntled outfielder, respectively. Clark, along with most of the important pitchers on that team, other than Blue, were already in the Giants' farm system when Lurie bought the team. Nonetheless, the strong 1978 team was, to a significant extent, a result of Lurie's and general manager Spec Richardson's effort to remake the team over the course of the preceding two years.

The real strength of that team was pitching. The staff that Vida Blue joined in 1978 included The Count, Ed Halicki, and Bob Knepper, all of whom were coming off of seasons where their ERA had been below 3.50. Knepper was a particularly promising young player as he began the 1978 season as a 24-year-old following a rookie year in which he had gone 11–9 with a 3.36 ERA. The two mainstays of the Giants' 1978 bull pen, Randy Moffitt and Gary Lavelle, were both also under 30 and had enjoyed strong 1977 seasons. Blue was the capstone to the staff, but most of the other important pitchers in 1978 had been drafted in the last years of the Horace Stoneham era.

A losing streak in early September finished off the Giants season. They were still only three games back after beating the Braves 8–5, buoyed by two home runs by Madlock and one by Evans, on September 8, but a week later, after dropping seven in a row, the Giants were nine games out with 14 left to play and essentially out of the race. Although the last few months of the season had not gone the way the Giants would have liked, it had still been a great year for the team—one that suggested a good future built around this strong nucleus of young players.

One of the strangest things about the 1978 season was how the Giants improved so dramatically, but it was equally surprising how quickly they reverted to mediocrity, finishing below .500 each of the next two years and one game above .500 in the strike-shortened 1981 season. The core of that

1978 team never contended again. Corey Busch, who began working for the Giants in 1979, sought to explain this by arguing that "the addition of Vida Blue created an energy level and an enthusiasm. . . . They caught lightning in a bottle . . . but it was put together pretty haphazardly."[11] Another reason why that group never contended again was that the starting pitchers were overused. Halicki and Montefusco wrestled with arm injuries and were never again effective over a full season. Even Vida Blue, after an off year in 1979, rebounded to be a very solid pitcher from 1980 to 1982 but was never again as good as he had been in 1978.

Knepper, the youngest of those four starters, regressed slightly following 1978, going 18–28 with a 4.37 ERA over the course of 1979 and 1980. Although he would never have a season quite as good as 1978, Knepper was one of the better left-handed pitchers in the National League from 1984 to 1988. Unfortunately, he had those good years with the Houston Astros, who acquired him in a trade with the Giants following the 1980 season. In exchange for Knepper, the Giants received an infielder named Enos Cabell who had no particular value, despite playing in 96 games and being the Giants' primary first baseman in a season that was shortened by about a third during the one year he played in San Francisco.

The Knepper for Cabell trade was a bad one by any measure, but it also captured the directionless feel of the Giants for much of the early 1980s. In 1982, in the first published *Baseball Abstract*, Bill James's annual baseball analytics series that helped revolutionize how baseball is understood, James wrote of Cabell: "How can you play full time if you don't do anything. The guy hit .255 (the league average was .255), hit only 2 home runs drew only 10 walks, had more caught stealing (7) than stolen bases (6) and played the least demanding position in the field. Badly. Why would a team keep somebody like that in the lineup."[12] Although this comment was aimed at Cabell, who James ranked as 24th among all 26 starting first basemen, at times in the early and mid-1980s this critique could have been applied to many players who passed through San Francisco. To the Giants' credit, Cabell was gone before the 1982 season began.

The offense was another story. Jack Clark was never quite as good as he had been in 1978 but remained a very good hitter, when healthy, for the rest of his stay with the Giants, and indeed for the rest of his career. Clark was traded to the Cardinals before the 1985 season. Evans also remained a very good hitter before departing for Detroit as a free agent following the 1983 season. Bill Madlock was sent to the Pirates midway through the 1979 season for a package of pitchers who, other than Al Holland, never quite made it with the Giants.

The oddest post-1978 story was that of Mike Ivie. By 1979, Ivie's bat was too good to keep out of the Giants lineup, so he started 76 games at first base, 24 in left field, and two at third base. Altogether he managed to come to the plate a career high 455 times and hit .286/.359/.547, leading the team in on-base percentage, slugging percentage, OPS, home runs, and RBIs. He turned 27 in August of that season and with McCovey showing his age, was poised to be the regular first baseman into the 1980s.

Ivie got off to a slow start in 1980 and even landed on the disabled list due to "mental exhaustion" in early June, but then, on June 25, he stunned the Giants and their fans by announcing his retirement. Ivie's announcement came just a few days after the 42-year-old McCovey announced he was retiring, so when the local media broke the news, some fans thought for a moment the media had mixed up the Giants' first basemen, but they had not. Ivie made this announcement only hours before that Wednesday night game was about to start, a game for which he had already been penciled into the lineup. Ivie's comments in the next day's *San Francisco Chronicle* were cryptic: "It's not that I'm unhappy, it's just that I figured its time for Mike Ivie to retire. And I'm walking away from a bundle of money. . . . I quit once before when I was 18 or 19. . . . So this is nothing new. Now I'm going in search of a nine to five job." The article also noted that Ivie's retirement would cost him about $1.5 million in salary he would not be able to collect.[13]

From the perspective of the twenty-first century, Ivie's words strongly suggest that he was wrestling with some combination of depression and anxiety that made playing big-league baseball very difficult, but back then few in baseball knew what to make of Ivie's decision, and even fewer were interested or knew how to get him the help he needed. Ivie's retirement was short-lived as he was back in the lineup on the 26th and played for the team until mid-September, when he wrapped up his season early due to a back injury.

The Giants did not know what to do about Ivie. Their manager, Dave Bristol, displayed nothing but insensitivity, asserting after the season was over, "we've got to get rid of the cancer on the club. . . . When he came back after that 'retirement' and we were on a winning streak, you could just see the air go out of the players. . . . He's got a lot of con in him too."[14] The team ended up trading Ivie to the Houston Astros and got one pretty good player, Jeffrey Leonard, and another useful backup first baseman, Dave Bergman, in return. Nonetheless, Ivie's early retirement, and battles with depression and anxiety, were a blow to the team that cost them one of their top power hitters. Ivie never quite overcame his psychological demons to become the player he could have been, and he bounced between Houston and Detroit through the 1983 season. He was never again even close to being as good as he was in 1978 and 1979.

The Giants team from which Ivie retired in 1980 was only slightly better than the 1979 version. Dave Bristol's 1980 Giants won 75 games, four more than in 1979, but finished in fifth place, 17 games behind the first-place Astros. Vida Blue bounced back from his poor 1979 season to reclaim his role as the team ace, going 14–10 with a 2.97 ERA. Bob Knepper, 9–14 with a 4.10 ERA, and John Montefusco, 4–8 with a 4.37 ERA, were the only other starting pitchers from 1978 who were still around. Gary Lavelle was still a valuable arm out of a bull pen that was now led by Greg Minton and Al Holland.

The offense in 1980 was a shell of the 1978 version, scoring only 573 runs, the lowest total in all of baseball. Jack Clark was again one of the best hitters in the league, with a slash line of .284/.382/.517, but injuries limited him to 127 games. Darrell Evans was his usual productive and reliable self, hitting .264/.359/.414. Bill North was once again very good in the leadoff spot, getting on base more than 37 percent of the time and stealing 45 bases in 64 tries, but the rest of the offense did nothing. Johnnie LeMaster and free agent bust Rennie Stennett were perhaps the least productive double play combination in baseball. Ivie stopped hitting during a difficult year. Milt May, Terry Whitfield, Larry Herndon, and a few others would have been useful role players on a better team but did not do much for the Giants.

The highlight of the 1980 season was once again a relatively early season game against the Dodgers. When the Giants hosted Los Angeles for a double-header on Sunday June 29, they started the day 32–39, 11 games behind the first-place Astros. The 50,229 fans who were at that doubleheader knew that it was a special day because it would be Willie McCovey's last game in San Francisco against the Dodgers. McCovey, who was 42 and had not hit well since 1977, had announced his retirement a week earlier.

The first game started out as a good pitching duel, as Dodgers ace Don Sutton and Bob Knepper, in one of his best starts of the year, were evenly matched through eight and a half innings, and the score was tied at three. By this time, Sutton was tiring, so Tommy Lasorda brought in Bobby Castillo, who had been one of the Dodgers' better relievers over the previous few seasons. Rennie Stennett, Rich Murray, and Johnnie LeMaster, three weak hitters, were due up for the Giants. Stennett singled, but Rich Murray, who was the brother of one future Hall of Famer—Eddie Murray—and was being asked to replace another—Willie McCovey—popped up to the pitcher and LeMaster struck out.

The right-handed Castillo needed one more out to send the game into extra innings, but Dave Bristol was not going to send Knepper, who was due up, to hit. The Giants skipper really only had one option and 50,000 fans knew it. The not-quite-ageless Willie McCovey made his way to the plate to the applause of Giants fan, applause that was part hope and part gratitude for all the great moments and great baseball "Stretch," as McCovey was known, had provided for us. The great, left-handed pull hitter went to the opposite field but managed to hit the ball hard enough for a game winning double. McCovey would go on to play four more games, including two at the 'Stick, but for Giants fans that pinch hit double was the memory that we wanted to preserve of the man who is still perhaps the most beloved player in Giants history.

The two players from that 1978 team who remained with the Giants the longest after that season were Greg Minton, an excellent reliever who had only pitched 15 innings for the team in 1978, and the player who had been the starting shortstop for that 1978 team, Johnnie LeMaster. In 1978, LeMaster was the weakest offensive link in the lineup. Chris Speier, who had preceded LeMaster as the Giants' starting shortstop, described LeMaster to me as a "really a good shortstop a good defensive ballplayer," but quickly added that "the poor kid couldn't hit a lick."[15] Speier's description of LeMaster, at least with regards to his hitting, was accurate. In 1978, LeMaster hit .235/.293/.335, but those numbers don't quite capture how poor of a hitter he was. Over the course of that season, LeMaster hit a grand total of one home run while driving in only 14 runs in over 300 plate appearances. LeMaster did not really compensate for his meager power with any speed, as he stole only six bases in 1978. Moreover, he was caught stealing six times, so his impact on the bases was also negative.[16]

LeMaster was the Giants' starting shortstop through 1984, before being traded to the Indians early in the 1985 season. He never really improved his hitting, and his 1978 season was one of his best, if that is the right word, with the bat. During his time with the Giants, LeMaster hit .225 with a total of 21 home runs over parts of 11 seasons. While nobody could defend LeMaster's hitting, his defensive value was more debatable. Some, like Speier, who played 1,900 big-league games at shortstop, thought LeMaster was a fine defender, while others viewed him as a subpar fielder whose poor defense was overshadowed by his inept offense.

Bruce Jenkins was in the second category regarding LeMaster's defense:

LeMaster, he was a comical figure among Giants fans. He couldn't hit at all and he wasn't that great of a fielder. Not if you saw Ozzie Smith. . . . It said something about the Giants as a mediocrity that he was the shortstop. . . . He didn't do anything particularly well. I felt bad for him because the fans were all over him. . . . He was a good-hearted guy. . . . He rolled with a million punches. . . . It was an era that lasted a little too long for my liking.[17]

The data suggest that Jenkins's opinion is closer to being right. LeMaster never won a Gold Glove, although given that his career overlapped entirely with that of Ozzie Smith, it is not exactly fair to hold that against him. However, his 0.3 defensive WAR and 61 fielding runs allowed with the Giants, as well as a fielding percentage that lagged slightly below that of National League shortstops overall during those years, all indicate he was not a great defender.

LeMaster was not a key contributor on that 1978 team. By the time the season ended it was reasonably clear that if the team was going to take another step forward in 1979, they either needed real improvement from LeMaster or to somehow upgrade at shortstop. LeMaster never got better, but the team stuck with him for seven years. LeMaster became a symbol of the team's ineptitude from 1979 to 1985. After Madlock, Montefusco, Ivie, Knepper, and Clark had been traded away, McCovey had retired, Evans departed via free agency, and Blue was traded away and then reacquired by the Giants, LeMaster was still there, failing to hit and never becoming an elite defensive shortstop.

LeMaster is not remembered now as the second to last Giant standing from that 1978 team, but for something he did in July of 1979. Even relatively early in his career, LeMaster had become a target of fans' frustration and was frequently and lustrously booed by Giants fans, so one day he came out for his pregame warmups with a jersey that, instead of having his last name, simply bore the word "Boo" on the back. The fans mostly appreciated what they perceived to be a gesture of humility and humor on the part of their not-so-beloved shortstop. This gesture also likely reflected more than a little frustration on LeMaster's part. Giants clubhouse man Mike Murphy recalled the incident in a 2019 interview and suggested LeMaster "just wanted to change his life a little bit." Murphy quickly also added of LeMaster, "he was a good kid."[18]

Three years into the Lurie ownership, Moscone's efforts in 1976 were looking like a major accomplishment, in part because of the team's strong 1978 season. The 1.7 million fans the Giants drew that year was extraordinary by any measure, but it also relieved Moscone of a commitment he had made in 1976 that might otherwise have come back to haunt him. Moscone had agreed at the time that if the Giants did not draw an average of one million fans a year during the next three years, meaning the 1976 through 1978 seasons, the city would not sue to keep them if they decided to leave. This meant that if the first three years of the Lurie ownership did not go well, he would be free to sell them to somebody seeking to move them to another city. The Giants great year in 1978 meant that in the unlikely chance that Lurie tried to move, the city could be free to explore legal recourse. After 1978, nobody was thinking about the Giants moving anymore—at least not for a few years. Most fans were looking towards 1979 and beyond with a sense of optimism.

In Corey Busch's view, the 1978 season helped Bob Lurie and the Giants strengthen their relationship with San Francisco, and San Franciscans to look at the Giants with a feeling of hope for the first time in years:

> The relationship between the city and the club changed when Bob bought the club. . . . A lot of people in the city realized how close they came to losing it. . . . There were a lot of people in the city who didn't want the team to leave. . . . The near miss in a way changed some attitudes. It was almost like there was a new beginning. '78 really helped because it brought a lot of excitement . . . bringing Vida over, the energy and all the rest of it, the great year they had in 1978 really opened people's eyes.[19]

NOVEMBER 1978

The 1978 Giants brought fans a lot of happiness and slowly began to solidify the bond between the post–Willie Mays Giants and the city of San Francisco. For much of that year, the Giants were the talk of the city, and, during the summer, of much of baseball. Given all that, it is somewhat striking just how quickly the team was forgotten. The fans who were there remember the team, but relatively quickly the memory of 1978 faded into the larger memory of the weaker Giants teams of the mid-1970s through the mid-1980s.[20]

The primary reason for this is, that in the two months following the end of the season, events in San Francisco rapidly overtook anything that had happened on the ball field that year. November is always a slow month for baseball. In those days, the World Series was over by the third week or so of

October. The trades, free agent signings, and other moves that feed the base-ball obsessive's appetite in the off-season didn't usually begin in earnest until the December Winter Meetings, so November is a natural time for baseball to recede into the background. November of 1978 was, in that respect, no different, but in every other way it was one of the most dramatic months that San Francisco, or any other American city, has ever experienced.

From the early 1970s, when Horace Stoneham began trading or selling off the cohort of Hall of Famers that had kept the team competitive throughout the 1960s, through 1977, the Giants' poor attendance was attributable to their poor play on the field as well as to Candlestick Park, but that only explains part of the story. Another reason the Giants struggled was due to San Francisco itself. The period from the mid-1960s through the mid-1970s was one of enormous transition for American society. The civil rights movement, the war in Vietnam, and Watergate radically transformed American politics. The rise of a youth culture, and alongside it a counterculture, changed American society in profound ways as mores about work, appearance, family, and sexuality began to fall away, and many struggled to create a new, freer, and more open society.

In many respects San Francisco was the epicenter of these transitions. The 15 or so years between around 1964 and 1978 saw the city change from a relatively conventional, if unusually beautiful, American city to a global center of the hippie movement and the gay rights struggle, an outpost of strong civil rights advocacy, radicalism of all kinds, and a hotbed of religious and cultural experimentation. These developments drew in some San Franciscans who welcomed these changes, but also engendered a strong backlash. In the 1970s, San Francisco was not yet the beacon of progressive politics and values that it became in the late twentieth century. Rather, it was a deeply contested and divided city.

In 1975, that division had played out in the dramatic mayoral election in which George Moscone, the mayor who by 1978 was partially credited with saving the Giants, narrowly defeated John Barbagelata in a runoff. Moscone was a progressive Democrat. His campaign promises to remake city govern-ment to look more like the people of San Francisco, strong support for gay rights and other civil rights movements, disdain for the business and real estate interests that had run the city for decades, and focus on the interests of the neighborhoods over downtown on development and other issues, made him almost a radical. Barbagelata, by contrast, was a conservative Republican who ran on a probusiness and a fiscally and social conservative platform that appealed to his white working-class base in the western part of the city, and to downtown and real estate interests who cared less about social issues but saw Moscone as a threat to the city's long-standing economic order.

These rapid transitions in San Francisco left little room for residents to pay a lot of attention to generally bad baseball teams playing in a bad ballpark in a distant corner of the city. Many of the newer migrants to the city, whether gay or straight, came seeking a new way of life that left little room for baseball. The Giants, like most teams, had no idea how to adapt to this. Baseball was an old and conservative institution that suffered as many parts of the country embraced the new and nontraditional. In no city was this contrast more dramatic than San Francisco.

The San Francisco of which Moscone became mayor in January of 1976 was extremely different from the San Francisco of recent years. While San Franciscans and visitors alike complain of the overheated economy that has led to a boom in population, increase in traffic and congestion, a huge increase in the cost of living, and many lower-income people being displaced, things were quite different in the mid-1970s. The city had been losing population for several decades, not least because of the departure of tens of thousands of high-paying, blue-collar jobs in the shipping and manufacturing sectors. Crime and drugs were ravaging the city while significant swaths of San Francisco, in areas like the South of Market district, were largely empty of homes or businesses.

There was also a lot of good news in San Francisco in the Moscone years. People who had been shut out of governance for decades were finally getting their voices heard at City Hall. The economy may not have been great, but the city was still affordable. New trends in everything from food to music to fashion that would later reshape America were beginning to transform San Francisco. A new civil rights movement, this one advocating for the rights of gays and lesbians, was growing in San Francisco and could count among its leaders a groundbreaking politician and Jewish New Yorker, who had moved to San Francisco in 1971, named Harvey Milk. And, in 1978, a very good San Francisco Giants team had been partially successful in bringing the city together while bringing fun and excitement to many San Franciscans.

Whatever optimism anybody in San Francisco felt when the season ended was cruelly wiped away by the events of that November. The month began with an election that did not feature many competitive races. California's governor, Jerry Brown, a native San Franciscan, was easily reelected while winning almost three quarters of the vote in his hometown. San Francisco's incumbent state and federal legislators, most of whom were Democrats, were almost all reelected easily. The campaign that had energized many San Franciscans the most that November was not between two people but around an initiative, Proposition 6, that sought to institutionalize antigay bigotry by making it legal for schools to fire any teacher who was gay or suspected of being gay.

The most active proponent of Proposition 6 was John Briggs, an assemblyman from Southern California who was hoping to ride antigay backlash to a higher profile in the state's Republican Party. The Briggs Initiative, as Proposition 6 was also called, led in early polls and over the summer was widely believed to be on the way to becoming law. However, in the last few months of the campaign, the anti-Proposition 6 forces began to grow. Most of the state's Democratic leadership, including Governor Brown and Mayor Moscone, campaigned against the bigoted initiative. Some prominent Republicans, including Ronald Reagan, the popular and very conservative former governor of California, also voiced their opposition to the Briggs Initiative, critiquing it from a small government perspective.

The politician who did the most, and was most visible, in the efforts to defeat Proposition 6 was a first-term member of the San Francisco Board of Supervisors. Harvey Milk campaigned throughout the state, frequently debating John Briggs. On Election Day, Proposition 6 was defeated statewide and drubbed in San Francisco. This was a big victory for Milk, who saw his national profile rise as a result of his efforts against Proposition 6.

Shortly after the election, the attention of San Franciscans turned further away from the Giants, but not towards politics, rather we began to focus on Guyana, a tiny country on the northeastern corner of South America. Most Americans, and even most San Franciscans, could not have found Guyana on a map on November 1, 1978. Those who had heard of it might have known that it was, along with Belize, one of two Anglophone countries in South America or that a few years previously many members of the Peoples Temple, a San Francisco–based church group that many thought had strange cultish overtones, had moved there seeking to build a socialist utopia in the thick Guyanese jungle. The leader of that movement was Jim Jones, a charismatic minister who had been deeply involved in civil rights and progressive politics in Indiana, northern California, and finally San Francisco, and had moved to Guyana himself in summer of 1977.

For about a year or so, news had been trickling out of Jonestown, the Peoples Temple outpost in the Guyanese jungle, that raised concerns back in California, the home state of most of the Peoples Temple members in Guyana. San Francisco, in turn, was the city with the strongest ties to the Peoples Temple.

Reports of members being abused or prevented from leaving the commune, extremely difficult working and living conditions, increasingly erratic and megalomaniacal behavior on the part Jones, and even the specter of a mass suicide ordered by Jones, had raised concerns back in the Bay Area.

After the election, Leo Ryan, who had been reelected to Congress from a district just south of San Francisco that happened to be very close to Candlestick Park, went on a fact-finding mission to Jonestown hoping to get some answers and ameliorate the concerns that many friends and families of Peoples Temple members had been raising with him. He did neither. His fact-finding mission started out well as he was allowed to address the members of the Peoples Temple and speak with them in semi-private settings. From these meetings he learned that many of these Temple members wanted to leave, so he sought to help them.

Jones was not amenable to this, likely because he knew that if some members left, the truth—that the Peoples Temple was an abusive cult and that Jones himself was a drug-addicted sexual predator who had exploited his members financially and otherwise—would become widely known. What happened in the days following Ryan's visit to Jonestown is remembered today, although often misunderstood and misnamed.

As Ryan, his party, and a small number of Peoples Temple members seeking to leave Jonestown boarded the airplanes to begin their journey back to California, Peoples Temple security teams, acting on Jones's orders, shot at the group, killing five people, including Ryan. One of the survivors was Jackie Speier, then an aide to Ryan, who decades later went on to serve in Congress as well.

As the news of the killing of Leo Ryan made it back to the United States, things in Jonestown moved quickly and in a horrific and murderous direction. Jones quickly gathered the entire commune and ordered them to drink punch laced with cyanide. Jones's orders were supported not just with words, but by his security team, who were ordered to shoot and kill anybody who did not drink the punch, which was made with Flavor Aid, a cheap powdered drink product similar to Kool-Aid.

The events at Jonestown are now remembered as a mass suicide, but that is not what occurred. Jones forced his victims to drink the poison, while those who refused were shot. This was mass murder, not mass suicide. The total number of victims exceeded 900, making it one of the biggest mass murders in history. Many of those victims had roots in San Francisco, while others had lived in San Francisco for a time and worshipped at the Peoples Temple headquarters on Geary Street, the city's biggest east-west thoroughfare.

The impact of this terrible event on San Francisco was immediate and profound. People in that city mourned the loss of friends and loved ones, looked for answers to figure out how this could have happened, and walked or drove by the Peoples Temple on Geary—that would remain there until it was damaged in the 1989 earthquake—while working through their feelings of anger, confusion, and shock. Suddenly the story of San Francisco in 1978 was not the renaissance of the Giants, but the Peoples Temple massacre.

Politicians, including the mayor, as well as journalists and other opinion leaders, sought to console the city while figuring out how to move forward. Given the scope of the Peoples Temple tragedy, it is little wonder that the small matter of the resignation of a disgruntled member of the Board of Supervisors on the grounds that he could not feed his growing family on his government salary, who within a few days had sought to rescind his resignation and get his old job back, was not of primary concern to Moscone and was not breaking through as a major news story.

Nonetheless, the question of what Moscone would do about the vacancy on the Board of Supervisors was extremely important. If Moscone reappointed Dan White, the supervisor in question, and then sought to rescind his resignation, the board would retain its 6–5 majority against Moscone's progressive agenda. This meant that the legislature, under the leadership of the centrist president of the Board of Supervisors, Dianne Feinstein, would continue to stymie Moscone's efforts to remake the city according to his progressive vision. However, if Moscone replaced the conservative White with a progressive, then he would have a working majority on the board and be able to pass a great deal of important legislation in the last year of his first term.

Several members of the board were encouraging Moscone to ignore White and follow his progressive instincts. These members, including Harvey Milk, were largely pushing an open door as Moscone was too smart of a politician to reappoint White. Over the weekend of November 25–26, fewer than 10 days after the killings in Jonestown, Moscone decided to appoint Don Horanzy, a progressive activist and employee of the Department of Housing and Urban Development, to White's seat.

Shortly before the press conference on Monday, November 27, when Moscone was going to announce Horanzy's appointment, Dan White, who had learned he was not getting reappointed, crawled through an open window in City Hall and walked into Moscone's office asking to meet with the mayor. After Moscone invited White into his office to talk, the former supervisor shot and killed the mayor. Then, he walked down the hall to Harvey Milk's office and shot and killed him as well.

These assassinations plunged a city that was already reeling into an even bigger crisis. The twin traumas of the killings in Jonestown and the assassinations in City Hall led to widespread anger, confusion, and fear as San Franciscans sought explanations and answers while worrying about how their city could move forward.

In the twenty-first century, the cliché of the sports team that helps a city work through a crisis or tragedy is reasonably well known. The Boston Red Sox winning the World Series in 2013, a few months after the Patriots' Day terrorist attack in Boston, the Houston Astros winning the World Series in 2017, a few months after their city had been devastated by a massive hurricane, and the Yankees winning the American League pennant, although losing the World Series in seven games to the Diamondbacks, a few weeks after the terrorist attacks of September 11, 2001, are examples of this.

In 1978, nothing like this happened. For Bob Lurie, who had worked closely and had a bond with George Moscone, the assassinations were a blow, but most of the players lived south of the city, affording them easier access to Candlestick Park, and had little connection with San Francisco. Almost none of the players from that 1978 team with whom I spoke mentioned the assassinations at all. The Giants strong season had been over for more than a month when these tragedies shook San Francisco. Moreover, the team was exciting and full of promise, but had also fallen out of the pennant race by mid-September, so the 1978 team was on the periphery as San Francisco sought to find a way to move forward after the events of November 1978. The city may have needed healing, but it did not turn to ballplayers or teams to help with that. It should also be remembered that the assassinations, particularly the killing of Harvey Milk, further divided an already divided city. While many of us grieved the loss of Moscone and Milk, White's angry homophobia and bigotry, and the actions he took in that regard, were popular with other groups of San Franciscans. Thus, in San Francisco of 1978, even something as seemingly simple as mourning the killings of two elected leaders was complex and politically charged.

November 1978 forever changed the course of San Francisco history. For many, Jonestown was seen as an extreme example of the idealism and rebellion of the 1960s gone deeply awry. This interpretation was never entirely fair or accurate as Jim Jones was hardly a Charlie Manson like figure luring lost hippie kids into his cult. Jones had spent his early years in Indiana and wore a suit, albeit usually with sunglasses even when indoors. Moreover, most of the members of the Peoples Temple were lower-income African Americans of all ages, not young white people who had come to San Francisco searching for answers. Jones was born in 1931, so he was not a baby boomer nor part of the generation that came of age in the 1960s and 1970s.

Jones had certainly traveled in progressive political circles, including providing political support for Moscone in the 1975 election, and being appointed to the city's housing commission by the new mayor after the election. His politics were far left on issues such as civil rights and economic policy, but he was more deeply rooted in American traditions of religious revivalism and hucksterism than in anything to do with the hippie excesses of the 1960s and 1970s.

The assassinations of Moscone and Milk were, in some respects, the actions of one reactionary, homophobic, deeply troubled, and not very smart man, but it was more than that. The assassinations occurred as a key vote regarding a federal consent decree that would have forced the police department to accelerate racial integration. Moscone and Milk backed the consent decree, but with White on the board, the decree was losing by one vote. Most of the police did not support the decree and were counting on White, a former police officer and their man on the Board of Supervisors, to help lead the fight against it. When White unexpectedly resigned, the police union leadership was among those most actively pushing him to get his seat back, because they knew that Moscone's appointee would cast his lot with Milk and the other progressives in support of the Mayor's efforts to integrate the police department.

Thus, White's actions were also part of the broader context of struggles over things like reforming the police. That was very important to many parts of the coalition, including people of color and gay San Franciscans who had helped elect Moscone. For Milk's gay constituents, who had been victims of wanton police violence for years, police reform was particularly important. This was an issue that divided San Francisco, but democracies, cohesive polities, and functioning cities do not solve those divisions with bullets to the heads of elected leaders. The killings angered San Franciscans, particularly those who were supporters of Moscone and Milk, but it also frightened many because it showed just how quickly the city could unravel.

Where, then, did the Giants fit into the gestalt of San Francisco as the 1970s wound down? This was the question with which, implicitly, Lurie had been wrestling since buying the team in 1976.

The 1980 census showed San Francisco's population as just under 679,000, making it the 13th most populous city in the United States, with only about 22,000 fewer people than Indianapolis, then the 12th most populous city in the country.[21] San Francisco was not a particularly small city to have a big-league team at that time, as cities like Boston, Cleveland, and Seattle had smaller populations, but of the 24 teams playing in the United States at the time, 10 were in more populous cities than San Francisco. In smaller cities, sports teams sometimes can play a slightly larger role as there is less competition for entertainment dollars and frequently more of a need for civic pride. No matter how poorly the Yankees or Mets are doing, for example, New Yorkers never waver in their certainty that theirs is the best and most important city in the world. Things are a little different in Pittsburgh, where, for example, in 1979, the World Champion Pirates brought the country's 30th largest city together and were a source of pride for all Pittsburghers.

San Francisco has always been different. In the 1970s, it was a smallish city with a strong big city attitude. While the Giants had been the talk of the town during the spring and summer of 1978, San Franciscans didn't need a baseball team for them to believe their town was an important and special place. This also meant that the ability of the team to play a healing role, or even to find its role, was difficult.

The Giants had struggled with finding their identity in San Francisco since the late 1960s, when a baseball team, even one with the great Willie Mays playing center field, seemed almost incongruous during and after the Summer of Love. By the mid-1970s, Horace Stoneham had more or less given up and was looking for a way out. The team was doing so poorly that Stoneham was forced to trade several of his well-paid stars while the city's attention was rarely anywhere near the Giants. The changes, divisions, and in November 1978, violence and killings, that were always part of life in San Francisco during those years didn't make things any easier for the Giants.

DIANNE FEINSTEIN

The psychological impact of Jonestown and the City Hall assassinations lingered over the city for years, but the political impact was immediate. Moscone was replaced as mayor by the president of the Board of Supervisors, Dianne Feinstein. Feinstein, who had come in third and missed the runoff in the 1975 campaign for mayor, while not a conservative in the national context, was substantially to the right of George Moscone. Dianne Feinstein became mayor in late 1978 and would go on to become one of the most important mayors in her city's history. In 1979, Feinstein was elected to a full term of her own, defeating conservative—by the standards of San Francisco—supervisor Quentin Kopp in a runoff. Four years later she was reelected easily, facing only nominal opposition.

While Feinstein's efforts to hold the city together during a time of extreme crisis and her decision not to roll back Moscone's efforts to make city government more diverse should be lauded, she followed a very different economic vision for San Francisco than her predecessor had. Feinstein was much closer to the downtown real estate and business interests against which Moscone had campaigned in 1975. Her vision for San Francisco included more development, a probusiness environment, and an emphasis on making the city a destination for tourists, conventions, and the like while moving past the hatred and bigotry that had been part of the politics of conservatives like Dan White and John Barbagelata. That model of social tolerance and support for business and real estate has more or less characterized San Francisco's approach to governance well into the twenty-first century.

All sports teams need to maintain good relationships with the governments of the cities where they play. Tax breaks, regulatory issue, transportation, and a myriad other quotidian challenges of running a team require liaising with, and remaining on the good side of, local government. However, in San Francisco as the 1980s approached, this relationship was particularly important because it was becoming increasingly apparent that something had to be done about the Giants home ballpark. It was becoming clear to most observers that the 'Stick was an obstacle that the Giants had to overcome. The freezing evenings, wind, remote location, and huge impersonal feel of the place helped drive attendance down and keep the Giants from genuine success in San Francisco.

During the 17 years Bob Lurie owned the Giants, San Francisco had four different mayors, but Feinstein was mayor for nine of those years. Because of the work Moscone and Lurie had done to keep the Giants in San Francisco, and because they were both seen as having played an instrumental role in that endeavor, the two had enjoyed a good working relationship. Nonetheless, the issue of moving the Giants out of Candlestick into a new home somewhere in San Francisco never came up when Moscone was mayor, but had he lived, and particularly if he had gotten reelected in 1979, it almost certainly would have.

Instead, it was Feinstein who was mayor when the 1980s dawned and the myriad problems of Candlestick Park could no longer be ignored. On the surface, Feinstein had a lot more in common with Lurie than Moscone had. Both Lurie and Feinstein were secular Jews who had ties to the city's old and influential German Jewish community. Both had grown up in comfort and privilege, although the Luries were a lot wealthier than Feinstein's family, and went to elite private universities—Feinstein to Stanford and Lurie to Northwestern. More significantly, they were both representatives of the wealthy communities that were part of the permanent government of San Francisco. Lurie was born into that as his father Louis Lurie was an extremely wealthy real estate investor, civic leader, and philanthropist. Feinstein, whose father was a doctor, did not come from quite that background, but through her studies at Stanford and before the Convent of the Sacred Heart, the city's most prestigious Catholic girls' school, Feinstein developed strong ties to those elites.

During most of Feinstein's nine years in City Hall, the Giants began to accelerate their quest to find a better place to play. In 1976, Lurie and Moscone had worked together in the context of a crisis to stave off the departure of the Giants for Toronto, which both men, along with a lot of other people in San Francisco, believed would have been terrible for their city. After a few years of owning the team, particularly after the 1978 season showed that San Francisco could fall in love with a post–Willie Mays Giants team, Lurie naturally began to turn his attention to ensuring a better home for the team. That quest would last for many years and would not be finally resolved until years after Lurie sold the team, but it began in the late 1970s and early 1980s.

Lurie and Moscone had a good working relationship forged by their cooperation under great pressure in 1976—Corey Busch described how keeping the Giants in San Francisco "made Bob a hero and made Moscone a hero"—but the assassinations of 1978 meant that Lurie's partner as he sought to find a ballpark suitable for the Giants would be Dianne Feinstein, not Moscone. Feinstein and Lurie, despite the similarities in their backgrounds, and their shared concern for the future of San Francisco, never enjoyed the relationship that Lurie and Moscone did. It is ironic that the mayor who critics saw as too beholden to real estate and one of the city's biggest and wealthiest real estate magnates struggled to build a productive and cooperative relationship, but they did.

Beginning in the early 1980s, the Giants began exploring three different paths to solving the problem of Candlestick Park. The first was to explore ways to improve Candlestick. There was not much that could be done about the ballpark because while improvements to concessions, clever marketing campaigns, or even putting a good team on the field could make a marginal difference, the real problem was the climate.

Busch, who joined the Giants' front office in 1979, summarized the extent to which the problem of the ballpark was always on the minds of the Giants management:

The ballpark problem was consistent. It was constant. It was pervasive. It was pervasive within the organization and it was pervasive amongst the fan base. . . . If the team was going to have any long term viability in the city, something was going to have to change regarding Candlestick. We didn't think renovating Candlestick, putting a dome on Candlestick was the answer. We believed that a ballpark closer to town that was properly designed and properly situated was necessary. We knew that if we didn't solve this ballpark problem that ultimately the team was going to leave.[22]

In May of 1981, the Giants issued a press release that stated, "San Francisco Giants President Bob Lurie announced today that the Giants have been actively exploring the feasibility of converting Candlestick Park into a domed, multi-purpose arena. . . . 'Our preliminary studies' said Lurie, 'have shown that from a physical standpoint, Candlestick can be converted.' . . . Lurie indicated that the next step will be to conduct a detailed economic feasibility study to determine if the project is financially possible."[23]

The idea of putting a dome over Candlestick Park may seem far-fetched, even absurd, from the perspective of today, but at the time it made sense to at least explore the idea. Domed stadiums were very popular in the early 1980s and had been relatively successful in Houston, Seattle, and elsewhere. Doming Candlestick would have been a reasonable way to solve the problem and would have not only helped the Giants and 49ers but would have also made Candlestick a more popular place for concerts and other major events. However, even to somebody with no architectural or engineering background, it was apparent that doming Candlestick would be a daunting and expensive task that would only solve some of the problems associated with the ballpark.

The feasibility study, led by Busch, worked for just under a year, issuing its findings in March 1982. The team then issued a

254-page report [that] not only contains an exhaustive analysis of all aspects of such a project, but also includes conceptual drawings and financial projections for an entirely new domed, multi-purpose stadium that could be constructed in downtown San Francisco . . . a fabric dome on Candlestick is structurally possible at an estimated cost of $60 million including related improvements but excluding interest. The estimated cost of building a new downtown stadium is $95 million excluding interest and land acquisition.[24]

In a 2019 interview, Lurie boiled down the findings of the study, which was submitted to Mayor Feinstein, by saying simply that "the cost [of doming Candlestick] was preposterous."[25]

Feinstein did not pursue doming Candlestick after receiving the report. However, in 1983, the mayor commissioned a study to see if Candlestick Park needed any seismic retrofitting and later commissioned some work to be done to make the ballpark safer should there be an earthquake during a game. Most people thought that given how frequently the 49ers sold out regular season and playoff games, she had done that with the football team in mind.

The Giants' study, although ostensibly about doming Candlestick, also presented another option, building a new stadium in a different location in San Francisco. This suggests that while the Giants were on the surface open to doming Candlestick, they probably always knew it was going to be extremely expensive and was less desirable than a new stadium, domed or otherwise, would be. Thus, the report laid the groundwork to pursue the second and third paths to solving the problem of Candlestick, building a new facility in San Francisco or building a ballpark close to San Francisco, most likely down the peninsula.

Although San Francisco had about 250,000 fewer people in 1980 than in 2020, there was still not a lot of empty space. San Francisco is only 49 square miles, making it the second most densely populated city, behind only New York, in the United States. This is in part because San Francisco lies on the northern part of a peninsula. It is surrounded by water on the west, north, and east, and mountains to the south. Therefore, the city has never been able to expand the way many Sunbelt cities, for example, can.

This meant that if San Francisco was going to build a ballpark in the city, the first and probably largest challenge was going to be to identify a space and purchase the needed land. It took another 15 years for the Giants to solve that problem, the same problem which had landed them at Candlestick Point in the first place.

Chapter 4

LABOR PROBLEMS

The Giants began to turn their attention to finding a new ballpark just as the early years of free agency had a very disruptive effect on what had long been a conservative institution. Players were moving from team to team more than ever, or at least that was the appearance. Salaries were quickly increasing, but at first primarily for players who reached free agency. There was something else about free agency that troubled the owners as well as many fans: If free agency could turn a team into a contender very quickly, as was the case with the Angels who won division titles in 1979 and 1982 relying substantially on free agent talent, it could also quickly devastate a team.

The best example of this was the A's, who in one off-season lost Rollie Fingers, Gene Tenace, Bert Campaneris, Sal Bando, Joe Rudi, and Don Baylor to free agency. The impact this had on the A's was quick, but not exactly long-lasting. In 1976, the team had broken their streak of five straight AL West titles but contended most of the season and finished 2½ games behind the Royals. Nineteen seventy-six was the ninth straight year the A's had played better than .500 ball. The team that had won 87 games in 1976 but lost all those players to free agency ended up winning only 63 games in 1977, the first of three consecutive years when they finished in sixth or seventh place. However, due to a strong farm system that produced, among others, Rickey Henderson, as well as some good trades and a new manager, the A's finished in second place in 1980 and won their division in 1981.

One of the reasons this decline was so abrupt for the A's was that the few times A's owner Charlie Finley tried to find a way to address this problem, by moves like selling Blue to the Yankees and Fingers and Rudi to the Red Sox,

Bowie Kuhn stopped him. Finley was not going to be able to sign all his A's stars after the season, but by selling these three would have freed up some money to re-sign, for example, Baylor, Campaneris, and Tenace or to invest in younger players. Today, it is relatively common for struggling teams to get rid of older, highly paid players or to trade players during the year before they became free agents, but Kuhn did not understand that. How the AL East would have looked in the late 1970s with these three players in the division is also fodder for great alternative baseball history. At the time, Kuhn's decision made intuitive sense, but from the perspective today it is less clear because vetoing the deal left Finley with nothing. Today, salary dumps at the trading deadline are very common, but in 1976 things were different.

Kuhn's decision to cancel the sale of three star players to two already good teams reflects the extent to which baseball people, including Finley, Kuhn, MLBPA leader Marvin Miller, and others, including fans and players, were trying to figure out this new world of free agency. Today, most fans understand free agency, arbitration, at what age players begin to decline in value, the damage a bad contract can do to a team, and the relative worth of a top prospect compared to a 30-year-old free agent, but well into the 1980s, most fans, and more than a few baseball executives, did not understand these things.

For teams like the Yankees and Angels and their fans, free agency was great. Between 1977 and 1981, the Yankees won four divisions, three pennants, and two World Series, only missing out on the postseason in 1979. That run of success was, in substantial part, due to Yankee owner George Steinbrenner's willingness to pay top dollar for free agents. Before the 1977 season, the Yankees inked Jackson and Don Gullett, a top left-handed pitcher from the Reds. The next year they went out and signed Rich "Goose" Gossage, the top reliever of the era and, somewhat inexplicably, Rawly Eastwick, another standout reliever. In 1979, they added a pair of elite pitchers: Tommy John, the star left hander on the Dodgers' team the Yankees had defeated in the two previous World Series, and Luis Tiant, who had been the ace of the Red Sox staff. In 1980, they only picked up two solid veterans in pitcher Rudy May and first baseman Bob Watson, but the next year they signed Dave Winfield to a record-shattering contract. Thus, in a five-year period, the Yankees signed three future Hall of Famers—Winfield, Jackson, and Gossage and several other big stars like John, Tiant, and Watson.

The Angels joined the American League in 1961. In their first 17 years, they finished over .500 only twice and never appeared in the postseason. In 1979, the Baylor, Grich, and Rudi triumvirate of free agents helped them win the AL West and make it to the playoffs for the first time. Three years later, Grich, Baylor, and a newer free agent acquisition, Reggie Jackson, who had signed a five-year deal with the Angels after his five years with the Yankees ended, helped the Angels win the AL West again and come within one win of their first World Series.

By the early 1980s, in part because of the Yankees' spending, fans of other teams were beginning to sour on free agency. Seeing a beloved young star leave for another team, or knowing that favorite players could leave once they were eligible for free agency after their sixth year in the big leagues, changed the relationship between teams and their fans. Today, most fans don't think twice about that, but at the time it was significant.

The Giants were among the teams who lost key players to free agency right away. One of the top players in the first free agent class was star Giants outfielder Gary Matthews. Between 1973 and 1976, Matthews, who turned 26 during the 1976 season, had emerged as one of the best young outfielders in the game, slashing .287/.367/.481 for those seasons, stealing about 13 bases a year, and playing a very solid left field. After the 1976 season, amidst charges of tampering, meaning that the Atlanta Braves may have begun negotiating with the star outfielder even before his contract officially expired, Matthews left the Giants for the Braves and remained a very good player for close to another decade. Fans of teams like the Giants or A's who were on the losing side of big free agent moves were exasperated by the new system, which they felt stripped their team of good players, leaving them nothing in return.

The view of many of these fans, while genuine, was problematic. After all, why is a player who plays without a contract for a year and simply has his contract from the previous year extended, the property of that team once the season in question ends? In most work environments where employees are given contracts, they are no longer considered employees of the firm once their contract expires. Matthews, for example, was not under contract with the Giants when he signed with the Braves, although he may have been when the negotiation started.

By the early 1980s, owners wanted to change this system in a way that would both bind players to their teams more while also keeping salaries down. Whereas the strike that led to the cancellation of the last third of the 1994 season and all of the postseason that year was due primarily to the owners' desire for a salary cap, in 1981 the key issue was compensation around free agency. The owners wanted to find a way for teams who lost a free agent to be compensated for their loss. This would make free agent signings feel more like trades and would therefore limit free agency, slow down the accelerating growth of salaries, or both. Naturally, the players were deeply opposed to giving up the hard-fought gains they had only recently secured.

THE STRIKE

Labor problems and the possibilities of a strike had been lurking around the edges of MLB since the late 1960s. In late spring of 1966, Marvin Miller had been hired by the MLBPA. Until that time, to the extent that the players were organized, it took the form of a company union that was heavily influenced by the owners. Miller recounted one of the ways this became evident when he interviewed for the job. After more than two hours of interviewing with a panel of players that included Jim Bunning, Harvey Kuenn, and Robin Roberts, Roberts told Miller, "'Most of our players are conservative. They don't know anything about unions. . . . The best way to combat this is to have a dual ticket, with you as director and a noted conservative as general counsel.' That's when he dropped then name of Richard M. Nixon. I sat stunned. 'Sorry,' I said instantly. 'It won't work.'"[1] The players quickly dropped that idea and hired Miller without Nixon as his deputy.

Miller used his position to advocate for the rights of players and to restructure the feudal system that had governed baseball up until that time. Key to this was ending, or at least reforming, the reserve clause. Miller's efforts to do this began with his support for Curt Flood's suit against MLB after the slick-fielding center fielder was traded from the Cardinals to the Phillies following the 1969 season. That legal action cost Flood his future in baseball but led to reforms, including no trade clauses for all players with 10 years of big-league experience who had been on their current team for five or more years. Miller had also led the players in a walkout in spring training of 1972 that lasted through the first week or so of the season.

The owners' initial fear that a union led by Miller would send salaries skyrocketing turned out to be legitimate, but they did not predict that increased salaries would help bring more money into the game, thus making all of them much richer too. There are very few people who played as central of a role as Miller, who held his position with the MLBPA until 1982 and died 30 years after that, in the creation of the modern industry of MLB, yet he is not nearly as well remembered as he should be.

The positions and goals of the two sides as the strike deadline of 1981 approached were relatively clear. The MLBPA wanted to keep the system the way it was. Free agency was working for the players as salaries were increasing, and it was beginning to work even for those players who did not become free agents, because the threat of free agency forced their current teams to offer more when negotiating longer-term contracts. Free agency also gave players more of an ability to choose where to play. An overlooked part of the early days of free agency is how many great players who began their careers in the 1970s chose to remain with their initial team. George Brett, Mike Schmidt, Robin Yount, and a few years later, Cal Ripken Jr., are examples of this. In more recent years, Derek Jeter, Mariano Rivera, Chipper Jones, and Craig Biggio all had Hall of Fame careers playing entirely for one team. By contrast, in 1972, the Giants had to trade Willie Mays, the greatest player in their team's history, a few days after his 41st birthday because the team was in dire financial straits.

The owners, however, wanted to weaken free agency, keep salaries from accelerating so quickly and, for some, try to return baseball as much as possible to the pre–Marvin Miller state of labor relations. Compensation for players lost to free agency was the key issue, but the two sides were far apart. Ownership wanted teams who lost a star free agent to somehow get another high-quality player in return. The MLBPA wanted to retain the existing system where there was no compensation to the teams who lost free agents. In this case it was the players, not the management, that wanted to keep the status quo.

Although the two sides were far apart in their initial demands, the issue lent itself to compromise because there were many possible ways to structure compensation. Teams losing a player to free agency could be directly compensated by the team that signed the free agent, draft picks could be used as compensation, a pool of compensation players could be created, or other methods could be established. Each of these possibilities, in turn, raised other questions: who would be in the compensation pool, how many players could a team protect, how high of a draft pick would they get, and how would different quality free agent players be treated in the system? These questions have never really gone away and are still frequently tinkered with today.

The question of compensation was so important, and so divisive, that in early 1980, the players almost went on strike largely over that issue. At that time, the basic agreement, the document that creates a framework for the work conditions and structures under which players work and negotiate with teams, had lapsed. There were a number of issues other than compensation that were resolved, but players and owners could not find common ground on that one issue. For example, some owners wanted a salary scale for players that would reduce the impact of free agency and make it more difficult for individual players to negotiate lucrative contracts, but ownership was persuaded to drop that idea. In 1980, a strike was averted not because agreement on compensation was reached, but because the players and owners agreed to postpone the most divisive issue for a year.[2]

The 1980 season came and went, but no progress was made on the question of compensation. That off-season, free agency continued as before. The biggest prize in the free agent market that year was Dave Winfield. Winfield had turned 29 just as the 1980 season wrapped up but had already played eight seasons with the Padres. He had been an all-star every year from 1977 to 1980 and could do it all on the field. A typical Winfield season was a batting average around .285, 20–35 home runs, 90 RBIs, and for good measure, 20 stolen bases and a Gold Glove for his splendid defense and great arm in right field. His career numbers of .284/.357/.464 through age 29, already with over 1,000 hits and 150 home runs seemed like a good down payment on a Hall of Fame career.

Winfield's free agency was significant for many reasons, but one of the most important was that there was little doubt where he would sign. The Yankees had been swept out of the ALCS by the Royals in 1980. Their owner, George Steinbrenner, who had been active since the beginning of free agency, wanted Winfield. The Yankees offer of $23 million over 10 years made the choice easy for the slugger. The contract the Yankees gave the former San Diego Padre was worth more than seven times what they had given Reggie Jackson only four years earlier. This was great news for Yankee fans, but not so much for the rest of baseball.

Winfield's decision to sign with the Yankees was a turning point in free agency because it made it hard to escape the conclusion that free agency was redistributing baseball's top talent not downwards, horizontally, or even randomly, but upwards. The Yankees were one of baseball's wealthiest and most successful teams playing in the country's biggest media market. Signing Winfield would only make them wealthier and more successful. This was the beginning of the era when some of the smaller market teams, like the Padres, who had been active in the early years of free agency, became less able to compete with the larger market teams.

Big market teams didn't face these problems. By 1981, the Yankees had made several free agent decisions that didn't work out. Pitchers Don Gullett and Rawly Eastwick were both injured too much to meaningfully help the team, but spending money on those players did not prevent the Yankees from remaining competitive in the free agent market. Most importantly, the Yankees almost never lost their top players to free agency. During the 1980s, they traded away a young Willie McGee and a young Fred McGriff, so while they made mistakes judging talent, money was never an issue. This critique of big market teams raises the question of how much about this was simply about stopping the Yankees and their owner, who was widely disliked throughout baseball. When I asked Corey Busch whether this was mostly about the Yankees, he told me that "it mostly was."[3] Bob Lurie expressed a similar recollection, saying that in those years, the Yankees "were always held up as the real bad guys"[4] regarding free agency.

Ironically, while Winfield played very well for eight of those 10 years, before injuries and a trade took him away from the team, the Yankees were not very successful during his tenure there. Winfield hit .290/.356/.495 with 1,300 hits and just over 200 home runs, winning five Gold Gloves and making the all-star team every year from 1981 to 1988. He was hurt for all of 1989 and was traded to the Angels early in the 1990 season. The Yankees made it back to the World Series in 1981 but lost to the Dodgers in six games. Winfield had one hit in 22 at bats in that series, provoking Steinbrenner to refer to him as Mr. May. From 1983 through 1988, the Yankees contended every year, but the team wouldn't make it back to the postseason until 1995, the year Winfield was finishing his long career, but with the Cleveland Indians.

The labor disputes of the 1990s, and many of the adjustments to the basic agreement in the last 25 years, have sought to address this question of how to limit the structural advantages of big market teams, but the Winfield contract helped raise the salience of this issue. The tension between big market and small market teams is, on the surface, relatively clear. Teams like the Yankees, Red Sox, and Dodgers play in massive cities with enormous fan bases, or in the case of the Red Sox, have an entire region to themselves. This means that, despite in some cases having to share this market with other teams, it is much easier for them to sell more tickets, get more advertising money from television and radio, and otherwise increase their revenue. This revenue is then easily translated into the ability to build strong teams through signing free agents and preventing homegrown talent from leaving through free agency.

Smaller market teams, like the Pittsburgh Pirates, Milwaukee Brewers, Kansas City Royals, or Cincinnati Reds face the opposite circumstance. Because they play in small markets, it is harder for them to sell tickets or generate television revenue, thus making it difficult to compete for top free agents or to retain their top talent. There is some truth to this analysis. The Yankees have been the biggest spender over the history of the free agent market while being able to retain players like Derek Jeter, Mariano Rivera, Don Mattingly, and Bernie Williams. They have also been extremely successful on the field. The Red Sox record is similar in this regard. However, for other big market teams, the story is not quite so simple. The Dodgers, Angels, Mets, Cubs, and White Sox play in the biggest markets, and have been good at times, but have not always been big powerhouses in the free agent era. Since 1977, these five teams have combined for six World Championships and 13 pennants. That is about what you would expect from a random group of five teams.

Although the Yankees have signed many of the highest profile free agents, many top free agents sign with small- or medium-market teams. In recent years, Robinson Cano (10 years/$240 million), Manny Machado (10 years/$300 million), and Bryce Harper (13 years/$330 million) signed as free agents with the Mariners, Padres, and Phillies, respectively. These are all small- or medium-market teams. This trend is not entirely new. For example, In the 1979–80 off-season, a year before the Yankees inked Dave Winfield, the biggest free agent contract was a five-year, $6 million deal for Nolan Ryan with the Houston Astros. However, in the 2019–20 off-season, the Yankees, badly in need of starting pitching, made it clear they wanted Gerrit Cole, a free agent who was one of the very best pitchers in baseball. The Yankees moved quickly, offering Cole a nine-year, $324 million contract. Cole, likely knowing no team would match those numbers, signed with the Yankees.

The specter of dominance by big-market teams was often a bogeyman that was used by ownership to gain leverage over the players, but there was nonetheless something to it. While medium- and smaller-market teams could sign free agents, even big-ticket free agents, they couldn't do it every year. This left little room for error. For example, the Giants decision to sign Rennie Stennett in 1980, or Manny Trillo a few years later, in another effort to solve the second base problem, didn't work out because those players were no longer very good, but the problem was exacerbated because those major signings meant the Giants could not compete for top free agents the following year. Similarly, the Giants had some ability to hold on to potential free agents like Darrell Evans in the second winter of free agency, but even Evans left via that route following the 1983 season. The Giants also lost Chili Davis, a slugging outfielder, at the prime of his career as he signed a three-year, $3 million contract with the Angels following the 1987 season.

For teams like the Giants, free agency during the off-season was more of a high stakes crisis to be managed rather than an annual shopping trip to improve the team, like it has been for the Yankees. During the first two or three winters of free agency, following the 1976 through 1978 seasons, Giants fans could look at the pool of free agents and fantasize about adding a big star like Pete Rose, Tommy John, Reggie Jackson, or Rollie Fingers, but by the time the 1980s began, that feeling had changed. The Giants and their fans no longer could look at the class of free agents and dream about how they would look in orange and black. Instead, most realized that the biggest prizes in the free agent market were going elsewhere. Nobody thought the Giants had a real shot at Dave Winfield, Phil Niekro, or Goose Gossage after he became a free agent for the second time following the 1983 season. The Giants made a strong bid for Steve Garvey, but thankfully he eventually decided that something about the ballpark, the money, or the team was unappealing and signed with the Padres. During these years, there was also a feeling that the Giants were vulnerable to losing top players to free agency.

In 1981, as the strike deadline, and the first major showdown around free agency, approached, little progress had been made, so on June 11, the strike began. The 1981 strike was, at the time, the longest in MLB history. Because it began in the middle of the season, the strike threatened to have a major effect on pennant races and the postseason. This became even more of a concern as the strike continued. Previous MLB strikes or lockouts had been brief, usually no more than a week or two, but it was clear that 1981 was going to be different. The dispute was essentially about one major issue that the two sides had been discussing fruitlessly for over a year.

The strike was settled at the beginning of August with an unwieldy compromise that was probably a slight victory for the owners. Free agency was altered so that some players who became free agents, defined as the top 20 percent at their position by a complex statistical formula, would be categorized as type A free agents. Teams who lost a type A free agent would receive a player back as compensation. However, that player would not necessarily come from the team who signed the free agent, but from a pool of players. Each team could protect 15 players from their roster, with the rest going into that pool. This was an odd and less-than-elegant solution because it offered no direct disincentive for signing free agents but created yet another way all teams could lose players. So, for example, if a Kansas City Royals player became a free agent and signed with the Yankees, the Royals could select a player from the Giants as compensation. In that scenario, there was little reason for the Yankees not to pay that player whatever was needed, while leaving small-market teams as vulnerable as big-market teams to the possibility of losing a player because the Yankees or Angels signed yet another free agent.

Once the strike was settled, the question of how to salvage the 1981 season came into sharper focus. About a third of the season had already been lost. Moreover, because of the long strike, players could not simply come back and begin playing right away. Baseball decided to resume play with the All-Star Game on August 9, because due to the strike the game had not been played on its originally scheduled date in July. The only Giant to make the all-star team was Vida Blue, who pitched one scoreless inning and was the winning pitcher for the National League.

Following the All-Star Game, the regular MLB schedule was resumed on August 10. However, MLB made one other important change. Instead of picking up the standings where they were, whoever was in first place when the strike was called would be declared winners of the first half. Then all teams would start with a record of no wins and no losses for the second half, with the winners of each half meeting in a best of five division series after the conclusion of the regular season.

Thus, the Yankees, A's, Dodgers, and Phillies had managed to clinch playoff spots during the strike, while other teams like the Reds and Cardinals, who were both in second place, just behind the Dodgers and Phillies, respectively, had nothing to show for their strong first halves. The Giants were one of the teams that benefited most from the split season format. They were in fifth place with a .458 winning percentage and already out of the race when the strike began in June. They were a very different team in the second half, playing at a .558 pace while finishing in third place, only 3½ games behind the Astros, the division winners of the second half.

The awkward system that emerged from the 1981 strike that called for the creation of a pool of players from which teams who lost players to free agency could choose, did not work well, but it ended the strike. Some good ballplayers changed teams because of this system of compensation. The system lasted from 1982 to 1985. Some of the teams that took advantage of this system included the Seattle Mariners, who, in 1983, picked up Danny Tartabull, a hard-hitting prospect who went on to a good major-league career, after losing pitcher Floyd Bannister as a free agent to the White Sox. However, Tartabull was chosen from the Reds, who had nothing to do with Bannister. A couple of years later, the Blue Jays lost Cliff Johnson, a veteran right-handed slugger, to the Rangers in free agency and in turn drafted Tom Henke from the Rangers. Henke went on to become an excellent reliever for several seasons with Toronto. The most famous player to change teams through this system was Tom Seaver, who was drafted from the Mets, during his second turn with that team, by the White Sox after the Pale Hose had lost Dennis Lamp, a pitcher, to Toronto.

The system was flawed in many ways. In addition to not penalizing teams for signing free agents, the formula for deciding which players were eligible for free agency was erratic. Some of the biggest stars of the era, including Gossage, who signed with the Padres following the 1983 season, Garvey, and Jackson signed big free agent contracts, but the teams that lost them to free agency—the Dodgers in the case of Garvey and the Yankees in the case of the other two—got nothing because, for whatever reason, these players were not considered type A free agents so the teams losing them were not eligible for compensation.

The nature of the compensation pool did little to stop wealthy teams from pursuing free agents because they rarely had one of their players chosen from the compensation pool. One exception occurred in 1984, when the A's lost Tom Underwood to the Orioles and selected Tim Belcher, a top pitching prospect who had only recently inked his contract with the Yankees. The Yankees protested, but Belcher went to the A's.[5] Belcher went on to a very successful 14-year career in the big leagues, primarily with the Dodgers and Royals.

During the 1980s and into the early 1990s, divisions between the large- and small-market teams, and equally importantly, the perceptions of these divisions, became more acute. In this respect, the 1981 strike may have led to 13 years without a major labor disruption, but it did not solve the problem as the owners saw it or bring about a durable agreement between players and owners around the issue of free agency. During those 13 years, labor issues were always on the table and the possibility of another strike was never too distant. In this regard, the seeds of the 1994 strike, which led to the cancellation of the last third of that season as well as the entire postseason, were sown in the failure to find a functional solution to the issues that first arose in the late 1970s and early 1980s.

FRANK ROBINSON'S GIANTS

Over the course of both halves of that 1981 strike season, the Giants won 56 games while losing 55, but they turned a corner in the second half. The strike had interfered with Frank Robinson's first year as manager, but in the second half Robinson began to do a bit better as the team began to play its best baseball since 1978. Robinson had been hired by Bob Lurie and Spec Richardson after Dave Bristol was fired following a disappointing 1980 season. Robinson had managed the Indians from 1975 to 1977 and would manage the Giants from 1981 through most of the 1984 season. After leaving the Giants, Robinson would manage the Orioles, the Montreal Expos, and the Washington Nationals.[6] Over his long career, Robinson managed over 2,000 games.

Robinson was a significant manager for two reasons. First, he was the only truly great player to have a real career as a manager. Robinson's accomplishments on the field are not as well remembered today, but he was an extraordinary player. He was the only player to win MVP awards in both leagues, with the Reds in 1961 and the Orioles in 1966. His 586 home runs were fourth on the all-time list when he retired. Robinson was a 14-time all-star who finished in the top 10 in MVP voting 10 times and was elected to the Hall of Fame during his first year of eligibility, while he was managing the Giants. Modern analytics confirm Robinson's excellence, placing him in the top 20 for WAR among nonpitchers, and in the top 30 in OPS+.[7]

Robinson's significance in baseball history goes beyond his greatness on the field. On Opening Day 1975, the Indians hosted the Yankees in Cleveland. Robinson batted second that day and was one for three with a solo home run in the first inning as the Indians defeated the Yankees 5–3. Robinson's home run was a nice touch given that he was the manager of the Indians as well. In doing that, Robinson became the first African American manager in Major League Baseball history. While it is important to recognize the significance of Robinson doing this, it should also be emphasized that this occurred fully 28 years after Jackie Robinson played his first game with the Brooklyn Dodgers.

When the Giants were looking for a manager to replace Dave Bristol, no National League team had yet hired an African American manager, so Robinson was the first African American manager in both the American and National Leagues. Bob Lurie shared an anecdote with me about his decision to hire Robinson that captures the discussion about race in baseball in the early 1980s: "I got a call from the owner of the Baltimore Orioles . . . and he said 'I read the paper and it indicated you might hire Robinson as your manager' and I said 'yes.' He said 'you can't do that' and I said 'why not?' and he said 'you can't fire him.' I said 'why not?' and that was the end of the conversation." Lurie's wife Connie clarified that the Orioles owner had meant that Robinson could not be fired because he was African American. Despite these racist warnings, Lurie hired Robinson.[8]

As a manager, Robinson brought an intensity and a focus on winning that the Giants had lacked for several years. Corey Busch suggested that this led to some problems between Robinson and his players:

> Frank was one of the greatest players of all time. Winning was his oxygen and he played with a controlled ferocity. He played hard. He played smart. And he played that way every inning of every game. As a manager, Frank had difficulty accepting anything less from his players. He knew the results from his players weren't always going to be like the results he achieved as a player, but he wanted the effort and the intensity. I think Frank understood intellectually he could not expect his players to play as he did, but that reality frustrated him. He was tough on his players because of that. Many responded well and many did not. As I watched Frank manage after he left the Giants, I saw a change that I think really benefitted him as a manager.[9]

Robinson had retired as a player following the 1976 season, but because of free agency, the game had changed an enormous amount between then and 1981.

Although he had never finished higher than fourth place in his almost three years managing Cleveland, as a player Robinson had been on two World Series–winning teams and five pennant winners. In San Francisco, like in Cleveland, Robinson simply did not have the horses to contend. Despite this, from the time play was resumed after the strike through the end of the 1982 season, Robinson had the Giants playing pretty good baseball. Given the players on that team, the .542 pace over that season and a third was very respectable and a reflection of Robinson's skills, and not least attitude, as a manager.

Robinson preferred veterans and many of them also indicated that they enjoyed playing for Robinson. Vida Blue pitched for Robinson in 1981 and described him as a "hard nosed guy who had this reputation for taking no prisoners. . . . And that was just him. . . . Deep down inside, I'm sure he wanted to tell the guys 'you're better than that.'" Blue also added that "It was nice to play for the first Black manager. That was cool. . . . He was a tough cat."[10] Dusty Baker played for Frank Robinson in 1984. By that time, Robinson's reputation as a tough manager had made its way around the National League, but Baker found there was more to Robinson than that. "We had a couple of run ins with the Giants when I was on the Dodgers so I thought Frank was this mean old, crochety, never smiled hard-ass. . . . I was so surprised that Frank wasn't the way he appeared on the opposite side of the field." Baker, noting Robinson's deeply competitive approach to the game, also added: "It was tough on Frank doing all that losing."[11]

Robinson's most successful Giants team was in 1982. That team relied heavily on veterans, in some cases, players Robinson had wanted on the Giants largely because of their approach to the game. One of these players was Duane Kuiper, a light hitting but good fielding second baseman who had played for Robinson in Cleveland. Kuiper was acquired following the 1982 season in exchange for pitcher Ed Whitson. By then, the Giants already had a better second baseman in Joe Morgan, but as Corey Busch told me, "Robinson wanted Kuiper."[12] Reflecting on his trade to the Giants, about which he was not happy at the time, Kuiper said "my relationship with Frank was really the only positive thing I could have seen about going to San Francisco."[13]

From 1972 to 1986, every National League team made at least one post-season appearance. The Cubs won the NL East in 1984, making it back to the postseason for the first time since 1945. The Padres and Expos, who had both begun playing in 1969, were in the NLCS in 1984 and 1981, respectively. The one National League team that did not win their division even once during this 15-year period was the Giants. The Giants had some real success in the late 1980s, but the period from 1972 to 1986 remains the longest the team has ever gone without making it to the postseason.

During that period, the Giants twice contended late into the season, in 1978 and 1982. Although the two teams were only four years apart, they were very different. Only three players, sluggers Jack Clark and Darrell Evans, along with dependable reliever Gary Lavelle, were important parts of both teams. In addition to these three, Johnnie LeMaster was the starting shortstop in both 1978 and 1982 but was not a valuable player either year. His .216/.267/.266 slash line in 1982 was dreadful even for the relatively low offensive era of 1982. Pitcher Jim Barr, who was a useful swingman capable of starting and relieving in 1978, played a similar role in 1982 after returning to the team following time with the Angels and injuries. Reliever Greg Minton pitched all of 15²/₃ innings in 1978 but by 1982 had become one of the top firemen, as elite relievers were still sometimes called back then, in baseball for the Giants.

Whereas the 1978 team was built around younger players like Clark, Bill Madlock, Bob Knepper, and Terry Whitfield that together suggested, albeit falsely, a bright future for the Giants, the 1982 team, particularly with regards to position players, had a much older feel. On that 1982 team that managed to stay in contention until the last day of the season, Clark was 26, still relatively young but in his sixth year as a big league starter. Evans was 35 and had been in the big leagues for well over a decade. Reggie Smith and Joe Morgan, the regular first baseman and second baseman on that team were, other than Clark, the best hitters on that team. Smith was 37 and Morgan was 38. Catcher Milt May had a decent year, hitting .261/.311/380, but he was already 31 and in his 11th year, and on his fifth team in the big leagues. Valuable bench players like Jim Wohlford, Champ Summers, and Duane Kuiper were over 30 as well. The starting pitchers in 1982 were a younger and less distinguished bunch that included people like Bill Laskey and Atlee Hammaker, but bull pen stalwarts included Gary Lavelle and Jim Barr who had been in the league since 1974 and 1971, respectively.

Joining Clark in what was one of the best young outfields in the majors were 22-year-old center fielder Chili Davis, who displayed power, speed, and strong defense while finishing fourth in Rookie of the Year voting, and left fielder Jeffrey Leonard, who hit a respectable .259/.306/.421. Leonard was 26 and had shown flashes of what he could do throughout his career, but by 1982 was demonstrating that the Giants had gotten the better of the Astros in the Ivie trade.

The starting rotation for that 1982 team was, like in 1978, very young, but for the most part consisted of journeymen like Rich Gale, who went 7–14 with a 4.23 ERA, and Renie Martin, who was 7–10 with a 4.65 ERA. However, the bull pen in 1982 was one of the best the Giants had ever assembled. Lavelle and Minton led a group that also included Fred Breining, Al Holland, and Jim Barr. All five of those pitchers threw over 100 innings with ERAs under 3.50. Minton's 10–4 record with 30 saves and a 1.83 ERA in 123 innings drew enough recognition for him to finish in sixth place in the Cy Young Award voting and eighth in the NL MVP voting. Modern metrics view Minton's 1982 season even more enthusiastically. The 5.4 WAR he had that year was the most ever by a Giants relief pitcher, and among the top 25 seasons by any reliever. Gary Lavelle, 37 years after that season and more than 40 years after 1978, was still proud of the Giants bull pens those years: "We probably had the best bull pen in baseball in '78 and '82. . . . We had Minton, myself, Al Holland back then [1982]. . . . A bull pen that shut down a lot of teams. . . . We were proud of that."[14]

The 1982 team did not get off to a great start. On July 30, after being on the wrong end of a four-hitter by Don Sutton and losing to the Astros, the Giants record stood at 48–53. With the season almost two thirds over, they were in fourth place, trailing the division leading Braves by 13½ games. Then, over the last 61 games of the season, Robinson's veteran team came together, and the Giants were one of the best teams in baseball, going 39–22, good enough for a .639 winning percentage.

Two months of great baseball put the Giants in the thick of one of the best three-team division races of the pre–wild card era. The Giants never got into first place, but they kept the pressure on the Braves and Dodgers, who seemed to be taking turns on top of the division. After defeating the Reds 11–7 on September 23, the Giants were still four games behind the division-leading Dodgers, but only one game behind the second-place Braves. Over the weekend of September 24–26, the second to last of the season, the Giants would be playing the Dodgers in Los Angeles three times with a chance to make up some ground.

On Friday night, the Giants started Rich Gale against the Dodgers' Bob Welch. Gale was not sharp but held the Dodgers to two runs over four innings despite allowing six hits and two walks. When Gale was lifted for a pinch hitter, Tom O'Malley in the top of the fifth, the Giants were trailing 2–0. However, O'Malley walked, putting runners on first and second for Chili Davis, who doubled them both home to tie the game. The Giants' bull pen took it from there as Al Holland and Greg Minton did not allow any Dodgers base runners the rest of the way. In the top of the eighth, Darrell Evans drove in Davis with a single and the Giants went ahead 3–2. That was the final score as the Giants cut the Dodgers lead over them to three games, and only two over Atlanta.

Saturday's starters were veteran Jim Barr against Dodgers ace Fernando Valenzuela. Barr pitched well, holding a strong Dodgers lineup to three runs in six innings, but Fernando was at least as good and after seven innings the Dodgers led 4–3. Once again, the Giants' bull pen, this time Lavelle, Andy McGaffigan, and Greg Minton shut down the Dodgers. Just like the previous evening, a late rally, this time capped off by a two-run single by Joe Morgan in the eighth inning, gave the Giants a lead. The Giants held on to win by a score of 5–4. Now the Dodgers led the Giants by two games and the Braves by one.

On Sunday, Fred Breining and Burt Hooton were locked in a scoreless pitcher's duel through four innings. This time, the Giants scored first with a three-run fifth inning that included a two-run home run by Evans. The Dodgers countered with one in the sixth inning and one in the seventh, but that was not enough. For the third game in a row, the Giants had beaten the Dodgers in Los Angeles by one run. The Dodgers lead had been cut to one game over both the Braves and the Giants as the last week of the season began.

The Giants kept it close over the next few games, so going into the last weekend of the season, the Braves were in first, one game ahead of both the Giants and Dodgers, who were tied for second. The Braves were set to spend the final weekend of the season in San Diego playing the Padres, while the Dodgers were preparing for a three-game set against the Giants in San Francisco. The

Braves could clinch the division by sweeping the Padres, but if they stumbled even once in San Diego, then either the Dodgers or the Giants could catch the Braves and tie for the division title by sweeping their series. If the Braves lost two or three times, it would be even easier for either the Giants or Dodgers to force a tiebreaker. For the first time in well over a decade, the Dodgers and Giants were playing meaningful games against each other in October. The oldest rivalry in baseball was at a fever pitch as that series in San Francisco began.

On Friday night, the Braves had their ace, 43-year-old knuckleballer Phil Niekro on the mound. Niekro was in his 19th season with the Braves. He was the last member of the Braves to have been with the franchise in Milwaukee. Among his teammates on that 1964 Milwaukee Braves team were four future Hall of Famers: Henry Aaron, Eddie Mathews, Warren Spahn, and Joe Torre. Niekro himself would end up in the Hall of Fame and was in top form that Friday night as he pitched a complete game shutout, allowing only three hits and walking none while striking out seven. Just in case there was any lingering doubt about Niekro's dominance, the great pitcher hit a two-run home run in the eighth inning to increase the Braves lead from 1–0 to 3–0. The final score was 4–0, bringing the Braves one step closer to the division title.

A few hundred miles up the coast, Jerry Reuss, the veteran Dodger lefty also pitched a three-hit shutout, although unlike Niekro, Reuss, who had pitched a no-hitter at Candlestick a few years earlier, walked three batters. The score of the opener of the Giants-Dodgers series was also 4–0, with all the Dodger runs coming on a grand slam by Rick Monday off of Fred Breining, the Giants starter that day, in the top of the eighth inning. The crowd that night was over 53,000, but many left with the feeling that the season was slipping away.

Things had not gone the way the Giants wanted on Friday night, but the Giants were still alive going into Saturday. If they won both their remaining games and the Braves lost both of theirs, the Giants would end up tied with the Braves for first place. On Saturday, the Giants and Dodgers were scheduled to play in the day while the game in San Diego was a night game. Attendance that day was 46,562, down a few thousand from the previous evening, but still very good.

In the top of the first at Candlestick, Giants pitcher Renie Martin walked leadoff hitter Steve Sax, but then picked him off of first base before retiring Ken Landreaux and Dusty Baker on fly balls. The Giants went quietly in the bottom of the first. Leadoff hitter Max Venable and then Joe Morgan both hit the ball to Ron Cey, who tossed it across the diamond to Steve Garvey for the first two outs. Jack Clark then struck out to end the inning.

And then, in the top of the second, the wheels came off of the Giants inning, game, and indeed the whole season. Steve Garvey led the inning off with a single, but Rick Monday hit into a force-out. At that point, with a man on first and one out, the inning did not seem to be off to such a bad start. A walk to Ron Cey followed by an error by first baseman Reggie Smith on a ground ball off the bat of Dodger catcher Mike Scioscia put a seal on every rock with only one out.

Robinson had seen enough of Renie Martin by then and brought in Al Holland to relieve him. Holland had come to the Giants in the Bill Madlock trade early in the 1979 season and by 1982 had established himself as one of the best lefty relievers in the game. His 7–3 record and 2.93 ERA going into that game reflected the fine season he was having in 1982, but things did not go so smoothly for Holland in this crucial situation. Shortstop Bill Russell greeted him with a two-run single. Bob Welch, the Dodgers pitcher, then tried to bunt, but could not move the runners over. There were now two outs, two on, and two runs in. One more out and the Giants would be out of the inning, behind by only two runs and still very much in the game, but Holland needed to get Steve Sax out first. Sax singled to left, driving in Russell and making the score 3–0. The final blow of the inning came next when Landreaux hit a three-run home run to put the game out of reach as the Giants were now trailing 6–0.

The Giants never got back in that game. They were behind 12–0 after six innings and lost by a final score of 15–2. With that loss, the Giants' hopes ended. Being mathematically eliminated from the race at home by the Dodgers was a tough blow and was felt intensely by Giants fan in and around San Francisco.

A few hours later, the Giants got a small piece of good news from San Diego. Former Giant, and longtime Dodgers nemesis, John Montefusco, now pitching for the Padres, had struggled against the Braves, only making it through three innings and leaving with his team behind 3–0. Atlanta held on to win that game 4–2, so with one day left in the season, the Braves were still clinging to a one game lead over the Dodgers.

Thus, while Sunday's game, the last of the series and the season, could no longer have an impact on the Giants' pennant chances, the team had a chance to achieve a goal that would bring some succor to their by now long suffering fans. If the Giants could beat the Dodgers, they could knock their archrivals from Los Angeles out of the race, thus doing to the Dodgers what they had done to the Giants the previous day. However, not only were the Dodgers playing well, but the pitching matchup favored Los Angeles for that final regular season game.

Starting pitching had been a weakness for the Giants all season as they relied mostly on young players on their way to undistinguished careers. However, the one standout in that pool of mediocrity was a 24-year-old rookie named Bill Laskey. By the end of the season, Laskey, albeit in a tallest building in Topeka kind of way, had become the Giants' ace. Laskey came into Sunday's game with a record of 13–12 and a 3.15 ERA. He was not the kind of pitcher to strike fear in opponents, but if he could keep the game close, and the Giants could score a few runs, the team's stellar bull pen could probably hold off the Dodgers, at least that was the plan.

The problem with that plan is that the Dodgers had a real ace going that day. Fernando Valenzuela had taken the baseball world by storm beginning in late 1980, when, as a 19-year-old, he pitched $17^2/_3$ scoreless innings at the end of the season. The following year, despite the strike, he pitched an amazing eight shutouts on his way to winning the Rookie of the Year Award, Cy Young Award, and finishing fifth in the MVP voting. Fernando, as everybody knew him, was not only a great pitcher but was the first Mexican American star in Dodger history and in 1981 had been the most famous and electrifying player in both Mexico and the United States. Unfortunately for the Giants, Fernando had proven in 1982 that his rookie year had not been a fluke. He solidified his place as the Dodger ace and as one of the game's most elite pitchers and came into the last game of the season with a 19–13 record and a 2.87 ERA.

Despite seeing their team eliminated the previous day, Sunday's crowd of 47,457 was even bigger than the day before. Many of the fans in attendance, including me, were there that day to recognize the great year the team was completing, but also in the hope that the Giants could knock the Dodgers out of the race. Neither pitcher was particularly sharp in the early innings. After an uneventful first inning, in the top of the second inning a Steve Garvey single, followed by a Ron Cey home run, put the Dodgers ahead 2–0. At that moment it looked like two long time Giant foes, including Garvey, who was always hated at Candlestick, might just give the newest Dodger phenom the runs he needed to keep the Dodgers chances alive. However, unlike the previous day, Laskey was able to limit the damage that inning, sandwiching a Bill Russell single between a pop-up by Scioscia and Fernando striking out for the final outs of the second.

The Giants struck back immediately in the bottom of the frame. A single by Darrell Evans followed by a double by Jeffrey Leonard and a semi-intentional walk to Bob Brenly loaded the bases. The Giants were almost in a position to break the game open with the bases loaded and no outs, but the next three batters, Johnnie LeMaster, Laskey, and Max Venable, a light-hitting outfielder filling in for the injured Chili Davis, were not good hitters. The Giants got a big break when LeMaster walked, sending Evans home. This put the score at 2–1, but more importantly, it meant that unless somebody hit into a double play, the Giants would at the very least be able to send Joe Morgan, who was hitting in his usual second spot that day, up with runners on. However, Laskey quickly hit into a double play that scored Leonard, but then Venable struck out. The score was now tied, but the Giants had not made the most of a big scoring opportunity.

They wouldn't get too many more off of Fernando. Over the next six innings the lefty gave up only two walks and no hits. Laskey also settled down, retiring the next 13 batters he faced, so through six innings the game was still tied 2–2. With only three innings left in the season, the Dodgers still had a chance as the seventh inning began. Around this time, the scoreboard let fans know that down in San Diego, the Padres had scored five runs in the bottom of the fifth to go ahead of the Braves 5–1 and were still leading by that score in the eighth. Giants fans who had their programs handy could also see that the Padres had brought in Dave Dravecky, a rookie lefty who had been very effective in 1982, presumably to finish off the game. By the top of the seventh in San Francisco, that Padres-Braves game was almost over, so we knew that unless the Giants could beat Los Angeles, the Dodgers would be heading to a one-game playoff against the Braves the next day.

The Dodgers had the middle of the order coming up in the top of the seventh. Laskey got Garvey to fly out to Clark, but the rookie pitcher was tiring. Following singles by Cey and Monday, Frank Robinson brought in Gary Lavelle, the Giants veteran lefty reliever. Dodger manager Tommy Lasorda countered by sending up José Morales, a 37-year-old, right-handed, pinch-hitting specialist who had already gotten nine pinch hits and four walks in 33 opportunities for the Dodgers that year, to hit for Scioscia. Morales managed to beat out an infield single, loading the bases with only one out. Robinson, aware of the importance of the game and the moment, brought in Greg Minton, who was the best relief pitcher on the Giants, and one of the best in baseball that year. "Moon Man," as the Giants fans called him, entered the field to the sound of 47,000 people yelling "Moooon, Moooon."[15]

Minton was a sinkerball specialist who almost never gave up home runs, so he was the right choice for a situation where the Giants needed a double play. However, Dodger shortstop Bill Russell did not hit into a double play—he struck out. Now with two outs and the bases loaded, Lasorda was faced with

a choice of his own. Fernando, his best pitcher, was throwing well, and probably had a few more innings to go, but with Minton likely to pitch the rest of
the game, the Dodgers were going to struggle to score runs. Moreover, even a
powerful Dodgers team, with sluggers like Dusty Baker, Garvey, Monday, and
Cey in the lineup, was unlikely to hit even a solo home run off of Minton. The
Dodgers' bull pen was not as good as the Giants' 'pen, but rookies Dave Stewart, Alejandro Peña, and Tom Niedenfuer were all finishing respectable, and
in the case of Stewart, excellent seasons. Terry Forster was a reliable, veteran
arm out of the bull pen as well. The Dodgers 24-year-old closer, Steve Howe,
was available too, but his career had already taken a downward turn due to
substance abuse problems with which he would wrestle for the rest of his life.

Lasorda had a tough decision to make. In those days, managers did not
have the kind of data available that they have today, so Lasorda went with
his ample gut and sent Jorge Orta, who had done little with the bat all year,
but who had been a very solid hitter over the previous decade with the White
Sox and Indians, up to the plate. Orta hit a ground ball to Joe Morgan at
second base, who tossed it to Reggie Smith for the final out of the inning and
the Giants were out of danger, for now.

Tom Niedenfuer, a 22-year-old fireballer who had been excellent for the
Dodgers all year, started the bottom of the seventh for the Giants. The first
batter for the Giants that inning was Bob Brenly. Brenly had started that day
because unlike the Giants other catcher, Milt May, Brenly was a right-handed
hitter and Robinson wanted more righties in the lineup against the left-handed
Valenzuela. Although he was already 28 years old, Brenly was also a rookie
in 1982. Brenly led off the inning with a single, and the fans had reason to
hope once again. Pinch hitter Champ Summers fell behind 0–2 but then
lined a double to deep right. Brenly, like most catchers, was not fast on the
bases, and with no outs was taking no chances, so he was held at third. Greg
Minton, who couldn't hit, was due up, but there was no way Robinson was
going to pinch-hit for his best pitcher, so Minton stayed in and struck out.
With two lefties, Venable and Joe Morgan due up, Lasorda then brought in
Terry Forster, one of the best lefty relievers over the previous few years, to
get the last two outs of the inning. Robinson countered by sending the righty
Jim Wohlford to pinch-hit for Venable, but just as the scoreboard showed the
Padres still leading 5–1 in the ninth inning, Forster struck Wohlford out. ·

This brought Joe Morgan to the plate. Morgan was one of the greatest
players ever to play the game. A two-time NL MVP and 10-time all-star, Morgan was one of those rare players who could do it all. He could hit and had

an extraordinary batting eye, as demonstrated by the almost 2,000 walks he drew over the course of his career. Morgan was a fast and very smart base runner and base stealer and an excellent defensive second baseman who had won five Gold Gloves at that position. Morgan was only 5'7" but had good power, hitting more than 20 home runs in a season four times. In 1982, he had been a valuable player for the Giants. Coming into the last game of the season, he was hitting .289/.399/.433 with 13 home runs, had maintained his usual excellent glovework at second base and, for good measure, had a rather extraordinary 24 stolen bases in 28 tries.

As Morgan came to the plate in the Candlestick afternoon, on October 3, 1982, Giants fans might have been reminded of a few other big October 3 moments in Giants' and Dodgers' history, one that occurred 31 years earlier when the Giants made their home in Harlem, not Bayview–Hunters Point, when a Scottish immigrant named Bobby Thomson hit what remains one of the most famous home runs in baseball history. Eleven years after that, also on October 3, the Giants had come back to score and beat the Dodgers in the top of the ninth of a final game of another three-game playoff to decide who would win the National League pennant. That rally gave the Giants their first, and as of 1982, only pennant in San Francisco.

There were few players in the National League who were better suited for such a big moment than the batter coming to the plate. Morgan had just turned 39 years old and had begun his big-league career when John F. Kennedy was in the White House. Morgan had seen plenty of big moments and had driven in the winning run in the top of the ninth of Game Seven of the 1975 World Series, so it was unlikely the pressure was going to get to him.

Forster had to pitch to Morgan because the on-deck hitter was Jack Clark, who, as usual back then, had been one of the best hitters in the National League in 1982. Clark was also a righty, so either Forster would have been removed from the game in favor of Alejandro Peña or been at a disadvantage against the powerful Clark. Therefore, Morgan was the man Forster had to get—and he almost did. Morgan fell behind 1–2, meaning Forster was one strike away from getting out of a very tough jam.

Forster never quite got that strike as Morgan clobbered his next pitch to deep right field. Dodger right fielder Rick Monday gave half-hearted chase and then watched the ball easily clear the fence. The Giants' broadcast, but not the Dodgers' one, broke away from the scene of Morgan rounding the bases to show Tommy Lasorda in the dugout rubbing his forehead in disgust and disbelief. That image remains a favorite video clip among many Giants fans. Morgan's big home run put the Giants ahead 5–2 and essentially knocked the Dodgers out of the playoffs. LA rallied for a run in the top of the eighth, but Minton shut them down after that, securing a 5–3 win for the Giants and the NL West title for the Braves.

Dusty Baker was playing left field for the Dodgers that day but had been a keen observer of the Dodgers-Giants rivalry since his youth in both Southern and Northern California. When asked about that 1982 Giants team, he described how "they [the Giants] signed our number one general. . . . Reggie Smith and Joe Morgan gave them a whole new attitude. Then they became tough." When asked specifically about Morgan's big home run, Baker simply said "that was heartbreak hotel. We were on our way to going to the playoffs again."[16]

Morgan's home run was one of the great highlights of a pretty rough 15-year period for the Giants. Larry Baer described how "everybody got very excited when Joe Morgan hit a home run to knock the Dodgers out. Didn't knock us in, but knocked the Dodgers out. That's almost as good and fulfilling as knocking us in." Only Mike Ivie's grand slam in 1978 rivaled it during that decade and a half era with no postseason appearances for the Giants. During most of the 1980s, Giants fans could debate which home run meant more for the team. Baer argued that Morgan's home run was bigger. "The Morgan home run because it was so decisive. IT KNOCKED THE DODGERS OUT. Ivie's home run was a really dramatic moment. We didn't win the division that year and it was earlier in the season."[17] There was always something bittersweet about this. Neither of these hits were part of a championship run. Ivie's was a late May home run for a team that ended up in third place. Morgan's was on the last day of the season but was hit only one day after the Dodgers had knocked the Giants out of the race. Morgan's home run meant the Dodgers were not going to the playoffs, but the Giants were not going either.

Fans of a team in the middle of a playoff draught of more than 15 seasons, and 20 years to the day removed from winning their last pennant, need to take their baseball pleasures wherever they can; and for Giants fans eliminating the Dodgers on the last day of the season was a pretty big one. Nonetheless, the intensity of that moment was also a reminder of the sad state into which the Giants had fallen.

By 1982, a lot was happening in San Francisco that pushed the Giants to the periphery of the vibe of the city. In the sports world, the football 49ers had won their first Super Bowl in January. That 49ers team featured all-time greats like Joe Montana, Ronnie Lott, Dwight Clark, and legendary coach Bill Walsh. They would go on to win three more Super Bowls over the next 10 years, so for most of the 1980s, San Francisco was a football town.

The early 1980s were also a difficult time in San Francisco in ways that had nothing to do with sports. The assassinations of 1978 still cast a pall over the city's political life. Dianne Feinstein, who had become mayor following the killing of George Moscone, had won a term of her own in 1979, and in 1983 would fight off a recall vote and then cruise to an easy reelection. Feinstein was a competent and smart mayor, but she was more conservative and less neighborhood-oriented than her predecessor. Under her leadership, the real estate and business interests that had long governed San Francisco reasserted their power. This gave San Francisco a and tougher less forgiving feel than had been the case during Moscone's three years in office.

When coupled with the cuts from Proposition 13, a statewide law passed in 1978 that capped property tax and therefore forced most California cities to make severe spending cuts, as well as the Reagan administration in Washington, this meant that San Francisco had fewer resources for lower-income people, neighborhoods, public parks, schools, and the like.

All of these conditions made life difficult for many San Franciscans, but then AIDS began to bring suffering and death to the city. In 1982, AIDS was not yet killing thousands of San Franciscans, as it eventually would, but it was a growing concern among gay people in the city. Over the next decade, AIDS would become the major public policy challenge in the city that had emerged as a global center of gay culture and politics. AIDS devastated gay San Francisco but also created political tensions and fear. Antigay sentiment increased as many Americans were grievously misinformed about AIDS. It also strained budgets of cities like San Francisco that were already struggling in a period of austerity from Washington, and in California, from Sacramento as well.

During difficult times like this, a winning sports team can sometimes unify the city by providing a welcome distraction and some badly needed good news. In the first seven years of the 1980s, the closest the Giants came to doing that was Joe Morgan's home run, a great baseball moment to be sure, but not exactly a World Series victory, or even a pennant. During these years, San Franciscans looking for a good news story generally looked to the 49ers, who would win a total of four Super Bowls between 1982 and 1990, not the Giants.

Above left: George Moscone, pictured here throwing out the first pitch at Candlestick Park early in the 1976 season, spent his first months in office that year working to keep the Giants in San Francisco. (Photo courtesy of Dennis Desprois). *Above right:* Bob Lurie was instrumental in keeping the Giants in San Francisco in 1976 and owned the team through the 1992 season. (©2020 S.F. Giants)

The Giants made their home in Candlestick Park from 1960 to 1999. It could be beautiful during the day there, but it got quite cold once the sun went down. (©2020 S.F. Giants)

Above left: John "the Count" Montefusco was the National League Rookie of the Year in 1975 and remained with the Giants through 1980. (©2020 S.F. Giants)

Above right: The Giants acquired Darrell Evans in a trade during the 1976 season. He was a very productive member of the team until he left as a free agent following the 1983 season. (©2020 S.F. Giants)

Left: During his eight full years with the Giants, Jack Clark was one of the best hitters in baseball. (©2020 S.F. Giants)

Johnnie LeMaster was the Giants' starting shortstop from 1978 to 1984. He never hit well, and his defense received mix reviews. (©2020 S.F. Giants)

In 1978, Manager Joe Altobelli kept the Giants in first place for most of the summer and helped excite a new generation of Giants fans. (©2020 S.F. Giants)

Willie McCovey was one of the most beloved players in San Francisco Giants history. After three seasons away from the team, he came back to the Giants in 1977 and remained with the team until he retired in 1980. (©2020 S.F. Giants)

Dianne Feinstein became mayor in November 1978 and remained in office through 1987. During those years, she sought to find a new home for the Giants in San Francisco. (©2020 S.F. Giants)

The Giants traded for Vida Blue during spring training in 1978. In the 1970s, he was one of the best and most famous pitchers in baseball. (©2020 S.F. Giants)

Frank Robinson was one of the greatest ballplayers ever. He managed the Giants for almost four years and kept them in contention until the last weekend of the season in 1982. (©2020 S.F. Giants)

Joe Morgan's home run on the last day of the 1982 season knocked the Dodgers out of the race for the division title. (©2020 S.F. Giants)

Jose Uribe was a fine fieldling shortstop during his eight years with the Giants. (©2020 S.F. Giants)

The Crazy Crab was the mascot fans loved to hate. (©2020 S.F. Giants)

When Al Rosen took over the Giants as general manager late in the 1985 season, the team's fortunes began to turn around. (©2020 S.F. Giants)

Bob Lurie finally got the general manager he wanted when he hired Al Rosen. The two were friends who worked together to build a winning Giants team in the late 1980s. (Photo courtesy of Dennis Desprois)

Above left: Roger Craig managed the Giants to a division title in 1987 and the National League pennant in 1989. (©2020 S.F. Giants). *Above right:* Will Clark's single to win Game Five of the 1989 NLCS was one of the biggest hits in Giants history. (©2020 S.F. Giants)

Dave Dravecky fought his way back from cancer to pitch for the Giants in 1989. (©2020 S.F. Giants)

Kevin Mitchell came over from the Padres in a mid-season trade in 1987. He helped the Giants to the division title that year. Two years later, he won the league's Most Valuable Player award and helped lead the Giants to the National League pennant. (©2020 S.F. Giants)

Just as Game Three of the 1989 World Series was about to start, San Francisco was struck by a major earthquake that caused billions of dollars of damage and forced the postponement of the final games of the World Series. (©2020 S.F. Giants)

Mayor Art Agnos and President George H. W. Bush discuss the damage following the 1989 earthquake. Standing between the two men is Nancy Pelosi, who was then serving her first full term representing San Francisco in Congress. In the background is the Golden Gate Bridge, which was not damaged in the earthquake. (George H. W. Bush Library and Museum)

Frank Jordan, in a Giants' jacket, spent most of his first year as mayor trying to keep the Giants from leaving. Peter Magowan led the ownership group that bought the team in late 1992. (©2020 S.F. Giants)

Roger and Carolyn, Craig, Al and Rita Rosen, and Bob and Connie Lurie. (Photo courtesy of Pat Johnson Studios)

Chapter 5

THE WORST GIANTS TEAMS EVER

In 1902, the Giants were playing in New York and had not yet become the powerhouse that would go on to dominate the National League in the first third of the twentieth century. They won only 23 of their first 73 games employing two managers, Horace Fogel and Heinie Smith, before bringing in John McGraw, who improved the team only slightly, but who, over the next 30 years, went on to become the greatest manager in Giants history, and one of the most important and famous managers the game has known. That 1902 Giants team, which finished in last place, 53½ games behind the pennant-winning Pirates, was led by two Hall of Fame pitchers, Christy Mathewson and Joe McGinnity, who pitched well but still managed a combined record of only 22–25.

Students of early-twentieth-century baseball might recognize the names of a few other players on that team, like Roger Bresnahan and Jim Delahanty. Delahanty was one of an amazing five brothers who played in the big leagues during that period. Jim was probably the second best of the five. The best was Ed, a slugging first baseman who died under mysterious and tragic circumstances as he fell, or perhaps jumped, off of the bridge over Niagara Falls in 1903 while he was still a productive player and only 35 years old. Roger Bresnahan was one of the best catchers during the early years of the twentieth century. Bresnahan was elected to the Hall of Fame in 1945. He is also credited with inventing shin guards for catchers. Most of the other players on that 1902 Giants team, like Joe Bean, Hal O'Hagan, Libe Washburn, or Henry Thielman, are almost entirely forgotten. The 1902 Giants were on the tail end of the worst three-year run in franchise history. Between 1900 and 1902, the Giants had a .378 winning percentage, but by 1904 won the pennant and established themselves as a force in the National League for many decades.

Fans of the Giants in the years following Morgan's big home run that eliminated the Dodgers on the last day of the 1982 season should have been grateful for that 1900 to 1902 run because other than that, the baseball the Giants played from 1983 to 1985 was the worst in franchise history. As in 1978, the 1982 team experienced a big setback, or perhaps a return to reality, the following season. By the end of 1982, Smith and Morgan were both gone. Smith became a free agent and signed with the Yomiuri Giants in Japan. Morgan was sent to the Phillies along with Al Holland for pitchers Mike Krukow and Mark Davis and highly touted prospect C. L. Penigar. Penigar never made it in the big leagues, but Krukow became a reliable starting pitcher for the Giants for several years and remains with the team today as part of one of the best announcing teams around. Krukow's partner in the broadcast booth is Duane Kuiper, Joe Morgan's backup in 1982. Before Krukow joined the broadcasting team, one of Kuiper's partners was Joe Morgan.

The 1983 team was not terrible, finishing only four games under .500, but it had a very different feel than the previous year. Jack Clark, Jeffrey Leonard, and Darrell Evans provided a solid middle of the lineup, combing for 71 home runs with OPS+ of 125, 118, and 150, respectively. At 36 years old, Evans had one of the best years of his career, hitting .277/.378/.516 while playing mostly first base, but it wasn't enough. Other than those three, the rest of the team was pretty terrible. Chili Davis suffered a sophomore slump, falling to .233/.305/.352 with only 11 home runs. Young Giants like Brad Wellman at second base and Tom O'Malley at third were, despite high expectations set by the team, pretty terrible. Wellman was spelled a bit by Kuiper, who was still very solid with the glove and, while unable to hit for power, had more value at the plate because of his .353 on-base percentage. Kuiper's lack of power was extraordinary. He came to the plate more than 3,700 times over the course of a 12-year career and only hit one home run, but that came while he was with the Indians, so during his four years with the Giants, Kuiper failed to his even a single home run.

One of the strangest stories of the 1983 season began when the lineups were announced on Opening Day. The Giants' leadoff hitter that day was not Duane Kuiper, whose ability to reach first and limited power would have worked well in the leadoff spot, or Chili Davis, who could get on base reasonably well, steal bases, and hit with power, or even Jeffrey Leonard, who was not a true leadoff man, but was a good hitter. Instead, Johnnie LeMaster was the first Giants batter of 1983. LeMaster had proven in his first six years with the Giants that he could not hit or draw walks, as demonstrated by his on-base percentage of .275 through 1982, but somehow Frank Robinson saw him as a leadoff hitter. This was a very puzzling move. LeMaster had been a subpar number eight hitter for most of his career, so the idea of giving him more at bats—and more important at bats—made no sense, but that is exactly what the Giants did. LeMaster led off in the team's first 11 games and a total of 136 times before the season was over.

LeMaster stole 39 bases in 1983 for the Giants while getting caught 19 times, so for the first time in his career the light-hitting shortstop demonstrated genuine speed on the base paths. The early 1980s were a time when stolen bases were having a resurgence as players like Tim Raines, Alan Wiggins, and most notably Rickey Henderson, were bringing excitement to the game by racking up big stolen base totals, so from this perspective the idea of moving LeMaster to the leadoff spot and having him run more made sense, but in the larger picture the move was not a good one.

The primary job of the leadoff hitter is to get on base, so the single most important indicator for evaluating a leadoff hitter is on-base percentage. In 1983, 65 players in the NL had enough plate appearances to qualify for the batting title. Of those, 47 had a higher on-base percentage than LeMaster. Another, Phil Garner, an aging infielder and future Giant, tied LeMaster at .317. This was a dismal figure for a leadoff hitter. Amazingly, only 33 players in the NL came to bat more than LeMaster that year. The LeMaster leadoff experiment allowed the shortstop to produce his most impressive offensive season, but on balance it was a failure as LeMaster was still unable to consistently hit big-league pitching.

The Giants struggles in 1983 cannot be attributed entirely to Johnnie LeMaster, but somehow the decision not just to bat him first, but to continue to do that throughout essentially the entire season, captured the feel of those mid-1980s Giants teams. LeMaster had been a Giant his entire career, but by 1983 he was a veteran who had shown what he could do—field a little and not hit at all. Despite this, the Giants asked more out of him and, not surprisingly, did not get that.

The Giants were asking LeMaster to do something, hit, that he had proven he could not do, but during this era they too frequently asked players to do things they no longer could do. From 1983 through 1985, bringing in veterans who were on the downside of their career was something the Giants did all too often. Players like Steve Nicosia, Mike Vail, Al Oliver, Manny Trillo, Randy

Lerch, Gene Richards, and Dan Driessen had long, and in some cases very good, careers, but were all well past their prime when they washed up at Candlestick Park sometime during this 1983 to 1985 run. These players might have had some value as role players on contending teams, but the Giants were asking them to be key contributors when they were past the point in their careers when that was possible. Even Vida Blue, who had been traded to Kansas City following the 1981 season, made it back to the Giants in 1985. He was, by then, approaching the end of a very good career but only went 8–8 with a 4.47 ERA. Some, like Dusty Baker, played well with the Giants, but they were, at best, stopgap solutions to much bigger problems. Baker described his experience playing on the Giants in 1984 after spending eight years, including four trips to the postseason, with the Dodgers by simply saying that "it was tough."

The 1983 season started out poorly for the Giants as the team dropped 10 of their first 13 games, but then they got hot as the early part of the season continued. As late as June 1, the Giants had a .563 winning percentage but were already 6½ games behind a very strong Los Angeles Dodgers team. However, from that day on the Giants played poorly, winning only 52 of the remaining 114 games. Nonetheless, the 1983 team had some strengths that carried over from 1982. The trio of Clark, Leonard, and Evans was one of the league's stronger middles of the orders. Greg Minton and Gary Lavelle were the nucleus of a bull pen that, while not as strong as in 1982, was still solid. The best news for the Giants in 1983 was that Atlee Hammaker, who had come over to the Giants from the Royals in the Vida Blue trade, developed into one of the league's top left-handed pitchers. His win-loss record was only 10–9, but he had a league-leading 2.25 ERA. Hammaker made his only all-star team that year and, unfortunately for the young lefty, was terrible in the two thirds of an inning he pitched. He gave up a solo home run to Jim Rice, the first batter he saw. A triple to George Brett, singles to Dave Winfield, Manny Trillo, and Rod Carew, with a couple of pop-ups mixed in, led to an intentional walk of Robin Yount. Then Fred Lynn hit a grand slam and Hammaker was taken out after giving up seven earned runs. His career All-Star Game ERA still stands at 94.50.

The Giants ended up in fifth place in 1983, but only 12 games behind the division-winning Dodgers. They were not a good team, but irrationally hopeful Giants fans could tell themselves that their team was only a few good players away from being back in contention. The problem was that the team's management seemed to believe that too. After the season, the Giants tinkered a little by signing Manny Trillo as a free agent. Trillo was a good-fielding, light-hitting second baseman. If Manny Trillo was an upgrade from Duane Kuiper, another veteran with a similar skill set, it was only a very slight one. Dusty Baker, a longtime Dodgers star who was reaching the final innings of his career, also signed with the Giants at the end of spring training.

The most significant move the Giants made in that off-season was to let Darrell Evans leave as a free agent. Evans, who signed with Detroit, had been the Giants best hitter in 1983 and had quietly been one of the best hitters in the game over the previous decade or so. In 1983, he played mostly first base and was one of the most productive first basemen in baseball. To replace Evans, the Giants traded for Al Oliver during spring training. The Giants gave up Fred Breining, Max Venable, and pitcher Andy McGaffigan for the 37-year-old Oliver. Oliver was, in many ways, the opposite of Evans. He hit for a much higher batting average but didn't do much else. Over the course of an 18-year career, Oliver hit .303 but only drew 50 or more walks in a season once, so his .344 on-base percentage was lower than the career .361 for Evans in that category. Oliver was not a real power threat either, topping 20 home runs only twice in his career. In 1983, he only hit eight dingers. Despite his flashy batting average, Oliver was not likely to replace Evans's value in the lineup. He didn't and was traded to the Phillies before the season was over.

Trillo, Oliver, and Baker provided little value to the Giants, although Baker was a good bat off of the bench in 1984, but more puzzling was why Giants decided to bring in relatively expensive veterans to bolster a fifth place team that had contended in 1982, in no small part because of the contributions of players like Joe Morgan, Evans, and Reggie Smith, who were no longer with the team. Part of the problem was that some of the young players the Giants had counted on in 1983 had failed or were failing their auditions. By the end of that 1983 season, it was apparent that Tom O'Malley and Brad Wellman were not going to good big-league players. Moreover, the Giants farm system was unlikely to provide any additional help in the immediate term.

Despite this, there were some good young players on that 1983 team around whom the Giants could have built. Hammaker had established himself as a top starting pitcher but lost most of 1984 to injury. The 23-year-old Chili Davis had slumped in 1983, but it was not hard to see he was going to have a very good big-league career. Similarly, the 27-year-old Leonard had proven himself to be a solid asset in left field. Jack Clark, the longtime right fielder, had been one of the best players in the game, if also one of the most unappreciated, but he was also only 27. However, after the 1983 season ended, the Giants sought to bolster this nucleus, not with other young players who could help in the longer term, but with veterans like Trillo, Oliver, and Baker, for whom there was no long term.

That strategy proved to be an abject disaster. The 1984 team wound up in last place, losing 96 games. It was the first time the Giants had finished in last place since moving to San Francisco. The franchise had most recently finished in last place in 1946 when they were still in New York. Their .407 winning percentage was also the worst of any San Francisco Giants team and the lowest of any Giants team since those 1946 New York Giants. That particular franchise record would only stand for a year. The 1984 Giants team, like most last place teams, also got their share of bad breaks. On June 22, Jack Clark was having, even by his standards, a great year, hitting .320/.434/.537, but he lost the rest of the season to knee surgery. Similarly, Atlee Hammaker, the young ace of the 1983 pitching staff, was limited to six starts and 33 innings due to injury.

Injuries and bad breaks were not the only cause of the team's problems in 1984, as the Giants also got some good breaks. Chili Davis proved that his off year in 1983 was indeed an aberration as he hit .315/.368/.507 while slugging 21 home runs. Similarly, Jeffrey Leonard had the best year of his career, hitting .302/.357/.484. Nonetheless, the Giants were in many ways just not a good, or well thought out, team in 1984. Joel Youngblood, a useful fourth outfielder and emergency infielder type, was cast as the starting third baseman after Tom O'Malley had not been able to win that job in 1983. Youngblood made 36 errors and had a fielding percentage of .887, only the second time a full-time player had a fielding percentage of under .900 since World War II. More contemporary defensive metrics are no less kind to Youngblood as his defensive WAR was negative 2.3 with negative 21 runs saved, meaning his poor defense cost the Giants an estimated 21 runs.

Youngblood was part of an infield that was one of the worst in Giants history. Al Oliver was the first baseman for most of the season. He hit .298 with no home runs but drew 20 walks to push his on-base percentage to a respectable .339. Trillo fielded decently at second base, but as expected didn't hit. LeMaster took a big step back from his season in the leadoff spot. In 1984, he hit .217/.265/.282. LeMaster was mercifully removed from the leadoff spot but actually had a better year on the basepaths, stealing 17 bases in 22 tries. Youngblood's defense overshadowed the reality that he also didn't hit much in 1984. His .254/.328/.358 numbers were very ordinary and did not justify getting his terrible glove in the lineup for most of the season.

By 1984, Frank Robinson was no longer able to help the Giants. He had made the team very good for the period from the end of the 1981 strike through the end of the 1982 season, but after that he became a poor fit for the team. As a manager, Robinson had always preferred veterans but by 1983 and 1984 was leaning on them too much. One hundred six games into the season, Robinson was fired. The Giants brought in Danny Ozark to finish the season, but Ozark couldn't do much either, leading the team to a 24–32 record for the remainder of the season.

The starting pitching, which had been a weakness for the Giants since the quartet of Blue, Montefusco, Knepper, and Halicki in 1978, was once again terrible. Without Hammaker, no Giants starter had an ERA under 4.00. To the extent there was an ace of the 1984 staff, it was either Bill Laskey, 9–14 with a 4.33 ERA, or Mike Krukow, 11–12 with a 4.56 ERA.

THE NADIR

Following the 1984 season, the Giants did little to improve on their 96 losses. They parted ways with several players who had played minor roles on the 1984 team, such as Joe Pittman, Bob Lacey, Randy Lerch, Steve Nicosia, and Gene Richards. During the off-season the Giants signed no free agents and made no major trades, although they sent aging reliever Gary Lavelle to the Blue Jays in late January. Then, in early February, just as spring training was about to start, the team made one of their biggest, and worst, trades of the decade.

Jack Clark had missed most of the 1984 season in part because he did not want to rush back after a knee injury, causing some tension between the player and manager Frank Robinson. However, by that point, Clark, who would turn 29 following the season, had been the Giants' best player for almost a decade. From 1975, when he had begun his career at 19 years old with 19 plate appearances at the tail end of the season, through 1984 when he lost most of the season to injury, Clark had hit .277/.359/.477 for an OPS+ of 134 bolstered by 197 doubles and 163 home runs. From 1977 through 1984, the years he was, when not hurt. a regular on the Giants, Clark had improved those numbers to .279/362/.481 for an OPS+ of 136 while accumulating 30 WAR.

In all of baseball during those years among players with 3,500 or more plate appearances (Clark had 4,166), only Mike Schmidt, George Brett, Eddie Murray, Dave Winfield, Jim Rice, and Keith Hernandez had an OPS+ better than or equal to Clark. Of that group, which included five future Hall of Famers, only Murray was younger than Clark. Clark's 30 WAR, a statistic that reflected both playing time and defensive value as well as hitting prowess, was 22nd in all of baseball for that period.

Despite his excellent numbers and consistent offensive production, Clark was somehow always underappreciated at Candlestick Park. The best players on bad or underperforming teams often confront this problem, but in the case of Clark, there was something more to it. Duane Kuiper, a teammate of Clark's from 1982 to 1984 and currently a Giants broadcaster, described Clark's great generosity with his teammates, recounting an anecdote about how Clark insisted that Kuiper use his new Mercedes 380 SL, orange because he played for the Giants, when the veteran infielder first joined the Giants in 1982: "He would give you anything if you asked for it."[1] Kuiper's longtime broadcasting partner Mike Krukow, who played with Clark on the Giants for two years, told me "Jack [Clark] could do everything. Just a magnificent baseball player. . . . He was an intimidating guy to pitch to. When I got to the Giants, he was the franchise basically."[2]

Gary Lavelle, who played with Clark during the entire time the slugging outfielder was with the Giants echoed these sentiments. "Jack Clark, who was one of my best friends on the Giants, just a great talent, had all the tools to be a Hall of Fame player."[3] Vida Blue was a teammate of Clark's from 1978 to 1981, and pitched against him in 1985 and 1986 when Blue was with the Giants and Clark was with the Cardinals, said of Clark "I'm not sure he knew how good he was. . . . I'd rather pitch to Mike Schmidt than Jack Clark. . . . Jack Clark, when he swung, he hit the ball hard. . . . I'd like to know what his exit velocity was when he just squared a ball up and hit it on the screws."[4]

Clark's former teammates had a difficult time figuring out why *he* had such a difficult time with, at various times, management, the media, and the fans. Blue said of Frank Robinson, who had been Blue's manager in 1981 and been Clark's manager from 1981 through 1984, "I don't think he knew how to handle Jack Clark."[5] Kuiper offered a similar explanation, describing the slugger as "a little bit misunderstood. . . . If he had something on his mind, he had to get it off his chest and that never sat well with management. It never sat well with whoever was managing him."[6]

By spring of 1985, it was clear Clark's years with the Giants were winding down. The team was anxious to trade him in the hopes of bringing some young talent into the organization. Clark had not gotten along well with Robinson over the last three years and was clearly ready to move on. The trade that sent

Clark, who had been in the Giants organization since he was drafted out of Gladstone High School in Covina, California in 1973, to the Cardinals, was not a good one for the Giants. Krukow described his feeling seeing Clark traded away: "I didn't think we got better when we made the trade. I didn't think we got enough for Clark because I thought he was one of the premier players."[7]

The package of players the Giants got never amounted to much. The key to the trade was David Green, a 24-year-old outfielder who had hit a little and had shown some power and speed the previous two years with the Cardinals. The Giants, who traded Clark in part because the outfield was crowded, decided to make Green a first baseman, a position he had never played at the big-league level. Green was terrible with the Giants in 1985, hitting .248/.301/.347 as their first baseman in 1985 and was sent to Milwaukee after the season.

The second key to the trade was Dave LaPoint, a 25-year-old left-handed pitcher who had been unremarkable but showed some promise in parts of five seasons with the Cardinals. LaPoint was an uninspiring 7–17 with a 3.57 ERA in 1985, his only season with the Giants. The other two players in the trade were Gary Rajsich, a 30-year-old outfielder who had not, and would never, establish himself in the major leagues. The only player of any value the Giants got from that trade was José González, who upon joining the Giants changed his name to Uribe González and then José Uribe. Uribe was the Giants' starting shortstop from 1985 to 1990 and a backup for the following two years. Uribe was an excellent defender but never hit much. In other words, the Giants had traded one of the best sluggers in the game for a good field, no hit shortstop and three marginal players who contributed almost nothing to the team.

Clark, for his part, continued to be an excellent hitter through the early 1990s and helped lead the Cardinals to pennants in 1985 and 1987. In 1987, he finished third in MVP voting in the National League and was the Silver Slugger first baseman, the position he began playing after leaving the Giants, in 1985 and 1987. He also had one last big home run that brought joy to many Giants fans, despite wearing a Cardinals uniform when he hit it.

In Game Six of the 1985 NLCS, the Cardinals were up three games to two, but with two out in the top of the ninth and behind 5–4, the Dodgers were one out away from tying the series and forcing a Game Seven in Los Angeles. With two out and two on base, Clark crushed a pitch from Dodgers reliever Tom Niedenfuer over the fence in left field. The home run put the Cardinals up 7–5 and the Dodgers on the brink of elimination. Cardinals closer Ken Dayley then retired the side easily in the 9th and the Dodgers were done for the year. 1985 was such a bad year for the Giants that for many fans that was the most memorable moment of the season. Jenkins's sentiments about Clark and that home run were shared by many Giants fans: "So much confidence and a little bit of swagger. . . . I just loved when he hit the home run against Lasorda and the Dodgers with the Cardinals. It was very Jack Clark."[8]

THE CROIX, THE CRAB, AND GUIDO

The Giants' poor play during years 1983 to 1985 raised challenges off the field as well. Attracting fans to Candlestick Park, or as Larry Baer phrased it "getting warm butts in cold seats at Candlestick"[9] was never easy, but having a consistently bad team only made it worse. In the late 1970s, the Giants had a little bit of an opportunity because the A's, with whom they shared the larger Bay Area market, were terrible. During those years, there were frequent rumors that the A's would be moving, most likely to Denver. For the Giants, seeing the A's go would have solved many of their problems as they would have become the only big-league baseball team in the Bay Area.

In 1980, that hope was dashed when the Haas family, like Bob Lurie's, a wealthy local family with strong ties to San Francisco, whose money came from making Levi's jeans, bought the A's. It also didn't help the Giants that in 1980 and 1981, with Billy Martin at the helm, and Rickey Henderson in left field, the A's were a good and exciting team, narrowly finishing in second place in 1980 and winning the division in 1981 before getting swept out of the playoffs by the Yankees.

From 1983 to 1985, the Giants could not sell tickets by promising fans they could see Brad Wellman or Johnnie LeMaster go hitless in four trips to the plate, or that they had a chance to see Randy Lerch or Renie Martin get knocked out of the game in the fourth inning, so the team had to find a different approach. This led to a period when the Giants engaged in a series of promotional strategies that were innovative, creative, funny, and may have even helped sell some tickets. For many observers and fans of the Giants, those promotions were more memorable than anything that occurred on the field between 1983 and 1985. Larry Baer, who worked for the Giants in the early 1980s after graduating from college described the Giants strategy during these years:

> You had to be creative. It became kind of a cult thing not unlike the Grateful Dead or punk rock or whatever things San Franciscans like, you know freezing at the 'Stick . . . The Croix de Candlestick campaign . . . we had a

lot of fun rolling it out . . . San Franciscans are different. One thing about San Franciscans . . . we celebrate being different. Not liking mascots . . . the Crazy Crab, which was an intentionally designed anti-mascot mascot. Being different, being kind of edgy. The Croix de Candlestick—even if the weather was bad—I don't think that would work in Philadelphia.[10]

Baer, who as a fifth-generation San Franciscan and a lifelong Giants fan has a pretty good idea of the culture and gestalt of the city and its team, elaborated: "The cookie cutter thing doesn't work because we like think the city has a lot of character. We like to think we are different. In many ways we are. . . . Its kind of like the *New Yorker* illustration. . . . I think San Franciscans are a fairly chauvinistic lot. . . . Willie McCovey was more loved than anybody because he came up here. . . . We feel like we've got an innovative culture."[11]

Two of the promotions mentioned by Baer captured the spirit of the Giants in those years when the team was pretty awful. The first was in 1983. By that time, the Giants has wrestled for years with the question of how to promote the team despite the freezing nighttime weather, including wind and fog in Candlestick Park. In 1983, Giants director of marketing Pat Gallagher, and John Crawford, an ad man who was advising the Giants, decided that rather than try to combat the reality of the climate at Candlestick Park, he was going to try to use it, to the extent possible, as a marketing tool.

Crawford and Gallagher's idea was that because by 1983 it was clear that nothing was going to be done about Candlestick Park, and equally apparent that every baseball fan, and even non-baseball fan, in the Bay Area was aware of the cold and wind at Candlestick, rather than hide from the ballpark's reputation, Gallagher made it a challenge. Fans who managed to stay to the end of an extra inning game at Candlestick would get an orange pin called a Croix de Candlestick. The pin featured the Giants SF logo embedded in snow and icicles and the words "Croix de Candlestick" across the top and "Veni-Vidi-Vixi" across the bottom. The latter was Latin for "I came, I saw, I survived." Giants fans could collect many Croix and wear them on their caps as a testament both to their loyalty to their team and to their ability to remain outside in the cold.

The Croix de Candlestick was heavily promoted in the Bay Area just before the 1983 season, so fans were very aware of it the first time a home game went into extra innings that year. Gallagher described what happened the evening of April 20, 1983, at Candlestick Park: "The first Croix de Candlestick night . . . we had about three or four thousand of 'em. The first night that we gave them away was a night game against the Dodgers. Jack Clark struck out to send the game into extra innings. . . . As soon as that happened people started cheering. It was a problem, almost a riot, at the gates because people expected them on their way out. . . . We had to figure out another way."[12]

Gallagher's memory is not entirely accurate. Clark did not strike out to send the game into extra innings. It was Tom O'Malley who struck out against Dodger ace Fernando Valenzuela for the last out of the ninth to send the game into extra innings. Clark grounded into a fielder's choice that sent pinch runner Max Venable home with the winning run one inning later.

Nonetheless, the problem Gallagher described was real. On a cold night, when people are anxious to get home and have little patience, the idea of simply handing out Croix de Candlestick pins was not going to work because it could not be done quickly enough. Following that game, the Giants switched to giving out vouchers after the game that could be redeemed for a Croix at a handful of Bay Area locations, including the Giants' store in downtown San Francisco. Unfortunately, this cheapened the Croix a little bit as fans simply needed a ticket stub from the extra-inning game rather than any proof that they had stayed until the game was over to receive their pin.

Even today, when attending a ballgame at Oracle Park, one sees many fans, usually well into middle age or older, with a Croix, or a few Croix, on their cap. While the Croix was an innovative and enduring promotion that drew attention to the team and helped brand the Giants in an unusual way, it is not clear that it sold any additional tickets. The simple reason for this is the obvious one. Extra-inning baseball games are not scheduled but occur organically. The Croix was not a giveaway like cap day or T-shirt day that might draw a few thousand more fans to a particular game. Nor was it something that enhanced the fan experience at every game, like better food or a new scoreboard, rather it was something that might happen at any given night game, but most fans knew was relatively rare. Roughly one out of every 10 games goes into extra innings, which means that if these events are evenly distributed between home and the road, and between night and day games, the Giants averaged around six extra inning night games a years. Therefore, the odds of getting a Croix were never very good.

The year after introducing the Croix de Candlestick, the Giants came up with another marketing idea that, while not as enduringly popular as the Croix, was, in its own way, equally memorable. To understand the true subversive only-in-San Francisco brilliance of the Crazy Crab it is important to understand two things. First, the early 1980s were a time when many teams were using goofy mascots. The most famous of these included the San Diego Chicken and the Phillie Phanatic. Across the bay in Oakland, there was no official mascot, but a long-haired, bearded, and frequently shirtless man named Krazy George, beginning in 1981, led fans in cheers, banged a tambourine with a mallet, and is said to have invented the wave. However, Giants fans were never the kind to embrace these kinds of mascots, not least because by 1983 or so, Candlestick Park, between the weather and the team, was the kind of place that required fortitude and determination, rather than light-hearted fun and games.

The second thing any native San Franciscan, or even tourist, other than those who observe kashrut or have shellfish allergies, can tell you is that the crab in San Francisco is delicious. Whether you're having them at a Vietnamese restaurant in the Richmond or Sunset Districts, dipped in melted butter down by the wharf, or as part of Christmas Eve cioppino, crabs are among the best fare that a city long known for excellent food has to offer.

The confluence of these two factors led the Giants to introduce a mascot, but one that the tough Candlestick crowd would jeer and boo, rather than celebrate. Pat Gallagher, one of the people behind the idea, described how the Crazy Crab came to be known:

In '84, we had this idea of this mascot that everybody would boo. . . . We're proving that Giants fans are made of a different grit, determination. They wouldn't put up with something as silly as chicken or any of that stuff, so we did this phony survey that said 63% of the people surveyed said they would boo a mascot. So, we came up with these TV spots with this guy with an orange crab outfit on the field. At that time we had no intention of putting this thing on the field, but the response to the ads was so great. . . . A week into it we said "what the hell, let's see what this thing looks like" . . . so we pushed him onto the field with that stupid music. People got up out of their seats and people booed. . . . It was so ridiculous, but it was great fun.[13]

Bob Lurie, who had hired Gallagher and approved the plan for the Crazy Crab, described how "this guy [the Crab] got pelted. . . . [It was] something for the fans to have fun with. . . . Some of the opposing players would throw things at the Crazy Crab." Lurie explained the thinking behind ideas like the Crazy Crab by saying simply "we were desperate."[14]

The Crazy Crab lasted through almost the entire 1984 season, usually making an appearance and dancing inanely to an equally inane tune that was played over Candlestick's public address system around the fifth inning. Giants fans dutifully, and with varying degrees of sincerity, booed the Crab. Many threw debris, usually, but not always, of a relatively harmless nature. The Crazy Crab was a genuinely unusual and even strange mascot, but it was a good reflection of a team that was struggling on the field, 13 years removed from its last postseason appearance and searching for an identity.

During the 1980s, the Giants drew a million or more fans every year but two. In 1981, they drew only 632,274 fans in a year when roughly one third of the season was lost to strike and the other two thirds occurred in the shadow of the looming or just completed strike. The other year was 1985. The Giants were terrible in 1985, going 62–100. That remains the only year in franchise history when the team lost 100 games. However, given how bad they were in 1984, when they lost 96 games, it is probably wrong to attribute the drop off in attendance from 1,001,545 in 1984 to 818,697 in 1985 simply to the quality of the team.

By 1985, the Giants had tried everything, except putting a consistently winning team on the ballfield, and they had been unable to meaningfully increase attendance at the ballpark or excitement at the ballpark in general. This led to another unusual marketing decision. Rather than try to turn the inhospitable nighttime conditions at Candlestick into an advantage, they tried to ameliorate that issue entirely by playing a schedule of only day games. They did not quite make this goal but managed to play 65 of their 81 home games in 1985 during the day.

The weather during day games at Candlestick was usually quite good and almost never as oppressively hot and humid as day games in the Northeast or Midwest during the summer, so the idea made some sense on paper. The day-game-heavy schedule was great for fans who were young people with nothing else going on once school got out and who had some spending money, seniors or other retired people, service sector workers whose days off were during the week, or tourists who were passionate baseball fans, but in general it was a bad idea.

The majority of fans were either in school or at work during weekday afternoons. This was particularly true during the first 10 and the last three or four weeks or so of the season when school was in session. The quality of the team was also an obstacle, but that was unrelated to when the games were played.

The bigger problem with this plan was that while it addressed the issue of poor weather at night, Candlestick Park's other major drawback, location, dissuaded fans from going there during the day. For most people in San Francisco, Candlestick was remote and ill served by public transportation, so going to a day game during the week meant traversing San Francisco twice during the busy workday, all but guaranteeing being stuck in traffic at least once. This problem was even worse for fans from Marin County, to the city's north, or San Mateo and Santa Clara Counties just south of San Francisco. These fans were very likely to be stuck in rush hour traffic after the game as they made their way home. Additionally, because Candlestick Park was in an area where there was not much else to do—the ballpark was surrounded by a parking lot, the bay, and a mountain—fans could not spend an evening out or meet friends near the ballpark after a day game. The Bayview–Hunters Point section of San Francisco was also a lower-income and heavily African American neighbor-hood in the 1980s, so many white fans felt unsafe in that area even during the daytime. This was in substantial part due to racist stereotyping, but it was a real sentiment for many.

The Croix and the Crab are memorable promotional ideas, but at the time they were understood largely as fun distractions that helped make another season of losing Giants baseball more tolerable. While it is possible that they helped generate some attention for the Giants, it is difficult to argue that they did much to raise attendance as the team finished 20th, 23rd, and 24th in attendance in 1983, 1984, and 1985, respectively.

In the bigger picture, it is not quite so easy to dismiss the impact of these two ideas because they helped rebrand the Giants and in doing that helped strengthen the connection between the team and San Francisco. These two in-novations, as well as the use of Don Novello's character Father Guido Sarducci on television ads for the Giants earlier in the decade, were an implicit recognition that the Giants did not play in an ordinary media market. San Francisco is a quirky, unconventional, fun-loving city where people have a complex relation-ship with traditions and convention. As the Giants began to understand this, they began to invisibly strengthen the bond between the city and the team. As Baer explained, "there's a lot of nuance to San Francisco. People are willing to have fun with the Giants even when the Giants aren't doing well."[15]

Baseball has always been a conservative institution and, for many, deeply associated with traditional American values and lifestyles. However, it would have been counterproductive to market it that way in the Bay Area. In the early 1980s, the Giants began to understand this and tried to create an image for the Giants that was consistent with the way the people of the city saw it.

More than 30 years later, following a period when the Giants were, for half a decade, the most successful team in baseball, the Crab, the Croix, and Guido Sarducci have been forgotten by most fans of the Giants and of baseball in general, who may have wondered what those orange pins on the caps of older Giants fans were, but their legacy was real. The 2010 team that won the Giants' first World Series ever in San Francisco was described as being made up of outcasts and misfits. San Francisco is the only big-league town where being described as outcasts and misfits is understood to be a compliment. Many residents proudly see themselves as such.

The best pitcher on that 2010 Giants team had long hair and had been busted for marijuana possession. Tim Lincecum was embraced by Giants fans because he seemed like somebody who could be part of San Francisco even if he were not a star ballplayer. Two years later, ace reliever Sergio Romo saved three games in the Giants' World Series sweep of the Detroit Tigers. In the bottom of the 10th inning of the fourth and deciding game, Romo struck out the side, freezing Tigers star Miguel Cabrera, who looked at a very hittable fastball down the middle for the final out of the game. At the victory parade in San Francisco, Romo, a heavily bearded and tattooed Mexican American, wore a long sleeve T-shirt emblazoned with the words "I only look illegal." This endeared him to Giants fans even more. It is hard to imagine fans of the Rangers, Tigers, or Royals, the teams the Giants beat in their three World Series victories, having a similar reaction if somebody on their team had worn a shirt with those words. Players like Lincecum and Romo helped establish the unique personality of those 2010 to 2014 teams, but the unique character of the team began in earnest during the first half of the 1980s.

TWO NEW FACES

In 1985, the Giants made some other personnel changes that marked the end of an era and made 1985 the dividing line of Bob Lurie's time owning the team. During the first decade of Lurie's ownership, the Giants were not a good team. From 1976 through 1985, the Giants finished over .500 only three times, including the strike year of 1981, and had an overall winning percentage of .468. From 1986 until Bob Lurie sold the team following the 1992 season, the Giants were a much better team, finishing over .500 in five of seven seasons for an overall winning percentage of .511.

One of the changes the Giants made was symbolic but, along with the Clark trade, marked the end of an era, albeit a largely forgotten one, in Giants history. For parts of 10 seasons, Jack Clark and Johnnie LeMaster had been teammates on the Giants. The underappreciated slugger and the skinny shortstop who couldn't hit and whose defensive abilities may have been underappreciated, or overstated depending on who you ask, had been mainstays on those Giants teams through the good seasons and the bad. By early 1985, Clark had many good years left but was anxious to get out of San Francisco. The trade of Clark for, among others, José Uribe, who was younger, a better hitter, and by 1985, a better fielder than LeMaster, made the longtime Giants shortstop very expendable.

LeMaster had once again failed to hit in 1984 and was slowing down in the field as well. Perhaps because he was a veteran, LeMaster started the first four games of the 1985 season while batting eighth, but he was never a regular after that. By May 7, roughly a month into the season, Uribe had won the shortstop job and LeMaster was sent to the Indians in exchange for Mike Jeffcoat and Luis Quiñones, players who even the most intense Giants fan can be forgiven for forgetting.

With LeMaster and Clark gone, the team still couldn't win many games, but change was beginning to happen. In late September, Lurie, having seen enough of the team's losing, fired general manager Tom Haller. Lurie's choice to replace Haller was an excellent one that changed the fortunes of the team. Lurie had known and thought highly of Al Rosen for several years, but Rosen was, in 1985, still with the Houston Astros. However, his time there was winding down so Lurie got permission from Astros owner John McMullen to talk to Rosen and hired him. Lurie gave full control of the team to Rosen with the caveat that he did not want to read about any moves in the paper—meaning Lurie was not going to stop Rosen from making any transactions, but that the owner wanted to be kept informed about what Rosen was doing. The two became close friends and spoke almost daily for the next six years.[16]

At the time Bob Lurie hired him, Al Rosen, who died in 2015, was an unusual baseball man but an extremely accomplished one both on the field and in the front office. Rosen had been one of the first great Jewish ballplayers, after Hank Greenberg, but before Sandy Koufax. Unlike Koufax and Greenberg, who had both grown up in New York City, Koufax in Brooklyn and Greenberg in the Bronx, the South Carolina–born Rosen had grown up in Miami. Like Greenberg, Rosen served in the military in World War II, spending four years in the Navy. Because Rosen did not go into the military as a famous ballplayer, he received no special treatment and saw a great deal of combat, including on an assault boat during the landing at Okinawa, one of the most intense battles of the war.[17]

Rosen was a proud Jew who, according to one biographer, "said that he was determined that every Jew in America would be proud of him because of his achievements. On one occasion, columnist and TV host Ed Sullivan wrote that 'Rosen was a Catholic because he always marked a cross on home plate each time he came to bat.' Rosen responded that 'it was not a cross but an x' and that he wished his name was 'more Jewish' so no one would mistake him for being Catholic." Rosen, like Greenberg before him, did not tolerate any anti-Semitic comments from opponents and was not afraid to physically confront bigots.[18] Rosen was not as big as Greenberg but had been an amateur boxer and knew how to handle himself in a fight.

Because of the war and the presence of standout veteran third baseman Ken Keltner on the Indians, Rosen got a bit of a late start to his career and only became a full-time starter in 1950 when he was 26 years old. He also retired at the age of 32 following the 1956 season. However, during those seven years he was a very good player. He was a four-time all-star and in 1953 was unanimously voted the American League MVP, leading the league in home runs, RBIs, slugging percentage, OPS, and total bases. A year later, following another standout season, the Indians interrupted the Yankees streak of pennants—1954 was the only year between 1949 and 1958 the Yankees did not win the American League pennant. In the eighth inning of Game One of that World Series, Rosen was on first base when Willie Mays made the most famous catch in World Series history.

After leaving baseball, Rosen worked outside of the game for years but returned to become president of the Yankees in 1978 and then moved on to the Astros. By the time Lurie hired him, Rosen was a well-respected baseball man. That reputation would only improve during his time with the Giants.

According to several players who were Giants when Al Rosen was president, Rosen brought the toughness he learned on the streets of Miami to his job. Will Clark described how "Al [Rosen] ran it [the team] with an iron fist. Al was very vocal and he was very, shall we say, seen. He would come in the clubhouse in a heartbeat and wear your ass out. In a heartbeat. If he had something to say, he was in that clubhouse. You got called in the office and he would let you know in no uncertain terms who was the boss and who was not."[19]

Dave Dravecky, who Al Rosen traded for during the 1987 season, described a different side of the Giants general manager, one that does not come across in the image of him as the tough guy that Clark and others described: "Al Rosen was absolutely amazing to me. I had so much respect and admiration for that man. It really was an honor to have been traded for by him knowing the kind of baseball man that he is . . . what he was building for the Giants. . . . What really has stuck with me is the relationship after. . . . Al Rosen, every time I saw him after that . . . he would always pull me aside. . . . Al Rosen means a lot to me."[20]

Rosen also understood how to build a winner. He had already won a World Series with the Yankees in 1978 and was determined to do the same in San Francisco. Rosen was an opportunist in that when he thought the team was close, he did not hesitate to make big moves during the season to make the team better. Rosen's approach was central to the Giants' success in the late 1980s. For Bruce Jenkins, the hiring of Rosen catalyzed the team's late 1980s renaissance: "Al Rosen, that was a brilliant move. . . . Within a year everything changed. . . . Everything came together there in a fantastic way."[21]

Lurie described Rosen's view on when a team should go for it, or in today's baseball parlance, be buyers at the trade deadline: "Al used to say, 'you never know when you're gonna win a championship and if you have an opportunity, you have to go for it', which is why he made those big key trades in '87 and '89. . . . His attitude was, 'if you've got a shot, you've got to take it. You never know when its gonna come around again.'"[22]

One of those players for whom Rosen traded during the pennant drive in 1987 was Kevin Mitchell, who came to the Giants along with Dave Dravecky and Craig Lefferts from the Padres. Mitchell, an African American player from San Diego who had begun his career with the New York Mets, had a different view of Rosen and one that goes to the heart of the complexity of racial politics in baseball in the 1980s.

Rosen's hard-nosed approach did not work well with the young Mitchell, so, as Mitchell explained, Rosen asked Dusty Baker to be a go-between: "Al Rosen stayed on my case every day. He would send Dusty over just to come talk to me. So I asked Dusty 'why do they keep sending you over here? Why don't they just talk to me personally?' But Al Rosen . . . he told the media that he had to go watch *Boyz n the Hood* to learn more about me."[23] Rosen died in 2015 before I began researching this book, but the extent to which the Rosen-Mitchell dynamic is about race should not be overstated. Rosen spent decades in baseball and was never connected to any racist or bigoted actions or remarks. Moreover, he had thought highly enough of Mitchell to trade for him in 1987.

Baker was a Giants coach when Mitchell was playing with the team and described Rosen as "tough, man. He taught me a lot. . . . He'd be harder on the team when you were winning than when you were losing."[24] Baker, like

Mitchell, is African American and as a player was a slugging left fielder too. Mitchell was perhaps a better hitter, but Baker was more consistent and better able to stay healthy. During more than half a century in baseball, Baker has earned a reputation as a man of great integrity and decency, who cared deeply about the men who played with or for him. When his former Dodgers teammate Glenn Burke, who came out publicly shortly after being run out of baseball for being gay in 1980, was dying of AIDS, Baker was the only one of Burke's former teammates to visit him. That is the kind of friend Dusty Baker was. Baker has also frequently worked hard to build relationships and mentor younger African American players, particularly outfielders. Baker himself was mentored in his first years with the Braves by a veteran African American outfielder, Henry Aaron, one of the greatest ballplayers ever.

Baker was also an advocate for Mitchell and recounts a story from 1988 when Baker began his tenure as Giants batting coach:

> I was the batting coach and Al Rosen asks us in a meeting, we've gotta get somebody to hit behind Will Clark. And I'd just talked to my dad about that, and my dad said "you don't need to go out and trade for anybody you've got the guy Kevin Mitchell." . . . I said [in the meeting] "we don't need to make a trade, give up anybody, we've got Kevin Mitchell." . . . He said "Kevin Mitchell, whose dumbass idea is that." I say "It's my dad's." He said "what's your dad know?" I said "my dad knows a lot about baseball. He coached me and about ten pros that came out of Riverside. My dad knows some baseball."[25]

This story also supports Mitchell's contention that Rosen was not a big supporter of the slugging outfielder

Given all this, it is no surprise that Baker and Mitchell were close. Mitchell described his relationship with Baker to me as being very important. "I think without Dusty there, a lot of us wouldn't have had any guidance. . . . It never stopped with Dusty. . . . Even to this day. He's still in my life."[26] Mitchell's warm feelings for Baker did not preclude him from chafing because Rosen sent somebody else to speak with him. This can be attributed to a misunderstanding as perhaps Rosen recognized the tension between him and Mitchell and sought out a respected intermediary, but Mitchell, as evinced by his alleged comments about *Boyz n the Hood*, a 1991 John Singleton film set in an African American community in South Central Los Angeles.

I could not find any evidence of Rosen saying this to the media, so he may have said it privately to Mitchell or to somebody else. Regardless, Mitchell's comments make it clear that whatever Rosen was trying to do did not sit well with Mitchell, who described such an occasion:

> I had a 104 temperature at Dodger Stadium. They pulled me into the office. They told me "Will Clark is playing." I told them "I'm not Will Clark," and Al Rosen stood up on me. And I stood back on him. And he started having chest pains. . . . So, I know Al Rosen lied to me, but he just didn't understand me. . . . Years later he softened. Because he always thought I would be caught up drinking, drugs and whatever. Then he saw me years later. . . . he apologized, cause now he sees me and my life . . . is different. I've got a good life I'm settled.

When asked the extent to which the tension between him and Rosen was racial, Mitchell replied "a lot. I still think it goes on."[27]

This is not to suggest that Rosen was a racist. Asking who was or was not a racist is generally an unproductive way to discuss race. Rather it is a reflection that racism was still part of baseball when Mitchell was playing and that the structures—white men holding the real power, and many players of color working for them in a deeply hierarchical structure within the context of a broader racist American society—created problems for African American players. That is not a surprise.

On September 17, 1985, Dave LaPoint had another uninspiring start, giving up four runs in the first and taking the loss in a 6–1 defeat at the hands of the Reds, dropping his record to 7–14 and the Giants to 56–88. Rosen had seen enough and fired Jim Davenport, a longtime Giants player and coach who had demonstrated no real ability as a manager in 1985. He was replaced by Roger Craig and the Giants' leadership team for the next several years was finally in place.

Roger Craig had been in baseball since the early 1950s. His first year in the big leagues was spent contributing to the 1955 Brooklyn Dodgers World Series victory, the franchise's only championship in Brooklyn. Craig was 5–3 with a 2.78 ERA in 21 games for that Dodgers team. He started and won Game Five of that World Series against the Yankees. Among his teammates that year, in addition to Jackie Robinson, Pee Wee Reese, Roy Campanella, and other stars from the *Boys of Summer* era Dodgers, were two other young pitchers, Sandy Koufax and Tommy Lasorda.

After coming to Los Angeles with the Dodgers in 1958, Craig was drafted by the expansion Mets, where he started and lost the first game in that franchise's history. He then bounced around the National League and pitched his final game in 1966 for the Phillies. Craig had managed the San Diego Padres in 1978 and 1979 but by 1985 had earned a reputation as one of the game's best pitching coaches in part because of his work with the Detroit Tigers, who won the World Series in 1984, as well as for his pioneering work helping pitchers develop the split-finger fastball.

Craig and Rosen would be the most successful and stable leadership team of the Bob Lurie era. Lurie not only had great confidence and trust in Rosen but viewed him as a friend. With the team in the hands of these two accomplished, respected, and competent baseball men, Lurie could focus his attention on finding a new home for the Giants, while enjoying seeing his team turn things around on the field.

A DOWNTOWN BALLPARK

As the Rosen-Craig era for the Giants was beginning, the Giants continued their quest for a new home, increasingly turning their attention to a downtown solution. Despite the talk of needing a downtown ballpark, the Giants never actually wanted a ballpark downtown. In San Francisco, downtown refers to the busy financial district where numerous office buildings, hotels, and the like leave little room for a ballpark. By downtown, the team, and its supporters, meant somewhere close to downtown and therefore closer to more of the city. Hunters Point, by contrast, was far away from major residential neighborhoods in the western part of San Francisco like the Sunset and the Richmond, and northern areas like Pacific Heights, Cow Hollow, the Marina, and North Beach.

Just south of downtown San Francisco lies a battery of neighborhoods, such as South of Market and Rincon Valley. This was a large part of the city that in the 1980s still had not recovered from the loss of manufacturing and shipping jobs in the period from 1950 to 1975, so there was empty space and buildings that could be torn down if needed for a new ballpark. By the early 1980s, South of Market was having a slight resurgence centered around a convention center, the Moscone Center, that was named for the mayor who helped develop it, but who was murdered before it opened. In 1984, the Democratic Party would hold its convention at the Moscone Center.

Somewhere in the South of Market or Rincon Valley area was the place where the Giants wanted to find a new home, but that was never going to be easy. Even in the early 1980s, finding and securing ownership of the land on which the stadium would be built, figuring out how to finance the ballpark, and working through all of the questions of land use regulations and the like were extremely difficult.

Finding land for a new ballpark, persuading the city to provide substantial funding, and taking care of all the regulatory issues are challenges every team in the United States face when they want a new place to play, but in San Francisco this was even more difficult. By the early 1980s, although Mayor Dianne Feinstein was, by San Francisco standards, a conservative, probusiness Democrat, the political sentiment in San Francisco had continued to move leftward. This meant that voters, and the legislators who represented them on the Board of Supervisors, were not inclined to subsidize or give tax breaks to wealthy men like Bob Lurie who wanted a to build a new ballpark for a baseball team.

Although the horrific violence of November 1978 had begun to recede into memory by the early 1980s as San Francisco was able to heal the psychic and other wounds from Jonestown and the assassinations, the new decade brought new, unforeseen, and devastating problems to San Francisco. The AIDS epidemic hit San Francisco harder and earlier than any other American city. AIDS devastated San Francisco's gay community, killing thousands in the prime of their lives and creating fear throughout gay San Francisco. In addition to those who died at the hands of this modern plague, the fear and confusion left in the wake of the spread of AIDS gave rise to increased homophobia as religious bigots suggested that AIDS was some kind of divine retribution by an angry god. This particularly venal and hateful notion was bolstered by a more quotidian homophobia, as straight people wallowed, often deliberately, in misinformation about AIDS, so they could further discriminate against gay people.

Dianne Feinstein was a smart, hardworking mayor who was not antigay, but given the lack of support from the Reagan administration in Washington, the city was overwhelmed as Feinstein sought to combat this disease that had such a huge impact on San Francisco. In that climate in the early 1980s, it is not hard to see why building a new ballpark was not the highest funding priority for the city or why calling for that funding was rarely a politically popular thing to do.

Since the A's moved to Oakland in 1968, baseball has stabilized at four two-team media markets, Chicago, Los Angeles, New York, and the Bay Area. The Bay Area has always been the smallest of these markets. In 2017, New York, Los Angeles, and Chicago were the three largest metropolitan areas in the United States, while the Bay Area was 12th.[28] In 1980, the Bay Area was 8th but still lagged behind the top three, which are the same today, by quite a bit.[29] This demographic reality had long made it difficult for both Bay Area teams to survive financially. The Giants had the advantage of being the first team in the Bay Area and of being directly identified with the biggest and most important city in the region, but by the early 1970s, the relative success of the two teams on the field had more than balanced that out. However, the collapse of the Oakland franchise as the stars of the 1971 to 1975 division-winning teams left by free agency or trades, shifted the balance of Bay Area baseball power, at least somewhat, back to the Giants.

A few years later, in 1980 and 1981, the A's experienced a bit of a renaissance built primarily around manager Billy Martin's aggressive style that made the team fun and competitive again. Although the A's marketed Martin and what they called "Billy Ball," the real star of that team was Rickey Henderson, an Oakland native who began his career with the A's in 1979 before becoming a regular in 1980. The young Rickey Henderson could do it all, field, hit for average, hit for power, and steal more bases than anybody in the history of the game. In the early 1980s, there was no more exciting player in baseball. From 1981 to 1985, the A's regularly outdrew the Giants every year. Thus, the assumption from the late 1970s, that if one team left the Bay Area it would be the A's, began to reverse itself in the early 1980s.

The baseball geography of the Bay Area has always been relatively clear. The A's base is the East Bay counties of Alameda, where Oakland is located, and Contra Costa, just north of Alameda. Giants fans are concentrated in the city of San Francisco and in counties further south on the peninsula, primarily San Mateo and Santa Clara. Marin, just north of the city and west of Alameda, is generally divided between the two teams. Given this, the failure of the Giants to find a downtown location in the early 1980s, as well as their strong fan base south of the city, led them to seek a new home somewhere along the peninsula south of the city.

This was the third option after doming or renovating Candlestick and finding a downtown home seemed to not work out. A new ballpark in either San Mateo or Santa Clara County made a lot of sense in some respects. The weather was almost always better on that part of the peninsula. Night games there in July and August would not be as cold and windy as in Candlestick, but warm and pleasant, ideal for baseball. Because Santa Clara and San Mateo Counties were heavily suburban, a good highway infrastructure already existed. That meant that the strong contingent of Giants fans who had been making the drive up to Candlestick from these suburban counties would have an easier time getting to the ballpark to see their team play. Moreover,

San Jose was one of the fastest-growing cities in the area, so the pool of fans south of the city would likely continue to expand.

All of those reasons made a lot of sense, unless you happened to be a San Franciscan. We understood the peninsula to be suburban, inaccessible, and inferior to San Francisco. If the Giants were to move there, they would potentially lose many of their most devoted fans who lived in San Francisco. Additionally, the paucity of decent public transportation to get from San Francisco to its southern suburbs, particularly from residential neighborhoods, meant that younger fans and many elderly fans who relied on the flawed but adequate Ballpark Express, operated by the city of San Francisco, to get to Candlestick, would no longer have a way of getting to games.

The politics of moving to Santa Clara county were also complicated. There was more space there than in the city, so that part of the process was, in some respects, easier. However, just as George Moscone did not want to lose the team to Toronto when he was mayor, no subsequent mayor wanted to see the San Francisco Giants move out of the city. The stakes were not nearly as high, but for a city with as substantial an opinion of itself as San Francisco, losing the team to the suburbs would still be a blow and not good for the political fortunes of any mayor. Because Candlestick was owned by the city, and the Giants had a lease there, the city had some leverage over the issue, but that probably would not have held up in court. Nonetheless, the city could slow down the process or create other problems for the Giants if they tried to leave. Bob Lurie described how, beginning in the 1980s, he "kept looking and hoping" for a site in Santa Clara that would work for the Giants, but added that "Dianne [Feinstein] was pretty much against everything outside the city."[30] Corey Busch offered some more insight into the constant exploration of moving the team south of the city, suggesting that Lurie had some concerns as well: "Our hearts were only in it maybe 99%. Those [possible sites south of San Francisco] were both refuges of last resort. We didn't want the team to leave the Bay Area, but . . . [Lurie] wanted the team in San Francisco. We believed in it because it was the only alternative we really had."[31]

Given all this, by the mid-1980s it was clear that renovating Candlestick to make it a warmer and better environment for baseball was not going to work, so there were really only two possibilities if the Giants were going remain in the Bay Area for the long term. They had to find a new home either somewhere south of Market Street in San Francisco or somewhere south of the city.

During the last decade Bob Lurie owned the team, the quest to find a permanent home for the Giants was rarely far from the minds of Lurie and the people who ran the Giants with him, Giants fans, or any of the three people, Feinstein, Art Agnos, and Frank Jordan, who served as mayor of San Francisco during these years. From a twenty-first-century perspective, the story of the Giants' quest to find a new home during the last 20 or so years they played in Candlestick Park seems complicated but understandable, but it didn't feel that way at the time. Throughout most of the 1980s, efforts to find the land and funding for a downtown ballpark, the search for a suitable home in Santa Clara Country, and talk of Lurie selling or moving the team out of the Bay Area seemed to be constant. Most of the time, it was difficult for an ordinary baseball fan to know what was likely to happen, which rumors could be trusted, and what the state of the negotiations were.

For example, after the 1985 Giants dreadful season, the front page of the *San Francisco Chronicle* reported to readers throughout Northern California that "San Francisco Mayor Dianne Feinstein yesterday threw her support behind Giants owner Bob Lurie's plan to buy out his Candlestick Park lease and move temporarily to the Oakland Coliseum." In the next sentence, the author of the story, C. W. Nevius, reported that "Oakland Mayor Lionel Wilson led a strong chorus of opposition to the proposed move."[32] The plan, if Wilson would agree to it, would have been for the Giants to play in Oakland until a promised downtown stadium was built in San Francisco.

About a week later, another Nevius article in the *Chronicle,* this one with a Denver byline, reported, "mention 'the Giants' here in the Mile High City and the response is cautious optimism." The article went on to describe how Denver hoped to woo the Giants for a few years while San Francisco pursued a downtown stadium. Nevius also noted that John Molinari, the President of San Francisco's Board of Supervisors, was bearish on the idea. The San Francisco politician told Nevius: "Perhaps as a very last-ditch thing I would take a look at it. . . . But it would have to be an 'everything's gone' sort of thing and we're not there yet."[33]

The speculation about where the Giants would play in 1986 occurred against the backdrop of continued discussion around a downtown ballpark somewhere around 7th and Townsend streets in the South of Market or Rincon Valley part of San Francisco. During 1985 and 1986, the papers reported that the ballpark was likely to be built. Some printed maps and diagrams of what the new ballpark would look like and how it would fit in to the surrounding area. Thus, Giants fans could distract themselves that off-season from the sad state of the team by wondering where the Giants would be playing in 1986 and beyond, while reading newspapers that seemed to be reporting different scenarios every few weeks.

Shortly before spring training began, the question of where the Giants would play in 1986 was clarified, although those familiar with the Giants in recent years probably knew all along what the outcome was going to be. On January 30, 1986, a headline above the masthead in the *Chronicle* announced: "Giants to Play at Candlestick." The article also noted that "what will happen beyond that [the 1986 season] is anyone's guess. Negotiations between the team and city officials over financing and building a downtown stadium will continue." In the next paragraph, reporter David Bush reminded readers that "The Giants . . . had been said at various time to be headed for Oakland, Denver, Vancouver B.C., Washington D.C., or Phoenix."[34]

Bush's article, and the resolution to the question of where the Giants would play in 1986, was almost exactly a decade after Lurie's purchase of the Giants in the face of a possible move to Toronto. In that decade, Lurie had kept his pledge not to take the Giants away from San Francisco but had not come meaningfully closer to solving the problem of Candlestick Park that had contributed to Horace Stoneham's need to sell the team to Toronto in 1976.

Given that the problems associated with Candlestick Park predated Lurie's purchase of the team, and that efforts to address those problems, in one way or another, all but defined the years Lurie owned the team, it is notable that during those 17 years, the Giants never played a home game anywhere but Candlestick Park. This was due, on the one hand, to Lurie's commitment to trying to keep the Giants in the Bay Area and, on the other hand, to the extreme difficulty of finding a solution to the problem of where the Giants should play.

Chapter 6

TWO ROOKIES AND A RETURN TO THE POSTSEASON

The 1985 Giants were a terrible team for many reasons, one of which was the appalling lack of production they got from the right side of the infield. Starting first baseman David Green, the prospect who was supposed to replace Jack Clark, hit .248/.301/.347 with a paltry five home runs. Backups Gary Rajsich, who was also part of the haul the Giants got for Clark, Dan Driessen, and Scot Thompson were even worse. At second base, Manny Trillo, while still able to make the play when the ball was near him, had at 34 slowed down in the field. Trillo's .227/.287/.288 slash line was even worse than Green's. Backup infielders Brad Wellman and Ricky Adams had proved they were no longer prospects by producing even less than Trillo. Veteran Duane Kuiper called it a career a few months into the season and transitioned to the broadcast booth.

Other than trading away Trillo and Green, the Giants did little outside of the organization to address these problems, but that did not mean the team did not have a vision. The plan was to give a couple of first round draft picks, one from the 1983 June secondary draft and one who was taken with the second overall pick in the draft in June 1985, as the Giants were stumbling through a terrible season, a chance.

Robby Thompson was the less heralded of the two prospects. He came to spring training in 1986 as a second baseman who was primarily known for his defensive skills. Thompson's goal that spring, as he told me was, "I'm going into spring training—what I wanna do, I wanna open up eyes. That was my main goal."[1] The infielder who had never played an inning above AA recognized that making the team was an ambitious goal and simply hoped to make a good impression and keep his career moving forward. Thompson miscalculated on two fronts. First, he was not aware of just how thin the Giants were at second base. Players like Brad Wellman, Mike Woodard, or Joe Pittman were not going to keep a top prospect off the team. Second, Thompson underestimated his own ability.

Thompson did more than open some eyes. He played his way into the starting lineup just a month before his 23rd birthday. Thompson had two and a half years of minor league ball under his belt by spring training of 1986, so was not particularly ahead of the pace that was expected of a good prospect. The same could not be said of the other rookie who opened some more eyes that spring training.

Will Clark had been one of the most famous college players in the country before being drafted by the Giants. He had also played on the 1984 US Olympic team, so he had about as high of a profile an amateur baseball player could have in the mid-1980s. Nonetheless, as spring training of 1986 commenced, Clark's entire professional experience consisted of 65 games in A ball. During those games, he had made an unmistakable impression, hitting .309/.458/.512 while playing his usual excellent defense at first base.

It is easy to overlook, but difficult to overestimate, the impact Clark had on the Giants. If Rosen and Craig brought a new attitude to the team's management, Clark brought that same attitude to the field. Clark was an intense competitor who when I spoke with him reminded me several times how he hated to lose. He was not the kind of player who was going to be happy as the star player making millions on a bad team, nor was Clark by disposition a kvetch. He was a hard worker with enormous talent who wanted badly to win and expected the same of his teammates—and he sure could hit.

Bob Lurie reflected on the competitiveness of probably the best Giants player over the course of his time owning the team: "His [Clark's] attitude was 'this is the seventh game of the World Series.' Every game was the most important game. He had that little bit of a high pitched voice and was always yelling and always making noise. . . . He kind of pissed off the other players, but they respected him because they knew how much he wanted to win."[2]

Clark and Thompson, who would go on to hold down the right side of the infield for the Giants for eight years, were both at their first spring training camp in 1986. Neither had played a game above AA in their brief professional careers, but they cut different profiles in that camp. Thompson, who just wanted to make an impression, described the two young prospects during spring training of 1986:

We were pretty much complete opposites with each other. I was kind of a prospect but not like this can't miss guy. Then we've got this guy who's a first round draft pick and played 45 games in the minor leagues . . . and is projected to possibly take over first base. All the confidence in the world. Cockiness. . . . Holy Cow, who is this guy? . . . We kind of blended together. . . . Made a good thing out of it. . . . We spent a lot of time in the first few years together.[3]

As spring training began, Green, Scot Thompson, and Gary Rajsich, the group who had been unable to produce at first base in 1985, were all gone. Mike Aldrete, a 25-year-old first baseman who had hit throughout his minor-league career, was getting a look as well, but everybody understood Clark was the first baseman of the future. Dan Driessen was still on the team, but his role had become that of pinch hitter and insurance policy in case both of the younger options stumbled.

Given how little the Giants got out of first and second base in 1985, Thompson and Clark were more than just a breath of fresh air, they represented the possibility of big upgrades at no cost at two key positions. Clark described to me the outcome of that spring: "Al Rosen . . . was like we can't do any worse than we did the year before, so we're gonna give some rookies a chance to make it. Robbie Thompson and I both made it out of spring training."[4]

In 1986, the new leadership of Roger Craig and Al Rosen was going to be in place for a full season. That and the two rookies who were playing their way into the starting lineup gave the Giants and their fans reason to believe that 1986 would be better than the previous year. It would have been hard for things to get much worse. One thing that was not going to change was that Candlestick Park would be the Giants' home. By the mid-1980s, the consensus that Candlestick was an inadequate home for the Giants had solidified, but there was still no more clarity about what to do about that reality.

Roger Craig had a few ideas about this. Mike Krukow, who played for Frank Robinson, Danny Ozark, Jim Davenport, and Craig during his time with the Giants and continues to announce Giants games, described Craig's approach to Candlestick: "His [Craig's] observations in 1985 were basically 'you know what? We hear more bitching in the Giants' clubhouse than anybody's clubhouse' which was right on. Then they went on to say, Roger Craig and Al Rosen, 'if anybody does not want to be here, we'll get you out, but this place should be the greatest home field advantage of all time' . . . and that was very true. Guys who continued being negative, they were gone." Krukow went on to say how that message was reiterated in 1986 and "by the time we left spring training, Roger Craig had worked his magic and I was on board 100 percent."[5]

Craig reiterated that message about Candlestick in spring training of 1986 because Clark also recalled how "Roger Craig had a big meeting. He said, 'I don't want to hear anything about the stadium. . . . It's our ballpark and we're gonna use it to our advantage. . . . We're not playing day games. We're playing night games. We're gonna play in the middle of it. . . . You guys better just suck it up. We're using it to our advantage. We're making the other team absolutely miserable."[6]

Vida Blue, who returned to the Giants in 1985 and was still on the team in 1986, remembered Craig's big speech a little differently. Saying of the turnaround Craig helped orchestrate, "Sometimes a change of managers can bring out the best in a player. Plus, the fact he's a disciplinarian 'hey I don't want to hear you guys quoted in the papers its cold out here.' Guys such as myself would always say 'but it's cold, Roger.' 'It's our home field advantage.' I'm like 'really?'"[7]

As the season approached, the Giants had a new right side of the infield and a new attitude, but other than that it was largely the same team that had lost 100 games the previous year, so whatever hope and optimism existed was tempered by some concern. Krukow described the sentiment that he and others had on the team in February: "At the beginning of spring training, we looked at the schedule and we were gonna open up in Houston, and in LA, six games scheduled. . . . So was a good chance of us being one and five or oh and six to start the year. That's what I thought going into spring training." Krukow's views changed by the end of that camp, but he added that outside the team "nobody expected us to do anything."[8]

In 1986, the Giants also introduced a new product to their fans. Through the early 1980s, Giants fans could listen to all Giants games on the radio station KNBR, but in most years only a handful of games, usually road games, were televised. In the early years of television, baseball executives believed that televising games was a bad idea because fans would not pay to attend games that they could watch on television for free. By the mid-1980s, this notion had clearly proven false as several teams broadcast many of their games and consistently drew better attendance than the Giants.

Accordingly, the Giants created one of the first Regional Sports Networks (RSN), partnering with the local NBC affiliate to create GiantsVision. Giants-Vision was a pay-per-view type product to which fans could subscribe and get different packages of games, but eventually all games were televised and broadcast. This product generated some income for the Giants but also proved to be a powerful engine for increasing interest in the team throughout the Bay Area.

OPENING DAY

The Giants opened the 1986 season against the Astros in the Astrodome, Houston's pitcher-friendly, domed ballpark. Seven of the players in the Giants' Opening Day lineup, Krukow, Bob Brenly, Chris Brown, Uribe, Dan Gladden, Chili Davis, and Jeffrey Leonard, were holdovers from 1985, but batting second at first base was Will Clark and batting seventh at second base was Robby Thompson.

A new era began when that team took the field. Actually, the new era began when Clark, the second batter of the day, stepped into the batter's box in the top of the first inning. The Astros' pitcher that day was the great Nolan Ryan. Ryan was 39 years old and had already won more than 240 games, struck out more than 4,000 batters, thrown more than 54 shutouts, and pitched five no-hitters. He was still a very good pitcher and still had his great fastball. Ryan would go on to pitch several more years, strike out more than 1,000 more batters, throw two more no-hitters, and win 80 more big-league games before finally retiring in 1993.

Ryan retired Gladden for the first out of the inning on a groundball to short, but then "Will Clark shows up. His first at bat in the Major Leagues in Houston. He's facing Nolan Ryan who's throwing about 118 miles an hour and he [Clark] hits one out with that distinctive style and kind of goofy look on his face like, you bet I did you sons of bitches. I'm here now and everything's gonna change. And it did. It wasn't just entirely him. He had a real swagger about him."[9] The Giants went on to win the game 8–3, with Robby Thompson getting a double as well. The two rookies had played well, but Clark and the Giants had made a statement to the rest of the league and helped put the previous three years unequivocally in the past. By the time the Giants got to San Francisco for the home opener, they were 4–2 and in first place in the NL West.

The Giants stayed in or around first place through July 20, when their record stood at 50 wins and 42 losses. They were unable to sustain that level of play throughout the rest of the season, winning only 33 of their remaining 70 games and finishing in third place, 13 games behind the division-winning Astros. Despite finishing relatively far out of the playoffs, 1986 was by most measures an excellent year for the Giants. In addition to finishing above .500 with 21 more wins than the previous year, the Rosen and Craig leadership team had successfully purged the feeling of being losers, or even laughingstocks, that had plagued the franchise over the previous three years. In this respect, the 1986 Giants put the rest of the National League on notice.

Two of the reasons for the Giants turnaround were the rookies on the right side of the infield. Clark and Thompson were valuable both at the plate and in the field. Both were excellent defenders who got better into the late 1980s and early 1990s, but they were already pretty good in 1986. Neither of them disappointed at the plate either. Clark, in a foreshadowing of what Giants fans would see over the next few years, shrugged off whatever pressure he felt as a 22-year-old who many believed represented the future for the franchise and hit .287/.343/.444 in 111 games. Thompson was a few steps behind Clark with the bat, hitting .271/.328/.370 in 149 games. This represented huge upgrades from Green and Trillo and their ineffective backups in 1985.

Clark impressed baseball writers so much that he finished fifth in the Rookie of the Year voting, but Thompson, in part because of playing in more games and his sterling defense, finished second. A team that can place two young stars in the top five of the Rookie of the Year balloting generally has a good future, and the Giants were no exception. One of the players who finished between Thompson and Clark was a 25-year-old who had played all over the field, while producing with the bat for the World Champion New York Mets. Within a year, Kevin Mitchell would join the Giants and add another big young bat to the lineup.

Another bright spot on that team was Mike Krukow, who was the ace of the staff and won 20 games but was already 34 years old. Vida Blue's 10–10 record did not reflect his full value to the team as he threw 156²/₃ innings with 3.27 ERA. Blue retired at the end of the season at the age of 36. The rest of the starting rotation was no better than ordinary, with less-than-memorable pitchers like Mike LaCoss and Roger Mason having mediocre seasons.

The lineup beyond Clark and Thompson had some strengths and weaknesses. Chili Davis had developed into a very good hitter but was no longer able to play center field and had moved over to right field. Chris Brown hit .317/.376/.421 and was beginning to look like the third baseman of the future. José Uribe provided his usual solid defense and forgettable offense at short. Bob Brenly had another good year behind the plate but was 32 years old. Dan Gladden in center field and Jeffrey Leonard in left field rounded out the outfield, but they did not have great years.

Nonetheless, the starting outfield, Chili Davis, Candy Maldonado, who had hit .252 with 18 home runs after coming over from the Dodgers in a rare trade between the two rivals, and closer Scott Garrelts presented a very good young nucleus around which a good team could be built. All that was needed was bounce back years from a few veterans and some good pickups from outside the organization.

Despite the needs of the team, Rosen and the Giants had a relatively quiet off-season. A number of second tier players were released or invited to the 1987 spring training, but the team made few major moves. The highest profile player that Rosen acquired was Chris Speier, a veteran who could play any infield position and had a good bat. Speier, who signed with the team as a free agent, had begun his career with the Giants and had been a teammate of Willie Mays when the shortstop was beginning his career and the great center fielder was winding down his tenure with the Giants. Speier was the perfect choice to back up a very good but young infield. Rosen seemed to be biding his time, almost like he wanted to see if the team would continue to make big gains before he made any big moves. However, according to Busch, Rosen was confident enough to predict at a preseason media luncheon that the team would win the NL West.[10]

THE FOURTH OF JULY

As the 1987 season approached, there was some optimism around the club. Robby Thompson recalled the feel as he prepared to begin his second year in the big leagues. "It's like wow, we're a good team. We got a lot going for us here."[11] The Giants' lineup on Opening Day 1987 looked a lot like it had the previous year. The batting order was changed around a bit as Will Clark was the leadoff hitter, but Krukow was back on the mound and Brenly was behind the plate. The only difference was that Chili Davis was in center instead of Gladden, who was no longer with the team. Candy Maldonado started in right field taking Gladden's spot.

A few months into the season, it looked as if the Giants had picked up where they had left off in 1986. Unfortunately, they picked up where they had left off in the second half of 1986. On July 4, behind a poor start by Atlee Hammaker, the Giants lost to the Cubs 5–3, putting their record at 39–40. With just under half the season gone, the Giants were a .500 team, five and a half games behind the division-leading Reds. The Giants were not quite out of the race but needed to do something if they were going to contend in 1987.

Five and a half games back at the halfway point of the season, particularly in those pre–wild card days, meant that to make it to the playoffs a team would both have to both play well and get a few breaks. Given that, making a big trade that, to some extent, involved forfeiting prospects for players who can make an impact right away was a gutsy move that could backfire. Al Rosen must have seen something in that 1987 team because that is precisely what he did.

Rosen celebrated Independence Day by sending three pitching prospects, 21-year-old Keith Comstock, 23-year-old Mark Grant, and 26-year-old Mark Davis to the Padres. The Giants also sent their starting third baseman, Chris Brown, who was slumping at .242./306/.424 after a very strong 1986, to the Padres. Brown was not getting along well with Giants management, so the Padres probably thought a change of scenery would help him. In exchange for those four players, the Giants received three players who would help the team right away.

Thirty-one-year-old Dave Dravecky had been an all-star for the Padres in 1983 and a valuable pitcher when the Padres won the pennant the following year. In 1986 and the first part of 1987, Dravecky had not been quite as good, but he was a veteran lefty who could still pitch. His 3–7 record with the Padres in the first half of 1987 was pretty dismal, but his 3.76 ERA indicated he still had something left as 1987 was a hitter's year. In addition to Dravecky, the Giants bolstered their bull pen in that trade by adding Craig Lefferts, a solid lefty reliever.

The Giants could part with Brown without concern because one of the players they got in that trade was another young third baseman, Kevin Mitchell. The 25-year-old Mitchell was in his second full year in the big leagues in 1987 and had just arrived in San Diego from the Mets in a big off-season trade. Mitchell had grown up in San Diego and was happy to be playing near his home. Dravecky described being brought into Padres manager Larry Bowa's office to be told about the trade and "wondering why this had happened. I wanted to settle in San Diego." Dravecky also recalled how "Kevin Mitchell was not a happy camper. He did not want to go." Dravecky then related how he and Lefferts spent the next hours speaking with Mitchell and helping him become comfortable with the idea of leaving his hometown.[12]

Although Mitchell was not initially happy with the trade to the Giants, the Giants believed his bat would be helpful down the stretch. Mitchell met the team in Chicago on July 5, where Roger Craig immediately wrote him into the lineup batting sixth and playing third base. Chris Speier, the veteran backup infielder, described Mitchell's first day with the team: "He [Mitchell] meets us in Chicago and his bats don't show up. . . . I stood really close to the plate so I went to a 33 inch bat which is short, but it was heavy. . . . I said 'here Kevin why don't you try this one.' Two home runs. I'm goin' 'it ain't the bat, Chris. It's not the bat.'"[13] Mitchell's home runs, along with 1²/₃ innings of shutout relief from Lefferts helped the Giants to a 7–5 win over the Cubs, but they did not gain any ground on the Reds, as they also won that day.

On the last day of July, Rosen made another move, sending Mackey Sasser, a minor-league catcher, to the Pirates for Don Robinson. Robinson was 30 years old and already in his 10th big-league season. Nobody would have called Robinson a star, but he was an extremely useful pitcher. He could start or relieve and could take on a heavy pitching load if necessary. Robinson was never going to be a top starting pitcher, but players like him, as the third or fourth man out of the bull pen and making an occasional start, can have a big impact on a contending team. Robinson had additional value because he was the best hitting pitcher of his generation. He could not hit well enough to be a starting outfielder or anything like that, but he hit better than more than a few middle infielders and catchers and was occasionally used as a pinch hitter throughout his career.

On August 5, a month after the big trade with the Padres, Dave Dravecky started for the Giants and scattered 10 hits but no walks and only three runs over seven innings. Mitchell had moved up to the number two spot in the lineup by then and went three for six. Lefferts pitched poorly in relief, contributing to the Giants losing to the Astros six to five. That loss dropped the third-place Giants' record to 53–55, five games behind the Reds. With the season now two thirds over, it looked like Rosen's big gambles were not paying off. The Reds were coming into Candlestick for a four-game series that the Giants had to sweep to revive their chance at making the playoffs. If they lost even two of the four, the race would be all but over.

On Friday, August 7, Mike LaCoss was sharp, throwing a complete game and only giving up one run. A solo home run by Will Clark in the fourth and a two-run blast two innings later by Mitchell, who had been hitting well ever since he got to the Giants, gave San Francisco a 3–1 win and closed the gap between the two teams to four games, but the defending NL West champion Astros were still only 3½ games back in second place.

The next night, Atlee Hammaker was scheduled to start for the Giants against Tom Browning for the Reds. Hammaker retired the side in the top of the first, yielding only a walk to Eric Davis. In the bottom of the first, Robby Thompson doubled, Kevin Mitchell and Jeffrey Leonard singled, and Candy Maldonado doubled, so four batters in, the Giants had a 2–0 lead. A run-scoring ground ball by Chili Davis and a sacrifice fly from Will Clark gave the Giants two more runs. Hammaker pitched a complete game, allowing only four hits and four walks, as the Giants breezed to a 5–2 win. That closed the gap between the two teams to three games and put the Giants in second place, meaning that Sunday's doubleheader would be extremely important. If the Reds could somehow sweep the Giants at Candlestick, they would likely knock them back out of the race, probably for good. A split, the most likely outcome of any doubleheader, would keep the race close, but a sweep by the Giants would put them one game out of first place and in the thick of the playoff hunt for the first time since 1982.

The Reds' starting pitcher for the first game of the doubleheader that day was Ted Power, a 32-year-old journeyman. The Giants were going with Mike Krukow. Krukow had been the ace of the staff in 1986 but was not having a good year thus far in 1987. Going into that game, Krukow's record stood at two wins and six losses with an ERA of 5.59. Despite his poor numbers, many of the more than 46,000 fans who came to Candlestick for the games that day had confidence in the veteran pitcher.

The first game started out much as the game the previous day had. Krukow easily retired the side in the top of the first. In the bottom of that frame, little used outfielder Eddie Milner led off with a walk and then stole second. He then came around to score on a ground out and a fly ball. With two away, Will Clark, who was emerging as one of the best hitters in the National League in his sophomore season, hit a two-run home run to put the Giants ahead 2–0. A Kevin Mitchell double followed by a Mike Aldrete single in the third extended the Giants lead to 3–0.

Mike Krukow picked a good day to find his old form and held the Reds to only three base runners and no runs through the first eight innings, so the Giants had a three-run lead going into the ninth inning. However, in the top of that inning, a leadoff single by Kai Daniels followed one out later, by a two-run home run by Eric Davis, the Reds best player, meant that it was suddenly a one-run game. Roger Craig was taking no chances and brought in the lefty to pitch to Dave Parker, who at 36 was still a dangerous slugger from the left side of the plate. Lefferts got Parker to pop up to Thompson. Seeking to keep the platoon advantage, Craig brought in Robinson to pitch to right-handed hitting catcher Bo Díaz. Díaz hit a grounder to Mitchell at third who threw it across the diamond to Will Clark and the Giants were only two games out. The two relievers that Rosen had acquired in the previous month, masterfully used by Craig, had played a major role in the big win.[14] At that moment, it was not so hard to see the logic of what Rosen and Craig had been trying to do in San Francisco, but there was still another game to be played that day.

The second game of the doubleheader had a familiar feel. The Giants got good starting pitching, this time from Kelly Downs, who pitched into the ninth inning while giving up only two runs. Once again, the Giants jumped out to an early lead that they never relinquished. The four runs the Giants scored all came in the bottom of the second, but unlike in the previous games, were due primarily to shoddy Reds defense. The Reds, perhaps showing some of the fatigue of the second game of a doubleheader on the road, made three errors, leading to three unearned runs in that inning. Once again, a newly acquired reliever, Lefferts this time, pitched well in the ninth. By the end of the day, only one game separated the two teams and, to the extent momentum exists in baseball, the Giants had it.

Over the next two weeks or so, the Giants and Reds alternated at the top of the NL West with the Giants leading some days, the Reds less frequently, and the two teams in a tie for first on some days. On August 21, Dravecky and Robinson pitched the Giants to a 6–3 win over the Expos and a one-game lead over the Reds.

On that day, Rosen added yet another veteran pitcher. This one did not come cheaply either. The Giants sent Jeff Robinson, a reliever who had a 2.79 ERA in almost 100 innings for the Giants in 1987, as well as a minor league pitcher named Scott Medvin, to the Pirates in exchange for Rick Reuschel. Reuschel, known as Big Daddy by all his teammates, was one of the most unusual pitchers of his era. He was also one of the best. However, by the time the Giants got him he was 38 years old, and while he could still be effective—he was 8–6 with a 2.75 ERA for the year when he joined the Giants—he had been slowed by age and injuries in the previous few seasons. Reuschel was a control pitcher who rarely walked batters, averaging roughly 2.37 walks per nine innings over his entire career, good enough to land him in the top 10 in the league in that category six times. In 1987, his 1.66 walks per nine innings led the National League. Because of his tendency to induce batters to hit ground balls, Reuschel seemed like a good fit for a Giants team that had standout defenders at first, second, and shortstop.

Reuschel was listed at 6'3" and 215 pounds for most of his career, but those measurements don't seem right to anybody who saw him pitch. Reuschel always seemed to be considerably bigger than 215 pounds. He was not exactly fat, but he also never quite looked like an athlete. He looked out of shape, like a middle-aged father of three who spent most of his time either at the office or driving his kids around and whose running shoes were gathering cobwebs in the garage. His physical appearance was heightened by his style. When Reuschel pitched, he did not look intense the way some pitchers do. He did not stare down opposing batters or strut around the mound but seemed to quickly and quietly go about his business.

Big Daddy was also one of the most underrated pitchers of his generation. Big Daddy was one of those players who are easy to overlook based on conventional measures. His career record of 214 wins and 191 losses with a 3.37 ERA is good, but not the kind of numbers that signals all-time great. However, two things must be remembered about Big Daddy. First, his best years were spent toiling for some pretty terrible Chicago Cubs teams. In fact, other than a few games in 1981 with the Yankees and the last few years of his career with the Giants, he always played for bad teams. The Cubs were not only bad, but they played in Wrigley Field, a hitter's park that hurt the numbers of all pitchers.

Reuschel ended up pitching for 19 years in the big leagues. He was the kind of pitcher who was very good for a long period of time with one extremely good year, 1977. For most of the rest of his career, he was among the best 15 or so pitchers in his league, while rarely being among the very best. He only made three all-star teams and only finished in the top 10 in Cy Young voting in those three years, but by the end of his career, he had a very impressive resume.

Based on WAR, the most comprehensive way to measure a player's total value, Reuschel was the 33rd best starting pitcher of all time. His 69.5 WAR exceeds that of Hall of Famers like John Smoltz, Jim Palmer, Don Drysdale, Carl Hubbell, and Don Sutton. He is one of only 46 pitchers to throw more than 3,500 innings with an ERA+ of better than 110. That is a fraternity of pitchers who were at least 10 percent better than the league average for a very long time. On a good team, a pitcher like that is a Hall of Famer, but languishing for bad teams he can be easily overlooked.

While many baseball fans may never have fully appreciated Reuschel, the same cannot be said for his teammates who saw how good he was on the mound, valued him as a teammate, and enjoyed him as a character. Mike Krukow had been Reuschel's teammate on the Cubs and understood what Reuschel could do for the Giants: "He was a great pitcher. Underappreciated pitcher. . . . One of the best pitchers in all of baseball. When he came over to San Francisco I thought he was the difference maker with us going to the playoffs."[15]

Kevin Mitchell first encountered Reuschel when the big pitcher was with the Pirates and Mitchell was beginning his career with the Mets. "

> When I was a rookie. We're in Pittsburgh. Big Daddy's with the Pirates. . . . Before I even met Big Daddy. . . . I'm on deck hitting for the pitcher. . . . I said "Is this guy gonna throw any harder? . . . I'm fitting to rake him." Wally Backman [a Mets teammate] said "you gotta go up there and face this guy. The ball moves like crazy." I said "dude, if he's throwing that slow, I'm fitting to bust him right now." And I got up there, the first pitch he threw me. That ball started way over there. It came in on my kitchen. Sawed me off so bad my hands swelled up.

Once Mitchell and Reuschel became teammates in San Francisco, Mitchell had a different perspective: "Big Daddy's the man. He is the man. . . . [on days when he was pitching] He'd sit over there reading his little book. . . . He was always reading. You know what he'd say 'just give me two runs.'" Mitchell also valued the veteran hurler's temperament because when Reuschel was pitching "nothing changed. . . . What you see is what you get out of Big Daddy. . . . He don't get mad. He don't do nothing. I wish everybody could be like that."[16]

Will Clark echoed his teammate Mitchell's views about hitting against Reuschel, "playing against him, you got your work cut out for you," as well as the value of having Reuschel as a teammate:

> You get him as a teammate, and you see how much of a professional he is. Big Daddy was as quiet as they came . . . He's a little hefty, a little rotund, but he's also probably the best athlete on the team, by far. At one point we had a bet going. We were gonna have a footrace with [speedy center fielder and leadoff hitter] Brett Butler and Rick Reuschel and I had my money on Rick Reuschel. . . . Roger Craig wouldn't let us do it. . . . You couldn't bunt on him [Reuschel].[17]

With Reuschel added to the rotation and the Giants in first place by one game, their chances looked very good, but there was still about six weeks left in the season. It took about five of those weeks, but on September 28, the Giants' 156th game of the season, behind solid pitching by Dave Dravecky and Don Robinson, and home runs by Robinson, Jeffrey Leonard, and Chili Davis, the Giants clinched the division and their first trip to the playoffs since 1971, when they lost to the Pirates in the NLCS.

Just two years removed from losing 100 games, the Giants had made it to the postseason for the first time in 16 years. Even in those pre–wild card days, 16 years was a long time for a team to be out of the playoffs. Since the Giants had last played a postseason game, every single National League team, and all but four American League teams, had been in the playoffs at least once. Only the Indians, Twins, and Rangers had a longer playoff drought than the Giants. The Mariners had still never made it to the playoffs, but 1987 was only their 11th season. The Twins were also playoff bound in 1987 as they would win the American League West.

After clinching the division, the Giants waited to see who their opponents in the NLCS would be. The Cardinals and Mets were locked in a battle for first place, but the Cardinals ended up winning the division, so the NLCS would be between the Giants and St. Louis. The Giants had won the 1987 NL West with a combination of powerful hitting, strong defense, and an excellent bull pen. If the team had any weakness it was a lack of a true ace in their otherwise solid pitching staff. The 1987 Giants were the most powerful since Willie Mays and Willie McCovey were playing for the team. Despite playing in a pitcher's park, they finished third in the league in slugging percentage, only .004 behind the league-leading Mets, and second in home runs, with only four fewer than the Chicago Cubs who played in Wrigley Field, long one of the best home run parks in baseball. Will Clark, who had a breakout season, hitting .308/371/.580, led the team with 35 home runs. Additionally, every starter except shortstop José Uribe hit 10 or more home runs. Backup infielder Chris Speier and backup catcher Bob Melvin also hit that milestone. The 205 home runs the Giants hit in 1987 was the most of any Giants squad since 1947.

As they had done in 1986, Clark and Thompson anchored the right side of the infield. Uribe, while not showing much power, played excellent defense and contributed somewhat on offense with his .343 on-base percentage. Despite his initial misgivings about being traded to San Francisco, third baseman Kevin Mitchell played very well after joining the Giants as their regular third baseman, hitting .306/.376/.530. Veteran catcher Bob Brenly had another strong season both behind the plate and with the bat. The starting outfield of Jeffrey Leonard, Chili Davis, and Candy Maldonado was one of the best in all of baseball. All three hit for power, had some speed, and could field reasonably well. Davis was developing an impressive ability to draw walks that, when combined with his power—he was second on the team with 24 home runs—would make him a very potent offensive force for the next decade.

The Giants bull pen was anchored by Scott Garrelts, a 25-year-old who from 1985 to 1987 was quietly one of the game's better relievers. Garrelts had logged 106⅓ innings in 1987 with a 3.22 ERA, 11 wins, and 12 saves. Garrelts was not an elite closer like the Cubs' Lee Smith or the Yankees' Dave Righetti, but he was dependable and durable. Garrelts was part of a deep bull pen that included midseason acquisitions Craig Lefferts and Don Robinson, both of whom had pitched well since joining the Giants.

To the extent the 1987 Giants had a weakness it was starting pitching. The starting rotation for the playoffs would consist of Dravecky, Reuschel, Krukow, and Hammaker. That was a group of good veteran pitchers, all of whom would have been strong number two or back-of-the-rotation starters, but going into the playoffs the team lacked a truly dominant starting pitcher.

Like all winning teams, the Giants were more than just a collection of good ballplayers having good years. Kevin Mitchell described the feel around the team he joined in July and helped get to the playoffs: "Wasn't no big-headed guys there. . . . Everybody picked each other up. I think Roger Craig had a lot to do with it." Mitchell also hastened to remind me of the impact Dusty Baker, then the team's batting coach, had on him and the team: "I think without Dusty there a lot of us wouldn't have had any guidance."[18]

Chris Speier was in his 17th big-league season in 1987 and was the most experienced player on the team. He described his feeling about coming back to the Giants before the 1987 season as being "like a kid in a candy store. . . . It was like oh my god I get to come back home, and it felt like coming home again." He described the feel around those late 1980s Giants teams: "Just coming to the ballpark, the feeling that we had and we were good. And we knew we were good. . . . I look back at that team on '87 through '89. We had really good character guys. . . . Krukow was there. Brenly was there. . . . Will Clark and Robbie Thompson, Jose Uribe . . . then they bring in Kevin Mitchell. It was a team."[19]

The Cardinals had won their division primarily with speed, defense, and pitching and looked like a very different team than the Giants. Their team total of 94 home runs was less than half of the number of home runs the Giants hit. More than a third of the Cardinals' roundtrippers came off the bat of former Giant Jack Clark, who due to injury would be limited to only one plate appearance in the NLCS. The Cardinals were built around speed and stole 248 bases, exceeding the Giants' total by more than 100.

The best player on each team told a lot about their team's style. The Giants best player in 1987 was a slugging first baseman who played strong defense but whose real value came from his bat. Will Clark's 35 home runs and OPS of .951 were good enough for 6th and 8th in the National League. Clark was a great player who could do almost everything, but he was not a fast runner and was limited to five stolen bases in 22 tries, a terrible percentage. The Cardinals best player by contrast was Ozzie Smith, a shortstop who is generally regarded as the greatest defender ever at that position. In 1987, Smith won his eighth of what would eventually be 13 consecutive Gold Gloves. Smith hit no home runs in 1987, but his .392 on-base percentage was quite good. Once he made it to first base, Smith stole 43 bases while only getting caught nine times. Will Clark would go on to finish fifth in the MVP balloting, while Smith would finish second. Smith's teammate Jack Clark came in third.

The Cardinals' pitching was comparable to that of the Giants. The ace of their staff was John Tudor, who went 10–2 in 1987 with a 3.84 ERA. They also had a conventional closer in Todd Worrell, who had 33 saves. The two teams were more or less evenly matched, but with Jack Clark out for the series, the Cardinals lack of power looked to be a problem as no other Cardinal had hit even 15 home runs during the regular season.

THE PLAYOFFS

The NLCS opened in St. Louis with the Giants sending Big Daddy to the mound against Greg Mathews for the Cardinals. Reuschel was not sharp that night, giving up nine hits and two walks over six innings and leaving with the Giants trailing five to two. Jeffrey Leonard hit a home run, but Ken Dayley bailed out Todd Worrell in the eighth inning by getting Will Clark to fly out with the bases loaded and the Giants down 5–3 for the final out of the inning. The score did not change in the ninth. The Cardinals, reflecting how their offense was built in 1987, got 10 hits on the day, including eight singles and no home runs.

That loss was particularly damaging because Cardinals ace John Tudor was scheduled to pitch in Game Two, with Dravecky going for the Giants. Dravecky, with some understatement, told me that in Game Two "I felt really good and I was locked in."[20] Dravecky was indeed locked in for his first playoff start as a Giant. He pitched what until then was the biggest game of his career, throwing a complete game, two-hit shutout. The Giants hit Tudor pretty well, winning handily by a score of 5–0 as both Clark and Leonard homered. That win put the Giants in good shape as they now were heading back to San Francisco for three games with the series tied at one game apiece.

On October 9, 57,913 fans came out to see the first postseason game in San Francisco in almost a generation. The Giants pitcher for Game Three of the NLCS was Atlee Hammaker, who had been 10–10 with a solid 3.58 ERA during the regular season. Joe Magrane, a 22-year-old rookie with a similar record of 9–7 with a 3.54 ERA, was the Cardinals' starter that day. The two southpaws were both making their first ever postseason start.

Through five innings, Hammaker was in control, allowing only two hits, no walks, and no runs. Meanwhile, the Giants went ahead 4–0 as Magrane proved no mystery to the Giants bats. Jeffrey Leonard continued his hot hitting with his third home run of the series in the third inning. Hammaker stumbled in the sixth, giving up a single to Ozzie Smith and a two-run home run to Jim Lindeman, but after six innings the Giants were still leading 4–2. Then, in the top of the seventh, the Cardinals rallied for four runs off of Hammaker, Don Robinson, and Craig Lefferts. It was a typical Cardinal rally as it included five singles, one stolen base, and no extra-base hits. The final score was 6–5 St. Louis as the Giants fell behind 2–1 in the NLCS.

Game Four was now almost a must win for the Giants. Veteran Mike Krukow, who had struggled with injuries through most of 1987, got the ball for the Giants. Krukow kept the Giants in the series by giving them nine very solid innings, holding the Cardinals to only two runs. A solo home run by Robby Thompson in the fourth and a two-run home run by Jeffrey Leonard, who was having a spectacular series, helped the Giants overcome an early 2–0 deficit. They held on to win 4–2 and tied up the series at two games apiece.

Big Daddy struggled again in Game Five, giving up two earned runs in only four innings, but five shutout innings of relief from Joe Price and a four-run fourth inning helped the Giants to a 6–3 win. Jeffrey Leonard was hitless in four at bats so, for the first time all series, did not hit a home run. Nonetheless, the Giants were heading back to St. Louis with a 3–2 lead and were only one win away from their first trip to the World Series since 1962.

Game Six, back in St. Louis, was a rematch of game two with Dravecky, who had pitched so well then, trying to maintain his mastery of the Cardinals. Tudor had been outpitched by Dravecky in Game Two and was getting one more opportunity to beat the Giants. Dravecky, who had told me he was locked in during Game Two, said that "but game six I was really locked in. . . . You're in that groove, you found that rhythm."[21] Despite that, as early as the bottom of the first, the Cardinals rallied as Tom Herr and Jim Lindeman singled with two outs, but then Dravecky struck out Terry Pendleton to extinguish that mini rally. With one out in the top of the second, the Giants had a small rally of their own as Will Clark walked and catcher Bob Melvin singled. Unfortunately, that brought up the bottom of the lineup and Tudor easily retired Uribe and then Dravecky to get out of the inning.

In the bottom of the second, Cardinals catcher Tony Peña led off. Peña was probably the best NL catcher not named Gary Carter over most of the previous five seasons and had been traded by the Pirates to the Cardinals just as the 1987 season was about to begin. Peña lifted a fly ball to right field. It was one of those plays that forces an outfielder to decide whether to dive for it or play it safe and hold the batter to a single. Maldonado did not make up his mind quickly enough and ended up making an awkward dive for the ball. Perhaps he lost it in the lights; perhaps he slipped on the damp turf; or perhaps he just misjudged it. Dravecky said of his former teammate, "the issue with Candy Maldonado and that ball in the lights, that can happen to anybody," and described what happened next as "the most freakish play."[22] Because of the turf at St. Louis's Busch Stadium, the turf around which the Cardinals had built their speed and defense oriented team, the ball took a big bounce over Maldonado, who was now sprawled on the right field turf. By the time Chili Davis, who was playing center field and backing up Maldonado, got the ball back to the infield, Peña, the slowest Cardinal in the lineup, was on third base with a triple.

Dravecky retired the next batter, Willie McGee, on a grounder to Mitchell that did not score Peña, bringing José Oquendo, a light-hitting backup who had played all over the diamond for the Cardinals in 1987 and was the right fielder that day, to the plate. Oquendo hit a short fly to right. Maldonado caught it cleanly and came up throwing. With the pitcher Tudor due up next it was likely that Peña would try to score. Sure enough, Peña tagged up and broke for home. Maldonado's throw was strong but a little bit up the line, allowing Peña to avoid catcher Bob Melvin's tag. Maldonado's two defensive miscues in one inning cost the Giants a run, but Tudor then struck out, so the Giants were only down 1–0.

Tudor and Dravecky then settled into a great pitching duel. Dravecky left the game for a pinch hitter in the seventh, after holding the Cardinals to just that one run, five hits, and no walks while striking out eight in six innings. Tudor matched Dravecky throughout the game, giving up no runs over 7⅓ innings. Peña's run in the second was all the Cardinals needed to win 1–0 and even up the series at three games apiece.

Manager Roger Craig was faced with a tough decision about who to start against the Cardinals and Danny Cox in Game Seven. Craig's best pitcher through the first six games of the series had been Dave Dravecky, but he had just pitched in game six. That left Craig with the lefty Hammaker or the veteran righty Krukow. Hammaker was on the full four days of rest, while Krukow only had three days off. However, in the 1980s, although most teams were using five-man rotations, it was not so unusual to use a pitcher on short rest. The Cardinals lineup had five switch-hitters, so there was no clear reason to use either a lefty or a righty.

The decision came down to a fully rested Hammaker, who would turn those switch-hitters into righties who would need an extra step to get to first base, or Krukow on one less day of rest. There were a few other factors too. Krukow was a veteran with a reputation as a team leader. He was the kind of guy who might just bring a little something extra to a Game Seven. Krukow had pitched very well in his NLCS start while Hammaker had not. Additionally, while Hammaker's numbers for the regular season overall were better than Krukow's, he had not been an effective pitcher since August. Both Hammaker and Krukow had six regular season starts after September 1. Krukow had a 2.43 ERA over that period while Hammaker's was almost twice that at 4.80.

Craig decided to go with the lefty Hammaker. Krukow reflected on what was ultimately a reasonable decision by his manager, while conceding that he wanted to pitch that game: "I absolutely wanted that game, but every starter on the team wanted the ball that day. Nobody had a problem with Atlee taking the ball."[23] Corey Busch noted of that decision, with some understatement, that "starting Atlee . . . will always linger as a question mark."[24] Bruce Jenkins was less equivocal than either Busch or Krukow:

> Roger Craig made the fateful decision to start Atlee Hammaker. . . . Krukow wanted to pitch that game. . . . Krukow's one of the greatest competitors the Giants ever had. . . . Atlee Hammaker was a real talented guy and people really wondered whether he had the stomach for a big game. This was the choice that Craig had to make and he didn't make the right one. When that team left San Francisco after Krukow's game [Game Four of the NLCS], they were over the moon. . . . They were gonna get to the World Series.[25]

As all Giants fans know, Hammaker was terrible that day, lasting only two innings and leaving with the Giants trailing 4–0. The Giants never fought their way back into the game. After a leadoff single by Kevin Mitchell in the top of the ninth, Leonard forced Mitchell out at second, Clark struck out, Chili Davis flew out to left, and the Giants season was over.

Hammaker became a scapegoat, just as Maldonado had in Game Six, for that Game Seven loss, but it should be remembered that Cardinals starter Danny Cox threw a complete game shutout. Hammaker pitched badly to be sure and still felt some of that frustration when I spoke to him more than 30 years after the 1987 season: "I felt bad. I didn't pitch well. . . . Very disappointing because we felt we were the best team."[26] Similarly, Maldonado made two poor defensive plays that cost the Giants a big run in Game Six, but the Giants offense was the real culprit. Coming back to St. Louis with a 3–2 lead, the Giants did not score a single run or even get an extra-base hit over the last two games of the series. Busch's succinct view of the 1987 NLCS was shared by many Giants fans as well: "The '87 postseason was a nightmare in so many ways."[27] The final two games of the NLCS cast a pall over what had been the Giants' best year since at least 1971.

The Cardinals won the NLCS with strong pitching and some timely hitting, but nobody was a true offensive star for the team in those seven games. Danny Cox and John Tudor had both pitched well, but both lost a game early in the series before their great starts in the final two games. Thus, voters were at a quandary for who would be the MVP of that series. They eventually settled on Jeffrey Leonard, the first player from a losing team to win such an award since Bobby Richardson in the 1960 World Series when the Yankees lost to the Pirates in seven games. Leonard hit a spectacular .417/.500/.917 with four home runs over the course of those seven games. He had also earned the ire of Cardinals fans with his one-flap-down home run trot in which he would jog slowly around the bases with one arm at his side after hitting a home run. Leonard was booed loudly and verbally abused during the final two games in St. Louis. That treatment did not seem to have much of an impact on Leonard who went three for seven with a walk over those final two games.

The Cardinals went on to lose to the Twins in seven games in the World Series. Many around the Giants felt that the Giants, with their home run power, would have been a stronger opponent for the Twins. Bob Lurie and Corey Busch[28] both assured me that the Giants would have won if they, rather than the Cardinals, had taken on the Twins in that World Series. The former owner and senior executive may well have been right, but that was cold comfort for a team that by the end of 1987 had gone a quarter of a century without a World Series appearance.

PROPOSITION W

Although the Giants played the 1986 and 1987 seasons at Candlestick Park, the idea of a downtown ballpark had begun to gain some more momentum during these years. It was apparent to both the Giants and their fans that renovating Candlestick was not a real option and that no matter how many clever gimmicks Pat Gallagher and others in the Giants' organization dreamt up, they could not stop the wind and the cold. The basic outline of the downtown ballpark that had begun to emerge a few years earlier was becoming clearer by 1987. The ballpark would be a baseball-only facility. It would not be as big as Candlestick Park and it would fit into the fabric of the city more elegantly. Candlestick was technically within the boundaries of San Francisco, but it was on a piece of land that was largely empty and not particularly urban feeling. The location of the new ballpark was probably going to be centered around 7th and Townsend, South of Market, just north of Potrero Hill.

The idea of a downtown ballpark was not without its problems. In addition to complicated issues of funding and priorities for the city, there were the more quotidian issues of parking and transportation. Because Candlestick Park was in a part of the city far from the center of town and where land was cheap, when the ballpark was constructed, a parking lot with space for more than 10,000 cars was built as well. Horace Stoneham had demanded this as part of the terms for any new ballpark. One of the reasons the Giants had struggled to draw fans during their last years in New York was because there was nowhere for fans to park near the Polo Grounds. Stoneham wanted to make sure that problem did not occur in San Francisco as well. The new ballpark was to be built in a part of the city that was already somewhat developed. The land around the proposed site of the ballpark was largely unused, but there was not enough space to build a massive parking area comparable to what existed at Candlestick.

However, because the proposed new location was closer to downtown, public transportation would be better than it had been at Candlestick, but it would not entirely solve the problem. In the 1980s, public transportation in San Francisco consisted of a large network of buses, Bay Area Rapid Transit or BART—which was designed to bring commuters in from the suburbs in the East Bay to a few areas in the center of the city—some bus and train service to and from the suburban counties, some rail-bus hybrids known as the Muni metro (Muni was short for municipal railway which ran the buses, too), and the cable cars, which had recently been revamped and were essentially for tourists, or people with a very short and specific commute, by the 1980s.

The new proposed location would be served by buses and the Muni metro, but the 1980s were a time when most people, particularly in California, were still very dependent on their cars. The better bus access would have been good news for many residents of the city, particularly those who did not have cars or were too young, or too old, to drive, but the location created significant problems for Giants fans from the peninsula or from north of the city in Marin County. Those fans, many of whom were among the team's most dedicated, numbered in the thousands and needed to be able to drive to the ballpark.

The scenario of thousands of cars approaching the ballpark for night games, just as the rush hour traffic of cars seeking to leave San Francisco for points south or east was starting, demonstrated one of the major shortcomings of the proposed site. However, advocates for this solution, including both Mayor Feinstein and the Giants, argued that improved public transportation would ameliorate the problem. Proponents of the new ballpark also stressed that while the location might not be perfect, the new venue would be a huge upgrade from Candlestick Park. Moreover, they pointed out, the alternative was that if a downtown ballpark were not built, it was almost inevitable that the Giants' days in San Francisco would soon come to an end.

By 1987, Dianne Feinstein's tenure in City Hall was winding down as well. Term limits precluded her from running for reelection that year. The mayor had been on Democratic presidential nominee Walter Mondale's short list when he sought a running mate in 1984, but by 1987 had begun to set her sights on the governor's mansion. Because Feinstein was not seeking reelection, San Francisco was preparing for its first mayoral election without an incumbent since 1975, the year George Moscone narrowly defeated John Barbagelata. In that election, the possibility of the Giants leaving had not been a major issue, but it became one as soon as Moscone took office. In 1987, the question of finding a better home for the Giants would be inextricably linked to the mayoral election.

The major candidates in that race were Art Agnos, a member of the state assembly, Roger Boas, a wealthy car dealer and former supervisor who had recently stepped down as the city's Chief Administrative Officer, and John Molinari, the president of the Board of Supervisors. The election quickly became a two-candidate race between Molinari and Agnos. Molinari, who had been a Republican but became a Democrat, was more conservative than

Agnos, enjoyed the support of Mayor Feinstein, and shared her sympathies towards business, real estate, and downtown interests. Agnos was considerably to the left of Molinari and had earned a reputation as one of the most progressive legislators in Sacramento during his decade in the assembly.

Although Agnos and Molinari were demographically similar—both were straight, white men—there were significant differences between them. Molinari was a conservative Democrat running, to some extent, to continue Feinstein's policies and approach. Agnos was a strong progressive who was, to a similar extent, running to finish what Moscone was unable to do in his three years in office. The 1987 election was not quite a rematch of the Moscone-Barbagelata runoff in 1975, but it was something of a referendum on the more conservative direction in which Feinstein had moved the city following Moscone's assassination.

Naturally, Agnos and Molinari had different views about the Giants and the question of the ballpark. By 1987, Feinstein was strongly associated with the downtown ballpark, so Molinari, who was running in large part to continue the Feinstein approach to governance, supported it. The ballpark, in addition to providing a home for the Giants, would reinvigorate a still underdeveloped downtown neighborhood, raising property values in the area and providing opportunities for business and tourism in that part of town. Agnos, like Moscone, had always been more oriented to neighborhood issues, so questions of displacing local low-income residents who lived around the proposed ballpark location, as well as traffic, parking, and, more generally, budget priorities for San Francisco, led him to oppose the ballpark. Agnos was a baseball fan and wanted to keep the Giants in San Francisco, but he was not amenable to Feinstein's proposal.

Agnos explained his opposition to the proposal as one based on both politics and location: "A lot of people thought [7th and Townsend] was an inappropriate place for a lot of reasons. . . . I didn't take a big chance [in opposing it]. . . . It was not a courageous move on my part. . . . I didn't suffer a lot. I had some blowback from people as I went to other parts of the city, the west and the northwest." The west and northwest have long been the more conservative parts of San Francisco. Agnos also added that "Feinstein didn't give a damn about the Giants. She wasn't a baseball fan and frankly just dismissed it. And most of us just dismissed Seventh and Townsend as a throwaway so she could say 'on my watch, we had a proposal.'"[29]

Feinstein may not have been a big baseball fan according to Agnos, but in a 2019 written interview she reminisced about the Seals and attending games with my uncle at the stadium on 16th Street. Over the years the team had a number of players who went on to the big leagues. The most famous were the DiMaggio brothers, but they were before my time. I certainly remember Lefty O'Doul, the manager, who was a real San Francisco legend. The city welcomed the Giants with open arms in 1958. You have to remember, we had the 49ers since the late 1940s, but baseball was still America's game. Getting Major League baseball on the West Coast was a really big deal.[30]

Molinari had deep roots in San Francisco and was from a prominent Italian American family in North Beach. Agnos was the son of a Greek immigrant and had moved to San Francisco as a young man around 1970. In an odd coincidence, Agnos grew up in Springfield, Massachusetts, which was home to a minor-league team affiliated with the New York and later San Francisco Giants. As a teenager, Agnos had the opportunity to see future Giants stars like Felipe Alou, Matty Alou, Tom Haller, José Pagán, and the great Juan Marichal play in his hometown. In fact, when Agnos met with Lurie during that election to explain his position, the future mayor told the team owner "Mr. Lurie, I was a Giants fan long before you became the owner or a fan of the team."[31] Although he did not start out as broadly known as Molinari, Agnos's progressive views, active campaign, and political skills made him the frontrunner by late summer of 1987.

Voters in San Francisco that year were not only going to select the mayor, they were also asked to determine the future of their Giants. Mayor Feinstein, with the backing of many of the city's supervisors, chose to place an initiative on the ballot that would seek voter approval for the downtown ballpark that Feinstein, Lurie, and others had been discussing.

At first glance, placing an initiative on the ballot on which it was known the two strongest mayoral candidates disagreed did not seem like a wise strategy because with Agnos campaigning against the ballpark, it would be tough to pass. Corey Busch recognized this in hindsight but sought to explain the Giants thinking at the time:

The '87 initiative was a mistake. We shouldn't have done it. . . . I thought that in the race for mayor . . . Molinari was supportive of the ballpark, Art was not. . . . We thought if we can get this thing on the ballot and it passes, if Molinari becomes mayor, that's his mandate. If Art becomes mayor then that's an indication from the people that they want him to pursue a ballpark.

. . . What went on the ballot was a non-binding, non-specific, no financing plan in the wrong spots. . . . It was just a mistake we shouldn't have done it.[32]

The initiative, which became known as Proposition W, asked the voters to vote yes or no on the question "Shall it be the policy of the people of San Francisco to build a baseball park at 7th and Townsend Streets at no cost to the City?" Proposition W significantly raised the stakes for the Giants. In the past, the idea of a new ballpark downtown had been just that, an idea, or perhaps a fantasy, but after November 1987 things would be different. If the initiative passed, work on the new ballpark would begin and the Giants would have a new home by 1990, at the latest. However, if voters rejected the ballpark, the Giants' days in San Francisco would likely be coming to an end relatively soon.

Mayor Feinstein supported the initiative but looked back on the proposal with mixed emotions while noting the complex political environment around the proposed ballpark:

> I didn't think it was the best solution. We didn't have all the i's dotted or t's crossed for the 7th and Townsend site. I urged the Giants not to go to the ballot, but they wanted to get to the voters while I was still mayor, rather than starting over with a new mayor in January 1988. There was opposition from residents on Potrero Hill, a mile or so away from the site, and that was the home neighborhood of Assemblyman Art Agnos, a leading candidate for mayor. His major opponent, Supervisor Jack Molinari, endorsed the ballpark measure. Agnos didn't and it became a big issue in the mayor's race. It probably ended-up hurting Jack's chances [in the mayoral election].[33]

The initiative did not call for massive public funding for the new ballpark, relying instead on private bonds and other forms of private funding. However, the ballpark would be expensive, and voters were wary of some of the cost associated with building the ballpark, acquiring the land, and other expenses being passed on to taxpayers.

Tucked away in a story announcing that the initiative was going to be on the ballot was a line that said "Feinstein said she would have preferred to wait to put the stadium on a less crowded ballot."[34] That sentence might have been missed by readers who were thinking about a new home for the Giants or wondering what the real cost would be, but with regards to the future of the Giants, it was a very prescient insight from a woman who has been one of the most successful politicians in San Francisco history.

Two years earlier, in 1985, San Franciscans voted for some members of the Board of Supervisors, some other minor local offices, and a handful of city and state initiatives. Two years before that, there had been a mayoral election, but Feinstein had faced no significant opposition. In both of those elections, turnout was low. In November 1983, 170,628 people had gone to the polls. Two years later, only 107,920 San Franciscans voted.[35] Those low-turnout elections tended to draw, on balance, a more affluent and conservative electorate, one that would have been more supportive of Feinstein and her ballpark proposal, but 1987 was shaping up to be different.

A contested mayoral race was likely to draw more voters than any odd-numbered year election in San Francisco since 1979 or even 1975. Moreover, Agnos's strategy was to mobilize large numbers of voters of color and progressive whites who were not particularly open to the idea of what they perceived to be a giveaway to Bob Lurie, one of the wealthiest men in the city.

Before the election, every voter in San Francisco was mailed an official voter guide. This booklet was designed to help voters navigate election day. It included helpful information like what day the election was and when the polls would open. It also included brief statements by candidates for office. The section on ballot proposals included a restatement of the initiative as it would appear on the ballot and an analysis by the "Ballot Simplification Committee." It then had statements in support and in opposition to each initiative. There were frequently numerous brief statements made by single individuals, groups of individuals, and the like.

The statements in support of Proposition W were signed by most of the most influential power brokers and organizations in San Francisco in 1987, including many names that would still be recognized by San Franciscans decades later. Dianne Feinstein, Bob Lurie, and Al Rosen wrote individual statements. Signers of group statements included San Francisco Supervisors Jim Gonzalez, Tom Hsieh, Willie Kennedy, Wendy Nelder, and Carol Ruth Silver, State Senator Milton Marks, Speaker of the Assembly (and future mayor of San Francisco) Willie Brown, Police Chief (and future mayor of San Francisco) Frank Jordan, as well as two previous police chiefs, labor leaders John Henning and Walter Johnson, George Moscone's widow Gina Moscone, Carole Migden, the chair of the San Francisco Democratic Party Central Committee, and two of her predecessors, a member of the San Francisco Republican Party Central Committee, Sheriff Michael Hennessy, Public Defender Geoffrey Brown, several longtime permanent government types, and activists including Arnold Townsend, Lee Dolson, Jim Rivaldo, Harold

Dobbs, Reverend Cecil Williams, former congressman John Burton, and the executive director of the Chamber of Commerce.[36]

Molinari made his position clear in the voter guide with an individual statement in favor of Proposition W in which he argued that "a new ballpark at 7th and Townsend will provide tremendous economic benefits for all of us, baseball fans and non-fan alike. Major league baseball [sic] is an important part of our economy, provides jobs and recreation for San Franciscans from all walks of life and contributes to San Francisco's stature as a world class city."[37]

There were some well-known signatories to statements opposing Proposition W, including mayoral candidate Roger Boas, Supervisor Richard Hongisto, and Supervisor Bill Maher, who each had individual statements, as well as the Sierra Club, but the remaining 15 statements were from a collection of neighborhood groups and activists with little citywide name recognition.[38] The last of these was signed by an alphabetized list of 61 activists and made its point very firmly and clearly:

> A 7th and Townsend stadium is an ill-conceived, unneeded, unwanted, under-funded, traffic, gridlocking, dollar devouring white elephant that would not work, not help the Giants, is not downtown and affords practically no parking.
>
> In the real world we would all eventually pay for not only the stadium itself, but also for the extra multi millions of dollars needed for new freeway exits, relocating the SP [Southern Pacific] depot, adding new Muni facilities, and shoring up subgrade land with a high water table.
>
> Vote No![39]

The first name on that alphabetized list of 61 activists was Art Agnos, the man who would become the next mayor of San Francisco and whose name just happened to begin with the letter A.

The vote on Proposition W was expected to be close, but the strong Giants season which ended just one win short of the World Series while setting an all-time franchise attendance record of 1.9 million, looked like it might help the chances of passing the initiative. For the first time in years, there was real excitement in San Francisco about the Giants, making it more likely that voters would decide to keep the team around, rather than lose them just as they were getting good.

By the time Election Day, November 3, arrived, the only question around the mayor's race was whether or not Agnos would get 50 percent of the vote and avoid a runoff. When the votes were counted, Agnos came up just a little short with 88,275 votes, good for 48.2 percent. Molinari was a distant second with 24.87 percent, but Boas had remained competitive with Molinari and received over 21 percent of the vote.[40] That, and the 3 or 4 percent of the vote that minor candidates got, was enough to force Agnos into a runoff with Molinari that was set for December 8. Agnos won that runoff handily and became mayor of San Francisco.

The same day the voters gave a big plurality to Agnos, but not quite enough to avoid a runoff, they voted against Proposition W. The final vote was not extremely close, with the no votes outpacing the yes votes by roughly 11,000 of the 177,000 votes cast, and the initiative failing by a margin of 53 percent to 47 percent. That was a defeat for Feinstein, Lurie, the Giants, baseball fans, most of the political establishment, and most of the city's business and labor leadership. It was a victory for neighborhood groups, environmentalists, and Art Agnos as he prepared to become the new mayor.

1988

Despite the two consecutive losses that ended the Giants' playoff run the previous year, the Giants could go into 1988 feeling good about their team and their future—at least on the field. Robby Thompson described the feeling that spring training as "the Giants got over the hump and we're on our way."[41] Will Clark echoed his teammate's sentiment, remembering how "that off-season [following 1987] that sort of set the tone. . . . We're here. . . . Now we just gotta make that next step."[42]

The team's two strong years in 1986 and 1987 marked the first time the team had won more games than they lost for two full seasons in a row since 1970 and 1971. They finished one game above .500 in 1981, but that was a strike-shortened year, so their 1981 and 1982 run did not occur over two full seasons. While the Giants were not necessarily favorites to repeat in 1988, they were expected to contend.

The Giants went into 1988 with largely the same team as the one that had come within one win of the World Series the previous season. However, on December 1, 1987, the Giants lost Chili Davis to free agency when he signed with the Angels just a few weeks before turning 28. Davis had been a very good player for the Giants, hitting 24 home runs with a .344 on-base percentage in

1987, but he was slowing down and had become a defensive liability in center field. Moreover, his 109 strikeouts in 1987, back when that was a lot, had kept his batting average to .250 and limited his overall value.

Rather than seek to replace the power they were losing when Davis signed with the Angels, the Giants went in a different direction that very same day and signed one of the game's premier center fielders. Brett Butler was a pro-totypical leadoff hitter. His on-base percentage was consistently better than .350 and had been .399 in 1987. Unlike Davis, Butler had limited power and had never, and would never, hit even 10 home runs in a season, but he was a much better defensive center fielder. He was also an excellent base runner who usually stole 30–50 bases a year. He was the ideal person for the top of a batting order that included sluggers like Clark and Mitchell.

The rest of the lineup looked very similar to the 1987 version, and it had many of the same strengths and weaknesses. Thompson, Clark, and Mitchell were all complete players who would continue to develop in 1988. José Uribe remained a good-fielding shortstop who provided little offense. Bob Melvin took over more of the catching from Bob Brenly, but neither of the two backstops provided much offense. Butler had a great year for his new team, playing excellent defense in center field, getting on base at a .393 clip, stealing 43 bases, and only getting caught 20 times, while leading the team with 109 runs scored. He solidified the center field and leadoff spots for the team. However, Maldonado and Leonard both slumped. Leonard's production fell off so much that he was traded to the Brewers in the middle of the season for infielder Ernest Riles.

As in 1987, the Giants' pitching, particularly their starting pitching, was not strong. Garrelts, Lefferts, and Don Robinson were at the core of a workmanlike bull pen, but the starting rotation was not consistent or particularly good, with some exceptions. One of those exceptions occurred on Opening Day in Los Angeles. The Giants' first day defending their NL West title from the previous season went very well. Steve Sax led off the bottom of the first inning with a home run, but that was the only run Dave Dravecky allowed as he cruised to a complete game, 5–1 victory.

Dravecky, the midseason acquisition from the year before who had pitched so brilliantly in the playoffs, began 1988 where he left off in 1987 and was beginning to look like the ace the team so badly needed. However, Dravecky struggled in his second start, lasting only four innings and giving up seven hits and three earned runs to the Padres. Six days later, he had a better game against that same Padres team, holding them to one run in seven innings.

Dravecky got shelled in his next start, giving up four earned runs in two innings. By now the Giants were concerned, particularly when their star lefty began to complain of stiffness in his throwing arm. After a good start against the Pirates, Dravecky was hit hard again, this time by the Cardinals on May 2, and he ended up on the disabled list for three weeks.

On May 28, the southpaw held the Phillies to one run in five innings in his first start back from the disabled list, but the Giants lost that game by a score of 4–3, dropping their record to an even 24–24. Despite their record, the Giants were still only four games out of first place. That was the last game Dravecky would pitch in 1988. The doctors examined and probed the pitcher to see what was wrong, but it was not until September when cancer was found in Dravecky's left arm. Although the doctors could save Dravecky's life, it was more or less clear he would never pitch again. This was a devastating blow to Dravecky and the Giants.

The loss of Dravecky was just one of many things that landed the Giants in fourth place, only four games above .500, by the end of the season, but there were some bright spots and reasons to be hopeful for the future. One was that at 39 years old, Rick Reuschel was having a renaissance. Big Daddy pitched 245 innings, his highest total since 1980, and won 19 games, his most since 1977. The late-season trade for Reuschel the previous year had been overshadowed by the bigger trade with the Padres several weeks earlier, but it was now possible that despite the terrible news about Dravecky, the Giants might have found their ace after all.

By 1988, the Giants and their fans were accustomed to first round draft picks winning jobs in the infield and becoming stars. Will Clark and Robby Thompson continued to be one of the best right sides of the infield in baseball, with Clark becoming a perennial MVP candidate as well. In 1986, a year after drafting Clark, the Giants drafted a shortstop from the University of Nevada, Las Vegas with their first round pick (third overall). Despite hitting very well in AAA in 1987, Matt Williams had struggled with the Giants, hitting .188/.240/.339 in 84 games with the big-league club. It was also becoming clear that Williams was not really cut out to be a shortstop. He was too big and not quite rangy enough. However, his sure-handedness, strong arm, and good instincts made him a natural at third base.

This created a problem for the Giants who already had a third baseman in Kevin Mitchell who hit .251/.319/.442 in 1988. The Giants, and particularly their new hitting coach Dusty Baker, saw a lot in the young slugger and were not anxious to trade him to make room for Williams, who had showed promise as a 22-year-old in 1988 but was still not quite ready. Al Rosen and Roger Craig were smart and experienced baseball men who saw what Mitchell and Williams could do, but getting them to that level would not be easy, especially given that they both played the same position.

Roger Craig sought to address this problem by moving Mitchell, who was faster than Williams, to left field. Mitchell was very athletic, had played all over the field for the Mets in 1986, and had the skill set to make the transition, but moves like that are almost never as easy as they look on paper. Craig needed somebody to help Williams with that transition. Fortunately, perhaps the greatest defensive outfielder in baseball history was available to help out. Willie Mays had recently been brought back to the Giants by Bob Lurie and was available to help the young Mitchell

Kevin Mitchell told me about the man who helped make a good fielder out of somebody who "wasn't the most graceful guy in the outfield, but I got it done" with a tone of appreciation and more than a little reverence: "He [Mays] took me to the outfield, spoke with me about going back on the ball, going to the corner and stayed on my case. . . . I mean cussin' me, everything else. I mean he was rough on me." Mitchell also mentioned how Mays showed confidence in him:

> He said he saw me years ago, a couple of years ago [earlier] in New York as a rookie as he was walking by the cages and he heard this loud noise coming off the bat. He thought it was George Foster. . . . He looked at me and he said, he saw this young kid with this loud noise coming [off the bat]. He said it was different than everybody else. And he said he told the Giants about me. "This kid is different." He said "this kid is different." I learned a lot from him, just attitude about the game. How to approach. He was the guy who took those light bats out of my hand and put a heavy bat in my hand.

For Mitchell, who had already been traded twice, did not get along particularly well with Craig or Rosen, and who had spent much of his career being moved to a different position, the confidence Mays showed in him was very meaningful.[43]

Mays was a presence in the Giants' organization during those years, speaking to young players at spring training, taking on some coaching tasks, and doing other tasks the team needed. Dravecky, for example, recalled how "when we would go to spring training and Willie was there, he would walk into the clubhouse, go into the trainer's room, and give all us pitchers grief."[44] However, Mays had not been a constant presence around the Giants for the previous decade or so. The reason for this is that, in a colossally stupid decision, Commissioner Bowie Kuhn banned Mays for life from all baseball activities because of his association with Bally's Casino in 1979. Mays' work at Bally's consisted not of gambling, or even going into the casinos, but of playing golf and otherwise interacting with high-stakes gamblers. The logic of banning one of the most beloved and recognizable living baseball players, whose ethics and integrity were impeccable, for a relatively minor infraction, reflects Kuhn's limited ability to understand baseball and the modern world in the 1970s. To make matters worse, Kuhn placed a similar ban on Mickey Mantle because of the great Yankees center fielder's association with Claridge Casino, which was similar to what Mays was doing with Bally's.

Former commissioner Peter Ueberroth, who took over for Kuhn in late 1984, described his decision to reinstate the two great players to me when me met in his Orange County office: "I asked for the files on Mickey and Willie. . . . I get the files and I come out here to home in Laguna Beach and I sit and read. I wanted to get away from the whole thing. . . . There's nothing in there at all. They never went into a casino. . . . And then I found out they had no benefits. They had nothing."[45] As soon as the ban was lifted, Lurie, understanding Mays's value both on and off the field, brought Mays back to the Giants.

MORE BALLPARK UNCERTAINTY

The Giants 1988 season was disappointing on the field, but by the late 1980s the uncertainty around the Giants future was as strong as at any time since the first few days of George Moscone's mayoralty. This made it difficult to appreciate the renaissance the team was enjoying. Despite finishing 11½ games behind the division-winning Dodgers in 1988, it was not a lost year for the team at all. The young core of Mitchell, Thompson, and Clark was bolstered by the addition of Butler, who immediately became the top-notch leadoff hitter the Giants had hoped they were getting when they signed him. Matt Williams still needed some seasoning in the minors but was likely to become a valuable player for the Giants in the near future. The pitching was still unsettled, but Reuschel had reemerged as an ace, and the bull pen had been solid.

Nonetheless, the defeat at the hands of the Cardinals in Game Seven of the NLCS and at the ballot box a few weeks later had set a tone for the 1988 season that the team never seemed to be able to shake off. Fans began to slowly accept that the Giants' time in San Francisco was heading towards the final inning. The idea of a downtown ballpark had not quite faded away, but unless the new mayor, Art Agnos, would get behind the idea, it seemed very unlikely. Meanwhile, places as disparate as Tampa, Sacramento, and Santa Clara County were making it clear that they would be happy to be a new home for the Giants.

Chapter 7

THE YEAR EVERYTHING WENT RIGHT
AND WRONG FOR THE GIANTS

The story of the Giants in the Bob Lurie years did not end in 1989, but even at the time it kind of felt like it did. It was the year everything went right for the Giants and for Bob Lurie, but also the year when some things went terribly wrong. It was a year with several different compelling Giants storylines as well as three of the most memorable moments in franchise history.

The lineup that Roger Craig used on Opening Day was the same one the Giants used for much of the year. The batting order did not remain precisely the same, but much of the rest did. The Giants had the same first four hitters in the season's first game, Butler in center, Thompson at second, Clark at first, and Mitchell in left, as they did in in 109 of their 162 games. The rest of the Opening Day lineup consisted of Candy Maldonado batting fifth in right, followed by Terry Kennedy, the catcher who was acquired in a trade with the Orioles in the off-season, Williams at third, Uribe at short, and Big Daddy on the mound. This lineup provided excellent infield defense, one of the top leadoff hitters in the league, a very solid middle of the order, and power in the three through seven spots.

The game started well for the Giants as Mitchell hit a two-run home run in the first inning. Reuschel gave up three runs in six innings, but that was good enough for the win as the Giants scored three in the top of the seventh. The final score was 5–3 in favor of the Giants with Mitchell driving in four of the Giants' runs. Mitchell's hot hitting had carried over from Arizona: "I knew I was in the zone in spring training. I hit half a dozen home runs in spring training."[1]

On April 26, the Giants dropped a game 3–1 to the Cardinals as their record slipped to 11–9. In the bottom of the first, Ozzie Smith, the light-hitting

Cardinals shortstop, came to bat against Kelly Downs. The switch-hitting Smith was batting left-handed against the righty Downs. The right-handed throwing Kevin Mitchell described what happened next:

> I had been playing with the weights that morning, so I was tight. We were supposed to be bunching Ozzie Smith . . . 'cause he liked punching that ball to left field. . . . He was batting lefty. . . . He sliced it down the line. . . . My mind was saying get to the line. Left handers' balls come back into play. It starts foul and comes back. . . . As I got over there, the ball was on my right hand. All I did was put my [bare] hand up and caught it. I didn't realize what I had done. I threw it in quick. I got in the dugout and I was leading off the inning. I ended up hitting a home run. . . . I felt that Ozzie Smith thought I was trying to show him up. . . . Willie Mays called me that night. He said "I didn't teach you that."[2]

Mitchell's one-handed catch, made almost nonchalantly as the left fielder actually overran the ball and then reached back and caught it with his right hand, remains a popular highlight widely viewed on YouTube and other platforms. It was a play that had no real impact on a game the Giants went on to lose, but it was nonetheless a great catch. It also may have been an omen that Mitchell, in only his first full year in left field, was having a charmed season.

During the first month or so of the season, Clark and Mitchell continued their hot hitting while Butler was enjoying another good year in center field and the leadoff spot. However, the rest of the team was not producing much at the plate and the pitching was still inconsistent. On May 5, the Giants lost another 3–1 game to the Cardinals as their record dropped to 14–15. Fortunately, no other NL West team was doing all that well either. The Reds were in first place, but the Giants, along with the Padres and Dodgers, were only two games back. At that point, the NL West looked like it was up for grabs as the last place Braves were only 3½ games behind Cincinnati.

The Giants then got hot, winning 24 of their next 38 games. The 38th of those games was on June 17 when the Giants hosted the Reds at Candlestick Park. The Giants' pitcher that day was Dennis Cook, a 26-year-old lefty who was making his second start of the season and pitching in only the sixth game of his career. Cook was sharp against the Reds, holding them to only one run in a complete game victory. The Giants' offense was now falling into place as Kevin Mitchell hit his 24th home run with one on in the third inning, and Brett Butler, never much of a power hitter, clubbed his second home run of the year. Altogether, the Giants scored eight runs, easily beating the Reds. With that win, the Giants, who had been in and out of first place for much of the last month, went ahead of the Astros by one game. They would remain in first place, although rarely by more than a game or two, for the rest of the season.

The next day, Al Rosen, seeing that this team had a chance to win the division, made a big trade, acquiring Steve Bedrosian from the Phillies in exchange for Dennis Cook, fresh off the previous day's strong start, third baseman Charlie Hayes, and Terry Mulholland. Bedrosian was a closer who had won the NL Cy Young Award in 1987. Despite that award, Bedrosian was a rarely a dominant closer. He walked too many batters and rarely pitched clean innings, but he was a proven closer, at a time when the proven closer paradigm was strong, and his acquisition definitely strengthened the Giants' bull pen.

A few weeks later, the Giants dropped the last game before the all-star break 6–4 to the Cardinals in St. Louis. That loss notwithstanding, the first half had gone as well as the Giants could have hoped. They went into the all-star break in first place, two games ahead of the Astros. Their .586 winning percentage was the best in the National League.

Three Giants would be starting in the All-Star Game in Anaheim. Will Clark, who was hitting .332/.418/.554 with 14 home runs at the break, had established himself as the best first baseman in the National League. Kevin Mitchell was having by some measures an even better year, as he had 31 home runs and was hitting .295/.378/.692 at the break. Rick Reuschel was going to start the game on the mound for the National League. His record stood at 12–3 with a 2.12 ERA. At the midway point in the season, Butler's .375 on-base percentage, Robby Thompson's solid hitting and defense, and strong pitching from Scott Garrelts, Craig Lefferts, Don Robinson, and the recently acquired Steve Bedrosian were also helping the Giants.

There were, however, some positions from which the Giants were not getting much production. Candy Maldonado was struggling in right, hitting .211/.296/.345. Tracy Jones was not helping in right either and was traded to Detroit for Pat Sheridan, who may have been a slight upgrade but still wasn't hitting enough for a corner outfielder. Third base was also a problem. Ernest Riles and Greg Litton had been sharing most of the time there, but neither was contributing much with the bat. Matt Williams had played a bit of third base too in the beginning of the year but was sent down to the minors in early May because he was not yet able to hit at the big-league level. On balance, the top of the Giants' order, Butler-Thompson-Clark-Mitchell was very strong, but the rest of the lineup was still a little thin.

Right field was a particularly acute deficit because on most teams it is a position that is expected to generate a lot of offense. The Giants tried unsuccessfully to acquire one more productive outfielder throughout 1989, but they had almost solved that problem years earlier, in June 1982, when they drafted a player straight out of high school. In 1989, Barry Bonds had not won any MVP awards or played on any all-star teams and was playing on a Pittsburgh Pirates team that went 74–88. Bonds was the Giants' second round draft pick in 1982 but had opted to go to college at Arizona State University. He was then drafted in the first round by the Pirates following his junior year there.

Baseball is full of might have beens and what ifs. What if the Red Sox had never sold Babe Ruth to the Yankees, if Roberto Clemente had ended up with the Dodgers as he almost did, or if the Yankees had traded Mariano Rivera when he was a failed starter before he was converted into the best closer in history? These are all fascinating questions, but for Giants fans, the question of what if Barry Bonds had signed with the team in 1982 rather than going to college is an intriguing one as well. Bonds would have fit in very well on that 1989 Giants team. He was not yet a great power hitter, but his .351 on-base percentage and 32 stolen bases in 42 tries, as well as excellent defense and, for good measure, 19 home runs, would have been a huge upgrade over Sheridan or Maldonado. Baseball has never worked this way and it is impossible to know how Bonds's career would have looked if he had signed with the Giants, but it is nonetheless a tantalizing question.

The All-Star Game did not go well for Reuschel, who gave up home runs to Bo Jackson and Wade Boggs, the first two batters he faced in the bottom of the first, the only inning he pitched. Clark and Mitchell were in the same three and four slots in the batting order in the National League's all-star lineup as they usually were for the Giants. In the first inning, Clark grounded out and Mitchell got an RBI single. In a hint of what was coming in October, the American League starting pitcher was Dave Stewart, the ace of the Oakland A's, so it was a Bay Area pitching matchup. Clark ended up hitless in two at bats, but Mitchell held his own, going two for four.

The Giants continued winning after the all-star break. The Bedrosian trade was the only major midseason trade the Giants made, but it was not until July 24 that the Giants' lineup was finally settled. On that day, Roger Craig put Williams, recently called back up from Phoenix, into the lineup at third base, batting sixth. The 23-year-old, three years removed from being the third overall pick in the draft, was finally ready. From that point in the season, Williams played sterling defense at third and, while still not hitting for a high average, was a formidable offensive weapon. His .500 slugging percentage over the rest of the season, largely on the strength of his 16 home runs, made Williams a genuine power threat and significantly lengthened the Giants' lineup.

If the 1989 Giants had been an ordinary team, Kevin Mitchell's one-handed catch would have still been a highlight that fans would watch for years, but two games in early August were much more powerful and profound, and they reflected that the Giants were a truly special team. Dave Dravecky's battle with cancer and effort to return, after missing the final four months of the 1988 season, had receded into the background during the 1989 season largely because the Giants were playing so well, but the southpaw was a valued teammate and an inspiration to many players and fans. In addition to that, Dravecky had been one of the best lefties in the league in the mid-1980s and had been almost unhittable in the 1987 NLCS. If Dravecky could come back, the top of the Giants rotation would include Dravecky and Reuschel, greatly improving the Giants' chances not just to make it to the postseason, but to win in October. However, Dravecky was battling cancer that had been found in his throwing arm: To come back from that would require a miracle.

Dravecky had missed more than a year but was nonetheless determined to pitch again. He began his rehab early in the 1989 season but found it frustrating as he was unable to throw with comfort at the speed needed. However, as the season continued, that began to change. Dravecky described how "I was out in San Francisco. I was starting to rehab and they were actually thinking about the possibility of me playing. . . . I couldn't feel like I could let it go. . . . It was May [1989]. . . . I went out to play catch with Atlee [Hammaker] and he goes 'look . . . air it out . . . just air the sucker out . . . the worst thing that could happen is you just can't do it' . . . boom. I let it go . . . and there was no pain. . . . Next thing you know I'm getting more velocity." With the confidence from that experience, Dravecky began his rehab in earnest, believing that he could make it back and contribute at the big-league level.

Dravecky's arm was beginning to feel better in May, but he was not quite ready to pitch yet. After a few more weeks of rehab, Dravecky was sent to the minors to work his way back to the Giants. He did well there and was brought back to the big-league squad, and on August 10 he was scheduled to make his first major-league start since being diagnosed with cancer. More than 34,000 fans turned up at Candlestick Park for a Thursday afternoon game between the Giants, who were leading the NL West by two games, and the Reds, who were in fourth place and no longer in contention.

The game received a substantial amount of media attention because of Dravecky's personal story. Dravecky's comeback was an extraordinary testament both to his determination and to the power of faith, particularly in times of despair. Dravecky was, and remains, a devout Christian. Giants fans were excited to see that Dravecky, who was well liked and had almost pitched the team to the World Series in the 1987 NLCS, was back, and they were also aware that if Dravecky could contribute over the next few months, then the team could possibly go all the way in 1989.

Although there was a lot of excitement around Dravecky's comeback, more experienced Giants fans were realistic about what they could expect. It was possible that Dravecky would only be able to go a few innings or that he would be completely ineffective. However, in the first inning, Dravecky retired the first three hitters, Luis Quiñones, Jeff Richardson, and Eric Davis on a flyout and two groundouts. Quinones was a little familiar to Giants fans as he had played with the team briefly in 1986 after coming to the team in exchange for Johnnie LeMaster in 1985. The game was off to a good start for Dravecky.

For the rest of the afternoon, Dravecky looked like his old self. Over seven innings, Dravecky allowed one hit, one walk, and no runs while striking out five. Dravecky had far exceeded anybody's expectations and seemed almost as dominant as he had been in the 1987 NLCS. The Giants went ahead 4–0, with the big hit coming on a two-run home run by Matt Williams. Dravecky struggled a bit in the eighth inning. First baseman Todd Benzinger led off with a single, but Joe Oliver followed by flying out. Third baseman Scotti Madison then doubled to left, but a good throw by Kevin Mitchell held Benzinger at third. This was the only real threat the Reds had mounted all day. Dravecky then struck out pinch hitter Ron Oester and was almost out of the inning, but Luis Quiñones then broke up the shutout with a three-run home run. It was suddenly a close game, but Dravecky got Richardson on a groundout for the last out of the inning.

Bedrosian pitched the ninth inning for the Giants, retiring the side in order. The Quiñones home run was a letdown, but the game had gone about as well as anybody could have hoped. Dravecky felt that way as well, telling me "now I'm in the saddle. . . . You're in the rotation. You've just thrown eight innings. . . . You're good to go."[3] The Giants felt the same way, believing that Dravecky would be the boost to their rotation that would all but guarantee a division title and very likely a more successful October than in 1987.

Dravecky made his next start on August 15 in Montreal. He was very good through five innings that evening, allowing only three walks and three singles. He was not quite as sharp as he had been over the first seven innings against the Reds, but again a two-run home run by Matt Williams, who was rapidly becoming a valuable part of the Giants' offense and infield defense, helped the team to a 3–0 lead by the middle of the sixth.

By now Dravecky was cruising, perhaps even a "little bit lazy."[4] Dámaso García, a light-hitting second baseman who had begun his career backing up Willie Randolph on the Yankees' World Series–winning team in 1978, and would only play in 12 more big-league games, led off the bottom of the frame with his 36th and final major-league home run. A home run from García's usually anemic bat was not a good sign, but the Giants were still winning and Dravecky still looked like he was pitching fine. Dravecky then worked the count to two and two before hitting the dangerous Andrés Galarraga with a pitch. It was clear by now that Dravecky was not quite right, but he stayed in the game to pitch to Expos star Tim Raines.

The next pitch was the last one of Dravecky's career: "I'd given up a run and Raines came up to the plate. . . . I rear back and I throw the pitch to Tim Raines . . . sinking fastball outside part of the plate. . . . All I hear is this incredibly loud noise. . . . I go reeling to the ground. Now I got Will Clark over me and he's telling me to breathe."[5] Bruce Jenkins was covering that game for the *Chronicle* and still remembers that moment: "It was like a gunshot. . . . You could hear it clear as day like a gun being shot in the forest. . . . Holy shit that's his arm."[6] The loud noise was Dravecky's left arm breaking. The video shows Dravecky falling to the ground as if he had been shot and then writhing in pain.

Dravecky's comeback had been cut short, but that it even happened at all after the doctors had told him he would never pitch again was extraordinary. Dravecky told me that Atlee Hammaker was his best friend in baseball. In addition to both being left-handed pitchers who played together from 1987 to 1989, Dravecky and Hammaker share a deep Christian faith, and even from talking to them both separately the affection and respect they have for each other is clear. Hammaker's description of Dravecky's comeback captures just how amazing it was: "For him to come back from [cancer], especially from the doctor's prognosis. To accomplish what he accomplished in the short time that he did it was not only inspiring. It was surreal. It was an amazing accomplishment. . . . He put time and effort in and trusted the process and then he went out there and competed."[7]

Giants fans who hoped that Dravecky would help the team win a championship had to accept that if the Giants were going to win, they would have to do it without a left-handed ace. Dravecky's cancer was so acute that in 1991 he had to have his left arm and part of his shoulder amputated because that became the only reliable way to contain the cancer. Despite this terrible setback, the Giants remained in first place, and while they never opened up a particularly big lead—they never led the division by more than seven games—they also were in control of the race for the last few months of the season. They ended up clinching the division on September 27 in a very anticlimactic way. They lost to the Dodgers and Tim Belcher 1–0, but that same day the second-place Padres lost to the Reds 2–1 in 13 innings and the Giants were going back to the postseason for the second time in three years.

The 92 wins the Giants accumulated in 1989 was the most of any Giants team during the Bob Lurie era and the most for any Giants team since 1966. The Giants won the NL West with a well-balanced team. The 699 runs they scored were second only to the 702 runs scored by the Cubs. The 600 runs they gave up were the third least, with only the Mets and Dodgers allowing fewer. Robby Thompson, in his fourth year with the team, was a good number two hitter and described the feeling of that 1989 team as "perseverance with that club . . . grinding, grinding. . . . Getting into the playoffs. . . . Everybody contributed any way possible."[8]

The Giants' offense in 1989 was built primarily around three players. Brett Butler led off, reached base at a .349 clip, stole 31 bases, and scored 100 runs. Clark and Mitchell were the most fearsome three and four hitters in the league. Clark hit .333/.407/.546, while Mitchell reached base slightly less frequently but hit for significantly more power, finishing at .291/.388/.635. The two combined for 72 doubles, 70 home runs, 236 RBIs, and finished first and second in the NL MVP balloting, with Mitchell taking home the award. Clark attributed his fantastic season to off-season guidance from the Giants' hitting coach: "I talked to Dusty Baker quite a bit and I made some adjustments in my swing and '89 I really stuck with those adjustments the whole year and I had a magical year. I was locked in the whole year. I was hitting balls right on the screws. . . . I stayed hot for six months [in 1989]. Even the outs I was making were loud."[9] Thirty years later, Baker spoke of his onetime mentee very positively: "Everybody knew Will could hit. Will knew he could hit. . . . And he played hard. I never saw him loaf. If he hit a popup to the infield, he'd always be halfway between first and second base or even second. He played hard. . . . You want Will the Thrill on your team if you're trying to beat somebody."[10]

Mitchell did not have one clear explanation for his extraordinary success in 1989 but echoed Thompson's sentiment about the team:

> I knew I was in the zone in spring training. I hit half a dozen home runs in spring training. . . . That '89 season, I was actually stronger at the end of the season. I could have went more. That's how good I felt. And not with weights. It was all swimming. That team I played on was the most exciting team I played on in a long time, besides playing on the Mets team that's a winner. . . .

The chemistry that we had there with Robbie Thompson, Uribe, Williams, Will Clark especially. . . . He made that team so exciting. He pushed us a lot too. . . . We considered him as a leader on our team.[11]

The rest of the lineup also contributed. Thompson was a very good number two hitter with a .321 on-base percentage, 12 stolen bases, and 91 runs scored. Matt Williams emerged as a legitimate power threat over the second half of the season and became a more than adequate number five hitter. The bottom half of the lineup was not quite as strong, with Candy Maldonado and Terry Kennedy both having off years, and José Uribe remaining a defense-first player. The team also had some depth with Pat Sheridan, Ken Oberkfell, and Ernest Riles providing versatility and veteran bats off the bench. The infield unit of Clark-Thompson-Uribe-Williams was sound defensively.

Rick Reuschel slowed down a bit in the second half but still ended up 17–8 with a 2.94 ERA. The rest of the rotation was not as strong or consistent. Don Robinson was effective as a full-time starter, going 12–11 with and a 3.43 ERA, while also hitting three home runs. The pitching find of the year was Scott Garrelts, who, after being primarily a reliever with the Giants since 1982, was converted to a starter and went 14–5 with a 2.28 ERA. Kelly Downs, Mike LaCoss, Atlee Hammaker, and several others, including Mike Krukow and Bob Knepper, who had come back to the Giants in August after eight and a half years with the Astros, filled out the starting rotation at various times during the season.

By the end of the season, the bull pen was also very good, with Craig Lefferts and Steve Bedrosian constituting a top lefty-righty tandem. The rest of the bull pen included LaCoss, Jeff Brantley, and several others. One of the best-known members of the bull pen for the first two thirds or so of the season was Goose Gossage. Gossage, a future Hall of Famer, had been pitching since the early 1970s and was already regarded as one of the best relievers in history, but he was 37 years old and had lost a little bit of his great fastball. Nonetheless, the Goose was a surprisingly helpful member of that bull pen, pitching 43²/₃ innings with a 2.68 ERA, while going 2–1 with four saves.

SUPERMAN DOES IT AGAIN

The NLCS was set to open on October 4 in Chicago. The Cubs won one more game than the Giants during the regular season and captured the NL East title handily, finishing six games ahead of the second-place New York Mets.

The Cubs, like the Giants, had a strong right side of the infield with Mark
Grace (.314/.405/.457) at first base and Ryne Sandberg (.290/.356/.497)
at second. Sandberg was a future Hall of Famer having an excellent season,
leading the team with 30 home runs, while Grace was, other than Clark, the
best first baseman in the National League in 1989. The two would both have
an excellent series in what Robby Thompson described as "two unbelievable
first baseman. . . . It was kind of like heavyweight battle."[12] Veteran right
fielder Andre Dawson, who would also end up in Cooperstown, was second
on the Cubs with 21 home runs, but the rest of the offense had some holes
as the Cubs got little production out of catcher, third base, or center field.

The Cubs starting rotation was probably better than the Giants. Their ace,
Greg Maddux, had been 19–12 with a 2.95 ERA in his third full season. Maddux would go on to become the best NL pitcher of his generation and one of
the very best in league history. In addition to Maddux, Rick Sutcliffe (16–11,
3.66) and Mike Bielecki (18–7, 3.14) were at the top of the Cubs' rotation.
Their deep bull pen was anchored by Mitch Williams, known as "Wild Thing,"
who saved 36 games in 1989.

Over the course of his 23-year career, Greg Maddux would start 30 postseason games, almost a full season's worth of work. Playing mostly in a good
period for hitters, Maddux held the best teams in baseball to fewer than 3.6
earned runs per game over just short of 200 innings. Game One of the 1989
NLCS was his first ever postseason start—and it was his worst. After three innings, Maddux had already given up four earned runs. However, Giants starter
Scott Garrelts got off to a rocky start as well, so the Cubs only trailed 4–3. Both
Clark and Grace had hit home runs in those early innings. Grace had also hit
a single and Clark a double, so the heavyweight battle, as Thompson called
it, was beginning quickly. Clark described his success in his first two at bats
that game: "First at bat was a sinker away, whacked it into left center. Next at
bat, I go to 3–2. I was looking changeup. I got a changeup, bam home run."[13]

Maddux struggled in the top of the fourth, giving up singles to Sheridan
and Uribe and a few batters later found himself facing Will Clark with two
outs and the bases loaded, but no runs in yet. This was a big moment for
Maddux. If he could retire Clark, he would be out of the inning and the Cubs
would still be in the game. However, if Maddux even gave up a single to Clark,
the Cubs would fall behind 6–3. Given this, Maddux and catcher Rick Wrona
discussed how to pitch to the very dangerous Clark. While the two conferred,
Clark watched intently. In fact, he watched so intently that he read Maddux's
lips, so when the inside fastball came, Clark was ready: "That was the read

the lips deal. I got the fastball in I was looking for. Turned on it."[14] When Clark turned on it, he sent the fastball clear out of Wrigley Field, giving the Giants an 8–3 lead. The final score was 11–3, with the Giants now only three wins away from the World Series. Looking back on that NLCS, Clark described "the Superman effect. Nobody's got kryptonite and you're good to go."[15]

In game two, Rick Reuschel, despite pitching in a ballpark he had called home for the first decade of his career, could not even get through one inning. The Cubs put up six runs in the bottom of the first and easily defeated the Giants 9–5. Will Clark was held to only a single in four at bats. Just like two years earlier, the series would go back to San Francisco with the Giants and their opponent tied at one game each.

Game Three saw another Giants pitcher, Mike LaCoss, get off to a poor start and surrender three earned runs before exiting the game in the fourth inning with no outs. However, a two-run home run by Robby Thompson in the seventh put the Giants ahead 5–4. The Giants held on to win by that score.

Game Four was a rematch between Garrelts and Maddux, and once again neither was particularly sharp. This time it was Matt Williams who hit a two-run home run in the fifth inning to give the Giants a lead. Four strong innings of relief by Kelly Downs kept the Giants ahead, but Downs left the game with two outs in the ninth after giving up a single to Ryne Sandberg. Steve Bedrosian then gave up a single to Lloyd McClendon and walked Mark Grace. With the bases loaded, the tying run on second, and the go-ahead run on first, Bedrosian struck out Andre Dawson for the final out of the game. The final score was 6–4, putting the Cubs on the brink of elimination. Bedrosian had reminded Giants fans that while nothing was ever easy with him, he usually got the job done.

Giants fans were excited about how the series had gone so far, but there was also an eerie sense of déjà vu. Two years earlier, the Giants had gone back on the road after going ahead 3–2 and lost the NLCS. Nobody wanted to see that happen again, but the Giants could avoid that possibility by winning Game Five and the pennant in San Francisco on October 9. The pitcher the Giants turned to for this hugely important game was Rick Reuschel. Despite his struggles in Game Two, there was no pitcher the Giants fans or players would have rather seen start Game Five. Thompson expressed this consensus view of Big Daddy: "This is the guy we want on our mound. This is the guy, keep the ball on the ground, keep the ball out of the air and guy with experience. Has been there and done that. . . . We were confident going in there with Big Daddy on the mound."[16]

The crowd of 62,084, roughly 61,000 of whom had better seats than mine, which was deep in the upper deck almost directly behind the left field foul pole, was one of the largest ever to attend a baseball game at Candlestick Park. It was a day game despite the 9th of October being a Monday. Presumably, that was because MLB did not want the NLCS to go head-to-head with Monday Night Football, as the Jets and the Raiders were scheduled to play later that evening. October 9, 1989, was also Yom Kippur, the holiest day in the Jewish calendar, but because San Francisco did not have a Jewish population comparable to that of Los Angeles or New York, few seemed to care about that—and it didn't stop me from going to the game. The game started at 12:05, rather than the 1:05 start that was more typical for day games at the 'Stick. This was good news for fans as it meant that the ballpark would probably stay warmer into the late innings. It turned out to be a beautiful day, one where all the stories about how cold Candlestick was at night seemed hard to believe.

Cubs manager Don Zimmer was a baseball lifer who began his career with the Brooklyn Dodgers in the 1950s. One of his teammates back then had been Roger Craig. The two young ballplayers became friends during their days in the Dodgers system and remained friends throughout their long careers. Zimmer even served as Craig's third base coach on the division-winning 1987 Giants team. Zimmer, who would coach well into the twenty-first century, fielded an odd lineup for Game Five. In an effort to get another left-handed bat against the right-handed Reuschel, Zimmer batted Marvell Wynne, a light-hitting outfielder who had hit .243/.274/.354 during the regular season, in the three spot. This decision made the usually potent middle of the Cubs' order seem less dangerous.

Reuschel projected his usual calm as he took the mound in the top of the first, but he surrendered a leadoff single to Jerome Walton and two outs later another single to Mark Grace that sent Walton to third base. He then struck out Andre Dawson to get out of the inning with no runs scored. In the top of the third, a dropped fly ball by Kevin Mitchell and a double by Ryne Sandberg gave the Cubs their first run of the day. Reuschel did not seem quite as sharp as usual, but he was pitching smart and getting the outs. A one run deficit was not at all overwhelming for the powerful Giants lineup, but Cubs pitcher Mike Bielecki was dealing as well.

Through six innings, Bielecki had only allowed two singles, one by Clark, and no runs, while seemingly cruising through the Giants' lineup. Slowly, fans began to realize that the Giants might have to go back to Chicago, and the bad memories of 1987 began to come into more acute focus. However, Reuschel was pitching one of the biggest games of his life as he evaded jams in the fourth and sixth innings. Through six and a half innings, the score was still 1–0.

In the bottom of the seventh, Will Clark, who was having a fantastic series, proved he had a little more magic in his bat as he led off the inning with a triple. Mitchell followed with a sacrifice fly and the game was tied.

The top of the Cubs order was due up in the first half of the eighth inning. Jerome Walton started things off with a walk and was bunted over to second by Ryne Sandberg. Taking the bat out of one of his best hitters' hands to give Marvell Wynne a chance to win the game was another questionable decision by Roger Craig's old teammate. Sandberg was clearly the better hitter, even getting the platoon advantage against Reuschel was not going to change that. In 1989, Sandberg had an OPS of .820 against righties, but Wynne's was only .590. In fact, Wynne hit lefties much better than righties in 1989. Zimmer's decision is indefensible from today's perspective, but in the late 1980s, bunting in that situation was still not altogether uncommon. Wynne could do little more than hit a grounder to Robby Thompson that moved Walton 90 feet closer to home but did not get the run in. Reuschel then wisely walked Mark Grace and got Andre Dawson out on a grounder to Will Clark. Going into the bottom of the eighth, the score was still tied at one run apiece.

One of the most important half innings in San Francisco Giants history began innocuously enough. Roger Craig sent Ken Oberkfell, a veteran left-handed hitter up to pinch-hit for Pat Sheridan, but Oberkfell lined out to left. José Uribe then struck out. Bielecki was still pitching well and the prospect of extra innings, or worse yet, a trip back to Chicago, began to settle over Candlestick Park. Then something strange happened. With two outs and nobody on base, Craig pulled Reuschel for a pinch hitter. It was a questionable decision because Reuschel had been pitching so well. The hitter Craig chose was Candy Maldonado, who had lost the right field job to Sheridan by the end of the season. Maldonado has been unproductive all year. Moreover, Maldonado was right-handed so did not even have the platoon advantage against Bielecki. Perhaps Craig sent the erstwhile right fielder up to hit in the hope that Maldonado, who always had some power, might hit one out.

He didn't. Instead, after falling behind 0–2, Maldonado worked a 10-pitch walk. This did not seem like a big deal at the time, but it ensured that, unless Maldonado was picked off or caught stealing, both Clark and Mitchell would bat one more time, probably in the bottom of the ninth. Brett Butler then fell behind 1–2 but also worked a walk, this one on seven pitches, as Bielecki was beginning to look less sharp. The walk to Butler changed the feel of the inning, suddenly the Giants were one batter away from having Clark up with a chance to win the game. Zimmer probably should have pulled Bielecki, who was clearly tiring after the walk to Butler. Nobody paid much attention to pitch counts then, but Bielecki was at 127 pitches at that point. He had also walked the two previous batters. Zimmer stuck with his gassed starter, who walked Thompson on four pitches.

By this point, the fans at Candlestick Park were on their feet sensing that the pennant that had eluded them since John F. Kennedy was in the White House, George Christopher was in City Hall, and before Will Clark had been born, was within reach. Will Clark, who was hitting .632 with six extra-base hits in the series up to that point, was coming up with a seal on every rock and two outs. Zimmer had finally seen enough of Bielecki and brought in Mitch "Wild Thing" Williams, one of the game's best lefty closers, to face Clark. Williams saved 36 games for the Cubs with a 2.74 ERA in 1989. During the regular season, Williams faced 87 left-handed hitters in 1989 and struck out 26 of them. Overall, lefties hit only .254/.345/.296 against Williams over the course of the year. Williams was the pitcher Zimmer wanted in this situation. Will Clark was the kind of ballplayer who loved the big moments—and this was a huge one. He described his thoughts to me when Williams was brought in: "Here comes Mitch Williams. I knew I was gonna face Mitch sooner or later."[17] Jenkins recalled that "trying to hit [Wild Thing] in any case was a real chore. To be a left-handed hitter against him was an exceedingly difficult thing to do."[18]

Clark recalled the first few pitches of that matchup: "He made some good pitches on me, gets me in the hole 0–2. I battle back, battle back, foul off a few pitches, take a pitch or two. I got a high fastball and I fouled it straight back. I was like 'whoa, I was on that one.'"[19] Williams was still ahead in the count, but he had not really thrown anything by Clark, who had fouled off four of the first five of Williams's pitches.

Since that Yom Kippur of 1989, the Giants have won four NL pennants and three World Series. In all those runs there were great pitching performances, big hits, and clutch defense, but no single hit, with the possible exception of Edgar Renteria's home run in Game Five of the 2010 World Series, was as significant for the franchise as what Clark did with that 1–2 count: "The next pitch was the same high fastball and I was able to get on top of it and get the base hit. Standing on first base all hell, I mean all hell, is breaking loose at Candlestick. 62,000 people are going absolutely nuts and all I could think about was my teammates, and I turn around and point at 'em. 'That's for you boys.'"[20] Giants announcer Hank Greenwald, calling the game on the radio, captured the moment perfectly, as he proclaimed "Superman has done it again."

Clark's single against Mitch Williams might be the second most famous and important hit in Giants history, behind only Bobby Thomson's "shot heard 'round the world" in 1951. Thomson's home run gave the Giants a walk-off win, before that term was coined, in the final game of a special three-game playoff between the Giants and their archrival Brooklyn Dodgers. That clutch home run is generally understood as one of the two or three most famous moments in baseball history. It not only captured the pennant for the Giants but assumed a larger role in baseball lore and even popular culture. Even today, millions of baseball fans have seen the video clip with Russ Hodges, the radio announcer that day, yelling "the Giants win the pennant" repeatedly as the ball clears the fence and Thomson rounds the bases.

Clark's single, while not quite as dramatic and barely resonating outside the Bay Area, effectively ended a 27-year period, by far the longest in Giants history, without a pennant. It came with two outs in the eighth inning of a nationally televised playoff game. Unlike Thomson's home run, which was hit in front of a crowd of only about 34,000—20,000 seats at the Polo Grounds were empty that day—Clark's single was hit in front of 62,000 fans desperate for a pennant. Jenkins concurred with that analysis, describing how "Will Clark just spanked that thing up the middle. He couldn't have hit it any harder. . . . I've never felt that way about any hit even through the three World Series [2010, 2012, and 2014]. . . . Really a singular event."[21]

Clark's single was the defining moment of the Giant's renaissance and completed their transformation from a team that lost 100 games in 1985 to a contender, a division winner, and finally, a pennant winner in only four years. At the center of that renaissance were Al Rosen, who had traded for Dravecky, Mitchell, Reuschel, and others while signing key free agents like Brett Butler, and Roger Craig, who had managed the team almost flawlessly while nurturing young players like Matt Williams and Robby Thompson as they made the journey from being high draft picks to big-league regulars and eventually stars.

No player had a bigger role in that renaissance than Will Clark. The first baseman who had been drafted number two overall was instrumental in changing the feel around the Giants. Clark's intensity and competitive nature made it clear that the Giants were no longer going to tolerate being losers, most known for their horrible ballpark. Clark was a magnet for the media and not only drew attention away from other young ballplayers seeking to make their way with the team, but also made it easier for veteran leaders like Mike Krukow or Bob Brenly to build a winning ethos. It also helped that Clark had hit from his first time at bat and rapidly became one of the best players in baseball. The single he hit off of Mitch Williams was the moment that sealed Clark's place in San Francisco baseball history, but his contributions to the Giants' winning ways began in spring training of 1986.

The line drive that Clark hit went right back up the middle, scoring Maldonado and Butler easily. Center fielder Jerome Walton bobbled the ball and then threw to third, just after Robby Thompson slid in safely to the bag. The Giants now led 3–1 heading to the bottom of the ninth, while the Cubs suddenly found themselves three outs away from elimination. With Reuschel out of the game, Craig turned the game over to Steve "Bedrock" Bedrosian, the closer who had been acquired midseason for just this type of situation, to get the final three outs. Corey Busch described the value of Bedrosian in this situation: "We had Bedrock. We had a guy coming out of the bull pen who we could really count on."[22]

Bedrosian was due to face Luis Salazar, Shawon Dunston, and Joe Girardi, not exactly the meat of the Cubs' order, in the top of the ninth. If anybody reached base, Mitch Webster, who entered the game in the bottom of the eighth as part of the double switch that brought Williams into the game, would bat, followed by the top of the order. Although the Giants were up by two, because Matt Williams had made the final out in the eighth, they too would be sending the weak part of their lineup to the plate in the ninth if it came to that.

Bedrock made quick work of Salazar and Dunston, needing only seven pitches to retire both of them. The Giants were now one out away from the pennant, but the slowly the unthinkable began to happen. A two-strike single by Curt Wilkerson, pinch-hitting for Girardi, followed by another single by Webster, put runners on first and second with the top of the order coming up. Jerome Walton lined Bedrosian's first offering to center for the Cubs' third consecutive single. The score was now 3–2 with two outs, the tying run on second, and the go-ahead run on first.

The next batter, Ryne Sandberg, was one of two batters the Giants did not want to see coming to the plate in this situation; the other was Mark Grace. A hit now would tie up the game and possibly deflate the Giants, who were now tantalizingly close to winning the pennant. The fans at Candlestick, and those watching and listening all over the Bay Area, had grown accustomed to the Giants never quite making it and were beginning to worry in earnest.

Robby Thompson described what was going through his head as he readied himself at second base: "I'm out there and I'm like this is what I do. I get paid for defense pretty much. . . . I'm like you know what, I want this ground ball right here. I don't know if he's gonna hit it to me, but I want it. If its anywhere in the vicinity, this game is over. . . . That's what was going through my mind, because if you have any doubts and don't want the ball, that's when some bad things can happen." Sure enough, Sandberg bounced the first pitch from Bedrosian back to Thompson. We Giants fans were relieved to see the ground ball to the second baseman as we had come to trust the steady Thompson's excellent glovework in his four seasons with the team. Thompson continued: "fortunately for me, it was hit to me and game over. And I fielded it and I'm bobbling it. I look back and I'm thinking was I saying I wanted it and then all of a sudden oh shit . . . here it comes. No, I really did. I wanted it. . . . It's just like a surreal moment. . . . That was so cool to get that last out."[23]

When Thompson fielded the ball and threw it to Clark—the bobble to which Thompson refers is not visible in the video, nor was it visible from my seat in the upper deck near the left field foul poll—Hank Greenwald again captured the moment beautifully, telling listeners "27 years of waiting have come to an end." The Giants were headed to the World Series for only the second time since moving to San Francisco. Over the course of that more than a quarter of a century since the Giants had last been in the Fall Classic, their old rivals the Dodgers had been there eight times, while seven other NL teams had been to the World Series at least once. The Giants, however, had not made it back since the heartbreaking loss to the Yankees in Game Seven of the 1962 World Series when Willie McCovey lined out to second base in the bottom of the ninth with the tying and winning runs on third and second.

The importance of that 1989 pennant to the city of San Francisco was profound. Once a proud baseball town, where the San Francisco Seals had been the flagship franchise of the Pacific Coast League for generations, and where Willie Mays, the greatest player of the postwar era, had roamed center field for almost 15 years, had become a baseball afterthought by the middle and late 1970s and again in the mid-1980s. Moreover, on several occasions, most notably in early 1976, it looked like the Giants would not be able to survive in San Francisco and would find a new home elsewhere.

While it would be inaccurate to describe San Franciscans as continuing to support the Giants by flooding into ballgames through thick and thin, the Giants were the city's team and, over the course of the three decades they had been in San Francisco, a core of deeply loyal and patient fans had emerged. Those fans who for years had braved the cold of Candlestick Park to watch uninspiring teams lose were finally getting their reward, as was the city more broadly.

Dave Dravecky had a special relationship with those Giants fans as they stood by him through some of the most difficult moments of his career and, indeed, his life: "I have been loved through the good, the bad, and the ugly of my story and it is these people here who have loved me well. . . . There's nothing like being part of this organization and being loved by these fans." Dravecky also understood that it was not always easy to be a fan of the Giants and that at times there were not too many people in that group: "When you were at Candlestick Park and it was freezing cold and there were 14,000 people that showed up. Those were 14,000 diehards that loved you even in the thick of that cold."[24] Dravecky's good friend Atlee Hammaker expressed a similar sentiment: "The people who came out were diehard fans. . . . Give credit to anybody who goes out there in that weather and enjoys the game."[25]

When Clark squeezed Thompson's throw for the final out, the loyalty of those fans was finally rewarded. Even at the time, the emphasis was on the Giants winning a pennant and a trip to the World Series. The last time the Giants had made it to the Fall Classic, they lost to the Yankees in seven games. The last time the Giants won the World Series had been in 1954 when they still played in New York.

For the fans, the NL pennant alone was, as Bob Lurie described it with characteristic understatement, "a monumental event."[26] The importance of the moment was not initially appreciated by the players. Chris Speier, who had begun his career 18 years earlier with the Giants and had finished his career during the 1989 season back with the team, was not on the playoff roster. He had been on the team for some bad years and for the near move to Toronto, but when asked if he had a sense of what this meant for the fans he replied simply "I don't think so." He then added insightfully, "I think players have a hard time understanding . . . how fanatical they can be."[27]

Thompson, who was part of the winning rally and fielded the ground ball for the last out of the series, reflected on whether he appreciated just what the pennant meant to the fans and the city: "At that moment, [I was] probably not [aware of what the pennant meant to the city]. After the fact . . . that's when it kind of kicked in to me. This team needs to stay here. . . . At that time, winning and beating the Cubs and those fans going nuts . . . we did it and so did these fans that stuck with us after that 1985 season. . . . Afterwards . . . you sit down, you think about it, you're having a beer and you're going that's just awesome for San Francisco."[28]

Despite the enormity of the moment in the history of the Giants, and the meaning it had for their most devoted fans, winning the pennant did not have the effect on San Francisco that it had on other cities. I remember going to North Beach to celebrate after leaving the game but finding very few people who seemed to share my joy. Bruce Jenkins had a similar recollection. "There wasn't a whole lot going on. . . . It just wasn't very visible. I went into Lefty O'Doul's [then the city's most famous and beloved sports bar] it felt just like a regular night with a bad turkey sandwich."[29]

There are several possible reasons for this relatively muted reaction to the Giants pennant. First, it was just the pennant, not the World Series. Moreover, their opponent in that World Series was going to be the Oakland A's, so not only were fan loyalties in the Bay Area, although less so in San Francisco itself, divided, but knowledgeable fans recognized that the A's were the heavy favorites. Second, by the late 1980s, the 49ers, not the Giants or the A's, were the marquee Bay Area sports franchise. That January, the 49ers had won their third Super Bowl of the decade and would go on to win another in January 1990.

There was another less tangible reason for the reduced enthusiasm. By 1989, casual fans, and San Franciscans who paid little or no attention to baseball, had grown tired of the constant discussions, debates, politics, and battles over the ballpark question and the Giants in general. Again, the team still had its fans, including thousands of very devoted ones, but its place in the larger San Francisco consciousness had become a source of fatigue for many.

For the players who had been together for several years, winning the pennant was a special feeling. It was an affirmation that the Giants were indeed the best team in the National League and a joyous payoff for years of hard work. For the fans it was something different. Many in attendance at the game, listening on the radio or watching on television, could trace their support for the Giants back years or even decades. Even by 1989, there were people in the Bay Area for whom being a Giants fan was not only an important part of their identity but had the same role in their parents' lives as well.

Within a few years, many of the players on that 1989 team would be toiling for other organizations. Brett Butler joined the Dodgers as a free agent following the 1990 season. Clark remained with the Giants through 1993 before signing with the Rangers as a free agent. Bedrosian was traded to the Twins after one more year with the Giants. Mitchell was sent to Seattle after the 1991 season. This kind of player movement is not unusual even for pennant winning teams. Players get old, can make more money elsewhere, or are sent away as parts of trades that are made with the hopes of improving the team.

This is also why almost nobody who was part of the Giants in 1989 was positioned to appreciate just how much that pennant meant to the team's fans. There were exceptions, including Bob Lurie, the team owner, who had worked so hard to keep the team in San Francisco. As a lifelong San Franciscan and baseball fan who began rooting for the Giants when they moved to San Francisco, Lurie was aware of what that pennant meant to the city. Clubhouse man Mike Murphy, who had been with the team since they first arrived in San Francisco, also appreciated the significance of winning the pennant: "It felt great. It felt wonderful."[30]

The die-hard fans who had suffered through years of cold evenings and too frequently lousy baseball at Candlestick had a different perspective. Unlike players, managers, and even executives, fans have a much longer and more enduring relationship with the team. While a player might not know for what team he will be playing in five years, most fans know for which team they will be rooting in five, 10, or 50 years. Devoted fans, like the core who stuck with the Giants in the lean years, do not change their team easily or, in most cases, at all. For them, their relationship with their team is a lifelong commitment, so they bring both the institutional memory and sentiment, and also belief in the future. For a player like Brett Butler, who played on several teams across a long career, or Matt Williams, who would play on several good teams, including a World Series–winning Arizona Diamondback squad in 2001, that pennant was one of many highlights of a great career. However, for fans who had been rooting for the team since childhood years earlier and had never seen the Giants in the World Series, that ball that Robby Thompson tossed to Will Clark was meaningful in a profound and powerful way.

THE BAY BRIDGE SERIES

The day before the Giants clinched the NL pennant, A's closer Dennis Eckersley struck out Junior Felix of the Toronto Blue Jays with two outs in the bottom of the ninth to secure a 4–3 victory for the A's in Game Five of the ALCS, giving them a 4–1 win in the series. That meant that, for the first time ever, the World Series would be played entirely in the Bay Area. The Series was referred to on official merchandise as the Battle of the Bay, but most people called it the Bay Bridge Series. The 1989 World Series was the first played entirely in one media market since the last of the Yankees-Dodgers matchups in New York in 1956.

The A's won 99 games in the regular season on their way to the second of what would become three consecutive pennants and were heavily favored to beat the Giants. They were a well-balanced team with no real weaknesses. Two of their players, Rickey Henderson and Dennis Eckersley, were in the prime of careers that would land them in the Hall of Fame. A third, Mark McGwire, had a Hall of Fame–worthy career but, because of his PED use, has never won election to that elite club.

The ace of that A's pitching staff, Dave Stewart, went 21–9 with a 3.32 ERA and was in the middle of a four-year stretch where he was one of the best pitchers in the game. Their number two starter, Mike Moore, had an even stronger 1989, going 19–11 with a 2.61 ERA. Bob Welch (17–8, 3.00) and Storm Davis (19–7, 4.36) rounded out the rotation. The A's' bull pen was even better. Eckersley, in an amazing display of control, struck out 55 batters in only 57 innings while walking only three. That contributed to his 4–0 record with 33 saves and a 1.56 ERA. Todd Burns, Rick Honeycutt, and Gene Nelson were the setup men in baseball's best bull pen.

The A's' pitching was good enough to have given up the fewest runs in the American League, but their offense was almost as good. The A's scored the fourth most runs in the AL despite playing in a tough park for offense. Only the Red Sox and Twins, who played in hitter's parks, as well as the AL East–winning Blue Jays, scored more runs than the A's. The A's offense began with Rickey Henderson, who had a .425 on-base percentage, 72 runs scored, and 52 stolen bases in 85 games after coming to Oakland in a midseason trade with the Yankees. José Canseco was held to only 17 home runs but hit .269/.333/.545 in an injury-marred season. The rest of the A's power came mostly from McGwire, who hit 33 home runs, and Dave Parker, who hit 22. Terry Steinbach, Dave Henderson, Carney Lansford, Walt Weiss, and Tony Phillips filled out a deep lineup that hit from top to bottom. In addition to their great numbers, the A's had something of an intimidating feeling about them as Parker, McGwire, and Canseco were towering and muscular men unlike most players of the era. In 1989, Will Clark was a better player than any of those three, but he looked small compared to the A's' top sluggers. Kevin Mitchell hit more home runs than anybody on the A's in 1989, but McGwire and Parker were both almost half a foot taller and 30 pounds heavier than Mitchell.

Mitchell himself described how the A's looked to the Giants as the World Series commenced: "Before those games even started, we was already intimidated as a team. . . . You look at those guys, those Bash Brothers [Canseco and McGwire] over there. Those guys were seven feet tall. We're like 4'7". That's how it looked, like we was overmatched. You had Dave Parker hitting home runs and taking a trot by our dugout like he was gonna high five us."[31]

The A's were a big, powerful, and physically intimidating team, but some of that was supplemented, so to speak. Busch phrased this aspect of that A's team as neutrally as he could muster, "that was a steroids club."[32] Two of the A's' biggest stars, Canseco and McGwire, wound up in the middle of the PED controversies that surrounded baseball in the late 1990s and early part of the twenty-first century. Many, including Busch, suspected their steroid use had begun by 1989.

Writing the day before the World Series was due to start, veteran *Chronicle* writer Bruce Jenkins compared the two teams on 11 criteria ranging from power to benches to starting pitching, and gave the A's the advantage in all 11 except for infield defense, which he rated as "even," and intangibles, which he rated "too close to call." Jenkins's analysis, while not encouraging for Giants fans, reflected a consensus among baseball writers and analysts.[33]

The first two games in Oakland did not go well for the Giants. In Game One, Dave Stewart held the Giants to four singles, a walk, and a Will Clark double as he threw a complete game shutout. The A's roughed up Scott Garrelts for four earned runs in four innings on their way to an easy 5–0 win. The next day was more of the same. Moore, Honeycutt, and Eckersley held the Giants to four singles, two walks, and one run while Reuschel gave up five earned runs in four innings as the Giants fell to the A's 5–1 and were down in the series two games to none.

BACK TO CANDLESTICK

After losing the first two games in Oakland, the Giants returned home for three games. The journey home was a short one, as the Oakland Coliseum is about a 30-minute drive from Candlestick Park when there is no traffic. Younger readers may not have experienced an absence of traffic in the Bay Area, but in 1989, unless it was rush hour, the drive between the two ballparks would have been smooth on most days.

The three games at home gave the Giants an opportunity to get back into the World Series. Winning even two of three would get the series back to Oakland, albeit with the Giants down 3–2. Mike Krukow, who by 1989 had moved from the field to the broadcast booth, described the sentiment that many on the Giants had as the series moved across the bay: "We felt . . . we were gonna be able to get back in the series with the A's, and it was our hope we could win the three game series [at home]."[34] Winning all three in San Francisco was extremely unlikely, but if they managed to do it, it would give the Giants a 3–2 edge as the Series moved back across the bay. The Giants had swept the home part of the NLCS, but the A's were a much stronger team than the Cubs had been. Even winning one game would avoid the ignominy of being swept in the World Series against their rivals from Oakland.

Because the World Series was being played entirely in the Bay Area, fans of both teams could easily attend games at either ballpark if they could get tickets. This meant that the crowd was less of a factor in the Giants coming home for three games, but they had some other advantages going into Game Three. Bob Welch, the A's' starter, was a very good pitcher, but he was a cut below Dave Stewart or Matt Moore, so the Giants had a chance to score a few more runs. Additionally, the games would be played without a DH. The Giants had no obvious DH on their bench and had used Ernest Riles, who had lost his job as starting third baseman to Matt Williams late in the season, in that role in the first two games. Riles had been hitless in seven at bats over the first two games, so losing his bat would not be a blow to the Giants' offense. The A's' DH was Dave Parker, who was their cleanup hitter. Parker was two for eight with one home run in the first two games. The A's offense would be weaker without him.

Since 1989, the Giants have represented the National League in the World Series four times, winning the championship in 2010, 2012 and 2014. Those three World Series included some very memorable moments, including: Edgar Renteria's three-run home run in Game Five of the 2010 World Series; Brian Wilson striking out Nelson Cruz for the final out of that game; Pablo Sandoval hitting three home runs in Game One of the 2012 World Series; Sergio Romo freezing Miguel Cabrera with a fastball down the middle of the plate for the last out of the 2012 World Series; Madison Bumgarner carrying the team to victory in 2014; and the miscue in the outfield that could have cost the Giants the game in the bottom of the ninth of Game Seven that year. None of those events are remembered nearly as well, particularly outside of the Bay Area, as what happened as the A's and the Giants were getting ready to play Game Three.

Through much of the twentieth and all of the twenty-first century, San Franciscans, knowingly or not, lived in the shadow of two major events that were central to the creation of the San Francisco the world knows. The first is the Gold Rush of 1849, which in a decade or two turned the city from an obscure Spanish outpost to one of the most vibrant, wealthy, important, and unusual cities in North America and the world. The legacy of the Gold Rush is still everywhere in San Francisco. The local football team is called the 49ers. A German Jewish immigrant who decided to make practical clothing for gold miners rather than mine gold himself founded one of San Francisco's best-known companies, whose impact has been global. People around the world wear Levi's, but few know that Levi Strauss started that company in San Francisco during the Gold Rush. More broadly, the Gold Rush made San Francisco an important international city, a center of trade and finance, and brought money into the city that fueled its development and growth in the second half of the nineteenth century.

The second formative incident was the earthquake of 1906, which locals refer to as the earthquake and fire, because much of the damage to San Francisco was done by the fire that followed the earthquake. The events of April 18 to 20, 1906, destroyed some neighborhoods and gave birth to others. For example, the Marina District is built almost entirely on landfill, much of which was originally from buildings that were destroyed in 1906. Because of that earthquake, San Francisco has very few old buildings, but more importantly, the possibility of another earthquake is always there in San Francisco and, to one degree or another, in the consciousness of all San Franciscans.

For decades after 1906, San Franciscans wondered when, not if, the next major earthquake, usually referred to as "the big one," would hit. At 5:04 P.M., moments before Don Robinson was to throw the first pitch to Rickey Henderson, the Bay Area got the answer to that question, and, because the World Series was televised nationally, the rest of the country got to see it in real time. Will Clark described the moment when the big one hit:

> I just got through running a sprint to center field and I was walking back and I just happened to look up in the stands and first I heard it before I saw it. It sounded like the F-15s flying over. . . . I looked up . . . and one of the light towers was swaying back and forth. I go "Oh no, this is not good." You could see it. You could literally see the wave coming through the stands . . . damn near knocked me down. After everything subsided, I made it back to

the dugout and the policemen that were there, that were with the team, their radios were going crazy.[35]

Robby Thompson, who, like Clark, was preparing to take the field in a few minutes, was also in the outfield preparing for the game:

I'm running sprints in right field. Whole starting lineup is out there. . . . All of a sudden, the ground literally, it was like a wave underneath the ground. It all happened so fast. . . . It seemed a lot longer. I'll never forget the clicking of the seats. . . . The light posts are going back and forth. . . . Where's my mom and dad, my sister, my wife. It's all a blur it happened so fast. . . . For us on the field, it didn't seem as impactful as it ended up being. . . . When it finally stopped 15 seconds later . . . they started playing that song "We Will Rock You," . . . the crowds doing that. . . . Then all of a sudden it gets quiet. They're getting the news that the Bay Bridge, part of it went down. . . . the Marina District's on fire. That was the first time at the professional level I ever went home with my uniform on.[36]

Kevin Mitchell also remembered the Queen anthem playing around the time of the earthquake:

Before the earthquake, I'm out on the field talking to Tony Phillips. May he rest in peace. I didn't know what was going on because they was playing that song "We Will Rock You." I thought people in the stands was stomping the stands until I saw right field. People started panicking and running. . . . As I walked over to the dugout, Willie Mays said "the bridge just fell." First thing I thought about was getting my grandparents out of here. They got stuck in an elevator [at the ballpark]. . . . As we was coming on the field there was a panic. We've got people trying to come into our dugout and take bats.[37]

Dave Dravecky was not on the playoff roster due to the cancer in his arm, but he was still with the team for the World Series: "Bob Knepper and I are sitting in the locker room. . . . All of a sudden, he looks at me and he goes 'lets get out of here.' . . . It was like a freight train had just come through into the clubhouse and I bolted into the parking lot."[38] Atlee Hammaker was in the clubhouse with Dravecky and Knepper and told me: "The ground was shaking. I didn't know what the heck was going on. . . . We go out into the parking lot where the press was. . . . The media tent was in the player's parking lot and I saw it [the ground] roll like carpet. . . . I've never seen anything like that and never have since."[39]

Mike Krukow was on the field and also reported the ground rolling beneath his feet: "I was just stepping out of the dugout to see where my family was. . . . And then here it comes. . . . It felt like a 600-pound gopher going 40 miles per hour beneath my feet. . . . I knew immediately we were having an earthquake. . . . And I looked up at the light tower behind the third base dugout . . . and it was torqueing. . . . This one didn't stop. It just kept on rolling. . . . We had no idea how big."[40]

Chris Speier, like Dravecky was not on the active roster for the World Series, but as a native of the Bay Area he had experienced earthquakes throughout his life, and perhaps because of that, he had a more light-hearted memory of the quake:

> The Gatlin Brothers are gonna sing the national anthem and I'm standing there right outside the dugout with Larry Gatlin and all of a sudden . . . it sounds as if everybody is stomping their feet. . . . I glance up and I see the tower going like that and I'm like "Larry, just relax. I think we're right in the middle of an earthquake." . . . It [the field] literally looked like an ocean and . . . [players] were rolling and stumbling. Larry's like two minutes away from going on. . . . Larry goes "fuck this." I have not seen him since. I don't know what happened to him. He ran straight down through those doors. That was it. . . . Everybody thought that the stadium was going. . . . I figured that's a sign for me to retire.[41]

Bruce Jenkins was up in the press box when the earthquake struck: "I remember the sound of it first. I heard this rumbling getting louder and louder. The earthquake was literally heading our way. 'What the fuck is that?' Lyle [Spencer from the *New York Post*] and I looked at each other. This is it. We're rocking back and forth. We can't keep our balance. We're grabbing a rail. This is it. This is the big one. We're going down. Nice knowing you. And then it calms down."[42]

Giants coach Dusty Baker was, like Speier, a native Californian and had spent most of his career playing for California-based teams. Despite having experienced earthquakes in the past, Baker still described October 17, 2019 as "the weirdest day of my life, damn near." Baker was having a pregame snack in the clubhouse when the earthquake hit: "I was eating banana nut bread . . .

[when] all this tons of cement up above, it liquified. The whole thing looked like Jell-O."[43]

Bob Lurie, as a lifelong San Franciscan born in 1929, had undoubtedly heard about the earthquake of 1906 in his youth from people who had lived through it, so he recognized what was occurring immediately, but, with the nonchalance of somebody who had experienced many earthquakes, did not immediately recognize the gravity of what had occurred: "I was going into the office. I knew it was an earthquake. Somebody came and got me and said Al Michaels wants to talk to you. I said 'I think we'll play.' . . . And then all hell breaks loose."[44]

By the time the World Series started, Lurie had already been working closely with San Francisco's mayor to bring a ballpark to an area just off the bay near the intersections of Third and King Streets. Art Agnos, who had been rooting for the Giants longer than almost any San Franciscan, albeit in the form of a minor-league affiliate in Springfield, Massachussetts, was not yet at the ballpark when the earthquake hit:

I was going to the World Series game out at Candlestick, but I was late because I was working at City Hall. . . . We were driving into the parking area
where the mayor's car is parked when I felt the earthquake shaking. . . . I
thought we were having flat tires. . . . Then I went into the ballpark . . . and
the place was rocking. The ballplayers were milling around down below. The
police were there. The crowd was very animated and [I was] trying to figure
out what to do next. . . . A police officer came up to me and said "Mr. Mayor,
you've gotta go. The bridge has fallen in."[45]

The earthquake that shook Candlestick Park, known formally as the Loma Prieta quake because the Loma Prieta mountain was very close to the earthquake's epicenter, was generally referred to in the Bay Area as the World Series Earthquake or some variation on that and was indeed "the big one." It was a recorded as a 6.9 on the Richter Scale, making it the most powerful earthquake to hit San Francisco since 1906, the one that had led to the destruction of much of the city. In the now more than 30 years since that World Series, San Francisco has not experienced a bigger earthquake.

Within a few minutes of the earthquake, news of the devastation it wrought, as well as rumors that, thankfully, turned out to be wrong, began to circulate. Word quickly got out that the Marina District, an affluent neighborhood in the northern part of the city that had once been a heavily Italian American, working-class neighborhood, close to where George Moscone had grown up, was badly damaged. Parts of the city built on landfill, like the Marina, were particularly vulnerable to earthquakes. In the Marina, some buildings fell, there were a few fires, and many buildings were quickly deemed unsafe by the city authorities and had to be evacuated.

The most famous resident of the Marina District in 1989, and perhaps ever, was not a politician but a ballplayer who had grown up nearby. Joe DiMaggio's home was one of the many that were damaged in the earthquake. A few days after the quake, he was seen and photographed standing in a line outside of Marina Junior High School waiting to see if he would be able to move back into his home.

Richard Ben Cramer, in his 2000 biography of DiMaggio, recounted an incident that occurred that night that demonstrates both the feel in the Marina District after the earthquake, as well as a less-than-flattering side of the greatest baseball player San Francisco's sandlots ever produced:

> By the time Joe got to the Marina, the streets were a horror show: buckled pavement, crumbling houses, broken concrete, glass, wires, fires. . . . On his block of Beach Street, there were three houses down in ruin, an apartment building was cockeyed, menacing the rest of the buildings. And amid the chaotic destruction, Joe's house was fine. . . . Maybe there were new plaster cracks. But nothing crumbled. Nothing burned. Nothing fell. . . . Joe took a minute to go upstairs, to his private quarters, and came back with his big right hand around the neck of a garbage bag. No, no, he said, he'd carry his own. He left the house without another glance around.[46]

Naturally, many wondered what DiMaggio had gone into his house to retrieve. It might have been his World Series rings, other items from his baseball career, a picture, or other ephemera from his marriage to Marilyn Monroe, but Cramer revealed that the "garbage bag . . . held six hundred thousand dollars, cash,"[47] mostly from autograph signings and other untaxed income.

The bridge that Agnos had been told had fallen was not the Golden Gate Bridge, the most famous and enduring visual symbol of San Francisco, but the Oakland Bay Bridge. The latter was a much less glamorous edifice connecting San Francisco to the East Bay, including Oakland. It was the bridge you would drive across if you were traveling between Oakland and San Francisco.[48] The news that the bridge had fallen evoked an image of a chunk of the roadway dangling over the water with cars falling into San Francisco Bay, but the reality was not quite that bad. Instead, the top level of the bridge collapsed onto the lower level. One person was killed, and the bridge rendered unusable for a month.

The damage to the Oakland Bay Bridge meant that just as the Giants and A's were playing each other in the World Series, it was more difficult to get from San Francisco to Oakland than it had been any time in the half century since the bridge was built. Halfway around the world, a few weeks after the earthquake, in an event unrelated to the World Series or the earthquake, the government of East Germany stopped preventing its citizens from crossing the Berlin Wall into West Berlin. This prompted Herb Caen, the legendary San Francisco newspaperman, citing one of the people who fed him quips and stories, to note that "Chris Nye asks, 'think you'd ever see the day when it's easier to get from East Berlin to West Berlin than from the East Bay to the West Bay.'"[49]

The Marina District and the Oakland Bay Bridge were among the highest-profile areas damaged by the earthquake, but the destruction went well beyond that. Throughout San Francisco, particularly in the northern and northeastern parts of the city where there was more landfill, buildings were damaged, and people lost their homes and businesses. The Embarcadero Freeway, which ran along the bay in the northeastern part, was structurally damaged. Oakland was hit very hard by the earthquake as several freeways were rendered unusable and buildings in many neighborhoods were either damaged or deemed unsafe until further inspection. As far away as Santa Cruz, a college town on the coast about 80 miles south of the city, there was widespread damage to the commercial area. Aftershocks throughout the region lasted for days, causing buildings and other structures that had initially been only slightly affected by the quake to become less safe. These aftershocks were unsettling for many people because it was a reminder of the potential for another quake.

One building that was not severely damaged during the earthquake was Candlestick Park. The attendance for the World Series game on October 17 is not known because the game was never played, but based on the attendance for the three NLCS games in San Francisco earlier that month, the number of guests and dignitaries who were at the ballpark but not counted in attendance statistics, and the fact that the earthquake hit just before the game while the park was already almost filled up, it is almost certain that there were at least 50,000 people at the game when the earthquake hit, but that number could easily be closer to 60,000.

Amazingly, nobody at the ballpark was killed or even badly injured. By 1989, most baseball players and fans recognized Candlestick as a cold, unpleasant place to play baseball. The Giants had spent the better part of the decade trying to find a new home. Giants fans who were also San Francisco voters were very aware of the heated campaign around various efforts to build a new ballpark, but when the earthquake hit, nobody thought about the cold and wind, where the Giants might find a new home, or whether the Giants would leave San Francisco. On the evening of October 17, baseball fans, and within minutes Americans who may have cared very little about baseball, were just grateful that the sturdily built, 30-year-old structure, buoyed by some preventative retrofitting a few years earlier, weathered the earthquake so well. It was Candlestick Park's finest moment.

Atlee Hammaker noted that after the initial jolt, which lasted around 20 seconds, the crowd at Candlestick was "pretty under control for the situation being what it was. . . . You'd think there'd be crowds just going crazy, but they were pretty under control." Hammaker also added a memory of "looking up and seeing a guy hanging on to a light pole trying to get the flags untangled before the earthquake hit and he ended up being on top of the light pole. That thing was shaking like a stick and that guy was holding on."[50]

Hammaker's observation was right. When the earthquake hit, there was not much panic in the ballpark. The crowd eventually evacuated the ballpark in a relatively orderly way. One of the reasons for this was that the crowd of Bay Area A's and the Giants fans were familiar with earthquakes. It is also possible that traffic on Bay Area highways and bridges was lighter than usual that day because many fans had left work early to watch the game or had gone straight from work to a bar to see the World Series on television. That too may have contributed to fewer deaths and injuries on many of the highways that were badly hit by the quake.

The earthquake was a major shock to the Bay Area, but overall, the damage was not as bad as it had been 83 years earlier. In the many years that passed between these two major quakes, the Bay Area had grown, more construction on landfill had occurred, and a network of freeways and bridges had been developed, so the potential for devastation was real. However, the region was also prepared. Emergency services were better, many buildings had been designed to sustain a relatively big earthquake, and more advanced communications technology meant people were less frightened, isolated, or vulnerable to rumors. This meant that the death toll was not as bad as many initially feared, and that many, but not all, buildings could be rebuilt relatively quickly.

Some decisions needed to be made as well. For example, San Francisco opted not to rebuild the Embarcadero Freeway that had been damaged in the earthquake, thus opening up the waterfront in the area of San Francisco that is now anchored by Oracle Park. Government officials had to focus on bringing in federal funds to help rebuild the area, helping those who were in need of urgent support, supervising emergency workers, and setting priorities for which repairs were most urgent. Mayor Art Agnos, who had spent much of his time over the previous months on the ballpark issue, had to turn his attention away from the World Series because the earthquake was now the top priority.

The future of the World Series was also in doubt. When Game Three was scheduled to start, the A's were up two games to none and looked like a team that was intensely focused on redeeming themselves following a loss in the previous year's World Series to a Dodgers team that had been generally viewed as inferior. After the earthquake, it was not clear what would become of the rest of the World Series. This problem was exacerbated because both teams made their homes in cities that had been damaged by the earthquake. Many parts of Oakland, including freeways in and out of the city, as well as numerous residential areas and the central business district, had been hit by the earthquake. Because of this damage, playing the rest of the games at the Oakland Coliseum was not an option either.

There were a few possible choices. One was to simply cancel the World Series and award the A's the championship based on their initial lead. There were a lot of problems with this solution. First, it was clearly not fair to the Giants, or even the A's, as winning only two games is not the same as winning a real World Series. It also meant that both teams would lose out on revenue they would have gained from hosting World Series games, and it would have been insensitive to the many fans of both teams who, due to the quake, were going through a difficult time.

A better solution would have been to simply wait until San Francisco and Candlestick Park were ready to host the World Series. This would give both teams a chance to win a legitimate World Series while providing people in San Francisco and Oakland with a needed distraction. It would also mean that MLB and the two teams would make some money. However, nobody was sure when the city and the ballpark would be ready to resume play as baseball was no longer a top priority.

Several Giants players used the days following the earthquake trying to help the recovery and rebuilding efforts and to raise morale in San Francisco. Will Clark recollected, "I went downtown and helped out as much as I could."[51] Mike Krukow remembered those days following the earthquake with some gravity, while drawing a contrast between the Giants and the A's, who went to Arizona for a few days to prepare for the World Series when it would resume: "It changed all of our lives. . . . What happened during that ten-day period changed my life. . . . We didn't leave the Bay Area, we stayed here."[52] Kevin Mitchell was forthright about how the earthquake impacted the Giants mindset and put them into an even deeper hole against a very good A's team: "I didn't think we was gonna play. . . . You've just had a lot of people being killed. The city was in rubbles. I didn't think it was a time to play. . . . A lot of players on our team, their mindset was gone already."[53]

Waiting until the city and the ballpark were ready may have made the most sense to the Giants and the A's, but the decision was in the hands of baseball's commissioner, Fay Vincent. Vincent had been in the job only about a month when the earthquake hit, having taken over from Bart Giamatti, who had died on September 1, 1989. The 51-year-old Vincent had spent much of his career as a corporate attorney and executive for Coca-Cola and did not have much of a baseball background. Vincent grew up, was educated, and spent most of his career on the East Coast, so he was perhaps not very familiar with the geography of California when he proposed his solution about finishing the World Series.

Art Agnos recalled meeting with the Giants and Vincent to discuss the plans for resuming the World Series:

> I got a call. . . . asked me to come to a meeting in Al Rosen's downtown condominium with Al Rosen, Bob Lurie, myself, and the commissioner of baseball and they asked me to come alone. To meet and talk about what happens the rest of the way. . . . The five of us, Fay Vincent, Lurie, Al Rosen, Corey Busch, and myself . . . got down to business pretty quickly and he [Vincent] said "what do you have planned for when we start the World Series. We've gotta get going pretty soon. It's been whatever days it's been without a game." Because we're in recovery and looking for survivors, et cetera, I said "I don't know when we're gonna start it. We've got to finish finding all the victims in both cities." I told him I didn't know when we would complete the process of finding the survivors and getting the city back in some stable condition. And, I didn't know what the condition of the ballpark was. So he says to me "Well, we can't let it go too long or else we'll lose the World Series, and I'd hate to be the first mayor in American history to be the cause of . . . the World Series not being completed." That kind of pissed me off because it was sort of a threat. . . . I said "well Mr. Commissioner, I'd hate to be the first mayor who resumed the World Series while we're still looking for dead bodies in both cities." That kind of chilled the atmosphere in the room.[54]

That is when Vincent came up with a proposal that was both foolish and insensitive. Agnos described what happened next: "He [Vincent] said 'Well, maybe we should go to San Diego and finish it there.'" Vincent decided to tell the mayor of a major American city that had just been devastated by a massive earthquake that he wanted to move the World Series a few hundred miles south to another city because it was more convenient.

Art Agnos was both a committed progressive and a big-city politician who could play hardball when necessary. He had won his first election campaign in a hard-fought primary where he ran against Harvey Milk from the left and went on to be reelected to the California State Assembly five times. In 1987, Agnos won a mayoral campaign that nobody had initially expected him to win, in part by working harder than his opponents. Agnos had also been shot in the chest at point blank range in 1973 by the Zebra Killers and was the son of a Greek immigrant who worked at his father's shoeshine stand as a boy. He was a tough man who had a reputation for speaking his mind, not taking criticism easily, and letting people know when he disagreed with them. If there was ever a moment for Agnos to give Vincent a piece of his mind, now was the time. The whole city would have supported him.

As mayor, Agnos was one of two principals from San Francisco in the meeting. The other was Bob Lurie, who by then had owned the Giants for more than a decade. Lurie and Agnos had been working together for much of 1989 to try to find a way to keep the Giants in San Francisco, but they were very different in both temperament and background. The soft-spoken Lurie was essentially a private man who had never run for office or sought publicity, but who had bought the Giants in large part because he wanted to make sure they didn't leave San Francisco in 1976.

Over the course of his life, Bob Lurie's contributions to the city of San Francisco were enormous. Had he not stepped forward in 1976, when no other San Franciscan did, the Giants would have gone to Toronto. In addition to saving the Giants, Lurie was a philanthropist who gave tens of millions of dollars to various charities. Players and others who worked with or for Lurie describe him as a level-headed, generous, and decent man.

Duane Kuiper told a story about an early encounter with Lurie after being traded to the Giants that captures the humility and gestalt of the man:

I'm in line [at the Giants store on his first trip to San Francisco after the trade] . . . and the guy standing in front of me is Bob Lurie. He's got stuff too. . . .

One, he's in line and two, he's paying. . . . I know now I'm getting into an organization where the owner is paying for his clothes and he's standing in line. . . . And he turned out to be literally one of the nicest, classiest guys in professional sports I've ever been associated with.[55]

Gary Lavelle, who pitched for Lurie's Giants for nine years, had similarly positive things to say about Lurie: "Bob Lurie deserves so much credit for what he did for the city of San Francisco and what he did for the Giants organization. A lot of the time, that's overlooked. . . . If I had a career to do over again, I would still want to be with the Giants."

Bruce Jenkins, who covered Lurie and the Giants for many years while writing for the San Francisco Chronicle, described Lurie similarly as a "very kindly, caring, good-hearted successful man, who didn't always make the right decisions, but made a lot of good ones. He was a fan who cared about the team. . . . [Unlike] Charlie O. Finley who was a complete lunatic and George Steinbrenner who was a tyrant. . . . An owner should be signing the checks, big picture, stay away from the nuts and bolts. And that's what I liked about Bob."[56]

Lurie may have been a modest and soft-spoken man, but he was also a San Franciscan who was loyal to his city and knew when his town was being offered a raw deal. Lurie's description of his response to Vincent's proposal is, as might be expected from the former team owner, understated: "Fay Vincent thinks its best that the World Series go to San Diego. And I went a little ballistic. After everything we've gone through, kept the team here, now you're telling our fans 'just, go to hell, you're not worth it, we're going to San Diego.'"[57] Agnos remembered what may have been Bob Lurie's finest moment more vividly. Vincent made his proposal "and that's when Bob Lurie popped out of his seat and said 'over my goddamn dead body are we going to San Diego. He said 'I didn't have the first World Series in [27] years to go to San Diego and finish it.'"[58] Lurie's words persuaded the commissioner and it was decided that the World Series would be completed in San Francisco, and if the Giants could win at least two of the three games, in Oakland as well.

The World Series finally resumed, at Candlestick Park on October 27, 10 days after the earthquake. More than 62,000 fans packed Candlestick Park to see the Giants play two of the most lackluster and forgettable games in their postseason history. Will Clark described how many of the Giants felt: "Here we are resuming the World Series in Game Three and I've never had 10 days off from baseball in my life, ever. . . . It literally was like spring training all over again. . . . The World Series lost a lot of its luster. I went from being locked in during the Cubs series to being lost, starting all over again."[59]

Game Three featured the same pitching matchup as Game One, and once again Dave Stewart outpitched Scott Garrelts. The final score was 13–7, but the game was never really even that close. Four of the Giants runs came in the bottom of the ninth when the game was already out of reach. The next day, Mike Moore, who had won game two for the A's, outpitched Don Robinson, who was making his first start of the series. Again, the final score of 9–6 did not reflect that the Giants were never in the game. They trailed 8–0 before even getting on the scoreboard in the bottom of the sixth. The Giants' four-run rally in the bottom of the seventh was not enough to make the game feel close.

The World Series had gone about as badly as it could have for the Giants. They were outscored by the A's 32–14. No team had ever been swept in the World Series with such a big run differential.[60] The defeat stung the Giants even more because it came at the hands of their cross bay rival, thus giving A's fans easy access to the Giants and their fans whenever they wanted to gloat. Jenkins summed up the impact of the earthquake and the sweep: "The earthquake was devastating in so many ways, but it almost rendered the World Series . . . a bitter memory in every respect."[61]

Frank Jordan, who was Chief of Police in 1989, was on the field when the earthquake happened and was deeply involved in the postearthquake recovery work, but he was also a lifelong San Francisco baseball fan who had been rooting for the Giants since they moved west. Jordan looked back on the final two games of the 1989 World Series in a 2019 interview and captured the feelings of many Giants fans at the time: "[Oakland's] two best pitchers were now fully rested and they did the same thing all over again. They beat us. Here we are as Giants fans rejected again, kind of always the bridesmaid, never the bride. Never could get that big victory we wanted."[62]

In the bottom of the ninth inning of Game Four with two away, Brett Butler hit a roller to Tony Phillips who fielded it and flipped it to pitcher Dennis Eckersley, who was covering first, for the final out of the World Series. The Giants' season, their most successful in 27 years, was over. The last game of that World Series was played on October 28, at that time, the latest in the year any big-league baseball game had been played. In a few days, the Giants would face another test—this one in front of the voters of San Francisco. And that is when an already unbelievable year for the Giants got even stranger.

PROPOSITION P

Because of the earthquake, the World Series ended only 10 days before the election, which was to occur only three weeks after the earthquake. Thus, the story of Proposition P, the initiative calling for a ballpark in the China Basin area of South of Market, involved a pennant race, a World Series, a mayor whose popularity had declined since his election, efforts by those who opposed the mayor to weaken him even more politically, political tactics used by those who opposed the ballpark that may have been illegal, and an extraordinary natural disaster.

Two years after being a vocal opponent of the idea of a ballpark at 7th and Townsend, Mayor Agnos became a strong advocate for a ballpark just a few blocks away. The proposal that Agnos and Bob Lurie worked out was to build a ballpark in a neighborhood known as China Basin, just a few blocks north of the previously proposed site. Instead of 7th and Townsend, this ballpark would have been a few blocks away, around where 3rd Street intersects with King and Townsend.

There were several clear advantages of this site over the previous one. Because of its proximity to the bay, it had the potential to have better views. The intersection of King and Third was also closer to downtown San Francisco and would be more easily served by public transportation. If you walk around that neighborhood today, you will find a ballpark. Proposition P sought to build a ballpark very close to where Oracle Park, the home of the Giants since 2000, and one of the very best places to watch big-league baseball in America, now stands.

Unlike 1987, 1989 was not a mayoral election year. In fact, there were no contested elections for any office in 1989, as City Attorney Louise Renne and Treasurer Mary Callanan were running unopposed. The ballot included 23 initiatives, but that was not unusual for San Francisco. This time, the ballpark initiative would be called Proposition P and was placed on the ballot by the Mayor. The basic agreement underpinning Proposition P was "a three-way deal between the city, Spectator [Management Group] and the Giants. Spectator would finance, by and large, a ballpark in exchange for the rights to build an arena."[63] The arena would be built just south of the ballpark and would be used to lure the NBA Warriors back to San Francisco from Oakland. This finally happened in 2019 when a new arena was built just south of Oracle Park.

The language of Proposition P was stronger and more precise than that of Proposition W two years earlier. Voters were asked "Shall the City enter into an agreement with Spectator Management Group, consistent with specified principles regarding the land acquisition, financing and construction of a new ballpark in the China Basin area, and shall certain zoning laws be amended to facilitate the construction of a ballpark in the area?"[64]

Whereas in 1987 Proposition W had, to some extent, pitted San Francisco's political establishment against a grassroots movement, two years later the leader of that grassroots movement, Mayor Agnos, was now one of the major proponents of the ballpark. Among those supporting Proposition P in the voter guide were: progressive supervisors Angela Alioto, Harry Britt, and Doris Ward; the League of Conservation Voters Willie Brown and John Burton; leaders of the San Francisco Democratic Party Central Committee, including Carole Migden, Adrian Bermudez Jr., Terrence Hallinan, and Aigar Jaicks; gay and lesbian activists including Supervisor Britt, Roberta Achtenberg, Larry Bush, Tom Ammiano, and Migden; as well as the chair of the Republican Party Central Committee. In addition, the Board of Supervisors collectively submitted a statement in support of the ballpark.

The arguments against the ballpark in the voter guide did not come from anywhere near as many well-known San Franciscan political figures. In addition to several local neighborhood activists, the only major political figures to submit statements were supervisor Richard Hongisto and former supervisor Jack Morrison. Morrison had been an ally of George Moscone when the two served on the Board of Supervisors together from 1964 to 1966 and had made an unsuccessful bid for mayor in 1967, but he had been out of office since the 1960s. Additionally, an organization called simply "grassroots" submitted 16 separate short statements to the voter guide, but as a whole those statements were not likely to be helpful as nobody knew who "grassroots" was.

Despite all the political firepower in favor of the ballpark, the vote was still always going to be close. A poll taken in late August showed the initiative passing 46 percent to 40 percent. That seemed like a comfortable lead, but the proportion of voters supporting the initiative was still less than half of all those surveyed. The breakdown of voters showed that men and voters under the age of 55 supported the initiative, while older voters and women were opposed to the new ballpark. Support for the ballpark increased with each income bracket. Voters making less than $20,000 opposed it 43 percent to 38 percent, while voters making more than $60,000 were for it 51 percent to 35 percent. These data suggested that, to some extent, even with the active support from the progressive mayor, there were still strong pockets of opposition among lower-income voters and women.[65]

Following the failure of Proposition W in 1987, the new ballpark initiative was understood by many to be the last best hope for keeping the Giants in San Francisco. A second defeat in two years would send a clear message that the Giants, after three decades in San Francisco, had no future in that city. If Proposition P were defeated, the voters would be rejecting a good stadium deal twice in a two-year period, but they would be doing more than that. They would be rejecting the deal supported by both the former centrist mayor and by the current progressive one. Moreover, they would be rejecting two deals that, on balance, were both better for San Francisco's finances than what most cities were doing to keep or gain a big-league team.

Proposition P was, like most matters of governance, a statement of priorities. Building the new ballpark was not going to be without costs, but it would bring economic development to a part of the city that needed it and had the potential to revitalize that area. It was also true that it would subsidize a baseball team, suggesting that baseball was more important than AIDS, homelessness, education, and other challenges facing San Francisco. Corey Busch, who was deeply involved in the effort to pass Proposition P, described the campaign against the ballpark: "It was traffic; it was financing; it was priorities of the city. . . . Still almost the neighborhood versus downtown kind of thing. . . . When in doubt eat the rich, so Bob [Lurie] was attacked as a wealthy guy."[66] The reality of the governance questions facing San Francisco was nowhere near that simple, but that was how voters in a city that was rapidly moving to the left saw it.

Another aspect of the campaign to defeat Proposition P was that because of Agnos's strong support for the initiative, those who wanted to see Agnos defeated in 1991, when he would be up for reelection, saw defeating the ballpark initiative as the first step toward achieving that goal. A big defeat for the mayor's favored project would show that he was not so popular in San Francisco halfway through his term.

One of those who wanted to see the mayor weakened was Quentin Kopp, who had served on the Board of Supervisors for well over a decade before being elected to the State Senate in 1986. Kopp had run for mayor as a conservative alternative to Dianne Feinstein in 1979 and lost in a runoff. He was hoping to finally get elected mayor in 1991. According to Busch, "Quentin Kopp came out against the ballpark initiative in '89 without knowing a damn thing about it and refusing several requests to get together so we could meet with him and present the plan. . . . He wanted to run against Art and he wanted this measure to lose because a victory in this would have been a real feather in Art Agnos's cap."[67] Kopp ultimately decided not to run in 1991, but others, like political consultant Jack Davis, who were anxious to defeat Agnos, also became involved in the "No on P" campaign. Bob Lurie and the Giants understood that if they couldn't pass Proposition P, they had to more actively consider what a future for the Giants outside of San Francisco might look like.

This was the context in which the election campaign was occurring during the fall of 1989. The slight margin in favor of Proposition P was more or less stable throughout October. With one month to go, it looked like a narrow win for the ballpark was likely. Then October happened. In October 1989, the Bay Area was the center of the baseball universe. The World Series was in the Bay Area for the sixth time, but this was the first time the entire World Series was played there. That also meant that 1989 would not be like 1987, when voters decided on Proposition W in the wake of a tough NLCS loss. When the Giants eliminated the Cubs on October 9, the election was less than a month away and supporters of the ballpark were feeling optimistic.

That optimism was tempered by the earthquake, which caused roughly five billion dollars of damage and killed 67 people, and was further undermined 11 days later when the Giants were swept out of the World Series by the A's. Therefore, the vote on the ballpark was not cast just in the afterglow of a Giants pennant, but also of a loss in the World Series and much more significantly the destruction caused by the earthquake. Those voters who thought San Francisco might have more important priorities than the ballpark before the earthquake now had even more reason to think that was the case.

That point was not lost on opponents of the ballpark proposal, but the politics were complicated for them as well. The earthquake had badly damaged the city. While the number of deaths was not as high as many feared "the big one" might cause, there was still a significant loss of life. There were also thousands of people in neighborhoods like the Marina who had, at least temporarily, lost their homes, and substantial damage to key pieces of local infrastructure such as the Oakland Bay Bridge and the Embarcadero Freeway. Repairing or replacing these roadways was going to be very expensive.

The earthquake also took an emotional toll on San Francisco and the whole Bay Area. Residents of the Bay Area, particularly those who have been there for a long time, know that earthquakes may occur and may, in some cases, cause a lot of damage, but few have any real plan for what to do when this happens. For most longtime residents, denial has been the most frequently employed strategy. That was the case on October 16, 1989, and is still the case today. It is how San Franciscans are able to move forward with their lives in the shadow of the inevitable big one, but that denial was no longer possible after October 17, at least for a while.

This meant that both sides had to approach the campaign with care. Proponents could not be seen as prioritizing a new ballpark just days after a major earthquake. This was particularly true for one of the biggest proponents of the downtown ballpark. As mayor, Agnos needed to focus, and be seen as focusing on, earthquake recovery, rather than a ballot initiative for a new ballpark.

Corey Busch described one major way the earthquake changed the strategy of the "Yes on P" campaign:

> We had a very sophisticated absentee ballot campaign and the day after the earthquake was the day our first absentee ballot mailing effort was going to hit . . . and the earthquake happened and we pulled it back. We didn't feel it was right to campaign for a ballpark in the immediate aftermath of this horrendous earthquake. Unfortunately . . . some of the mail actually did get mailed and that created a bit of a backlash. . . . For about two weeks we had no absentee ballot campaign and that was a major blow to our efforts, then money came in from Sacramento.[68]

Opponents of the ballpark had to be sensitive as well. If they focused too much on how earthquake recovery was too important to think about a new ballpark, they also risked being seen as using the earthquake for political purposes. However, because the opponents of Proposition P were behind in the polls, they had to be open to taking more risks—and they were. Those risks were even more tempting for opponents of the ballpark who were not San Franciscans.

A few days before the election, a piece of campaign literature landed in the mailboxes of thousands of Sn Francisco voters that played the earthquake card. Voters were asked how the city could be thinking about baseball and ballparks when it was still reeling, economically and otherwise, from the earthquake. It was soon revealed that the mailer had been paid for by a close associate of Gregg Lukenbill. Lukenbill was the owner of Sacramento Kings of the NBA and hoped to bring a big-league baseball team, likely either the Giants or the A's, to that city. If the ballpark initiative failed, Lukenbill figured, the Giants would be looking for a new home and would consider Sacramento.

Lukenbill's last-minute mailer outraged proponents of the ballpark, particularly Mayor Agnos. Many in San Francisco blamed the Sacramento magnate, his associate Maurice Read, and consultants Jack Davis, Rich Schlackman, and David Townsend, who crafted the mailer, for the defeat of Proposition P. These five men became known as the Ballpark Five and were indicted by San Francisco District Attorney Arlo Smith for campaign finance violations, but the case was later dismissed.

It is impossible to know the impact of the mailer funded by Sacramento interests, but when the all the votes were counted, Proposition P had been defeated by an agonizingly small margin. The initiative was defeated by 2,054 votes out of a total of 173,646 votes that were cast. That margin of 1.1 percent meant that the Giants' future in San Francisco was deeply imperiled with no clear next move for those who wanted to keep the team in town.

Had the earthquake not occurred just a few weeks before the election, the ballpark would have almost certainly been approved. Corey Busch still believed that almost 30 years after the vote: "In '89, we thought we had [the ballpark] solved and we did. . . . If it had not been for the earthquake, we would have won [the ballot initiative]"[69] When I asked Art Agnos whether he thought the initiative would have passed if not for the earthquake, he did not hesitate to give a direct one word answer, "absolutely."[70] This is not just the opinion of Busch and the former mayor, but was a widely, if informally, held opinion at the time and makes intuitive sense. The election was extremely close. If only 1,030 voters, roughly half a percent, changed their minds about the ballpark due to the earthquake, that would have been enough to change the outcome from passing to failing in the last days of the election. Similarly, the earthquake created problems for the proponents of Proposition P, who had a much stronger field campaign, to implement their absentee ballot program, which would have driven up the vote total for the yes forces.[71]

Agnos fleshed out the impact of the earthquake but also of the political context that may have also hurt Proposition P:

There was pennant fever, World Series fever and everything looked positive, and then comes the earthquake. The earthquake shook up the city, physically and mentally and psychologically. . . . What it did was give the opponents of the ballpark, and some of the opponents were not against the ballpark, they were against me, because they wanted to beat me . . . cause they were gonna look to beat me in the next election. . . . The city was so anxious, so disturbed at the damage and the effects of the earthquake. . . . It made them vulnerable to arguments from my opponents that weren't correct. Today we'd call it fake news. . . . They used the idea that I was gonna put money into the ballpark. The money I was gonna put into the ballpark as the public contribution was the federal money that was available only for this purpose. It could not be used for earthquake recovery. . . . So the opponent said "we need to use all the money we can get, from every source, to rebuild the city, not a ballpark."[72]

The failure of Proposition P to pass occurred in very unusual circumstances. Had the earthquake not occurred, the ballpark initiative almost certainly would have passed. Had the Giants beaten the A's, even with the earthquake, it probably would have passed. However, had the Giants lost to the Cubs in the NLCS or had a terrible 1989 season, the initiative might have lost regardless of whether or not an earthquake occurred. It is not easy to determine how the nexus of baseball and seismic events impact local elections—and there is little research on this subject. We cannot know what might have happened if October 1989 had played out differently, but we know the effect that electoral defeat had on the Giants and their owner.

Following the defeat of Proposition P, there was little appetite from either Agnos or Lurie to pass another ballpark initiative. Bud Selig described how the defeat of Proposition P "broke Bob's heart. And, frankly . . . it broke our hearts. . . . It was sad to watch." Selig also noted that Proposition P went to the voters only a few years before the construction of Camden Yards in Baltimore, which began a flurry of construction of downtown, baseball-only ballparks around the major leagues. Thus, as Selig noted in this respect, Lurie "was ahead of his time."[73] Politics is not baseball and two strikes was enough for the owner and the mayor. Lurie then turned his sights to points south on the peninsula, while Agnos focused his political energies on what was shaping up to be a difficult reelection campaign in 1991.

Lurie described the defeat of Proposition P as "really disturbing. . . . You get to a point where enough is enough."[74] For Lurie, two defeats were indeed enough. After 1989, Lurie never pursued a downtown ballpark again. Within months of the defeat of Proposition P, other cities, including Denver and New Orleans, began to explore the possibility of luring the Giants away from San Francisco. Thus, as 1989 wound down, the Giants were in the unusual position of being the defending National League champions, while also facing the possibility that they only had two or three years remaining in San Francisco.

The idea of the Giants moving down the peninsula had been discussed periodically for years. The logic of the idea was clear as the Giants had a big fan base in both San Mateo and Santa Clara counties, but the major drawback, that fans from the city might not be so happy to make the drive out of town to see a ballgame, was also evident. However, after the voters of San Francisco voted twice against a downtown ballpark, that drawback seemed less relevant, especially as in those days before the Bay Area traffic became as heavy as it is today, the drive was not really that much farther than going to Candlestick for many residents.

During the next three years, Santa Clara county was a tantalizing possibility that again led Bob Lurie to believe he could find a way to keep the Giants in the Bay Area, but he would ultimately find that it was no easier to find a permanent home for the team there than it had been in San Francisco. In the bigger Giants picture, the quest for a new ballpark was an important part of the last 10 years that Lurie owned the team and was the background upon which all of the Giants' successes and failures on the field occurred.

Chapter 8

TAMPA BOUND

At the dawn of the 1990s, the Giants still looked like a strong team. Will Clark, Robby Thompson, Matt Williams, and Kevin Mitchell were all under 30 and, with the exception of Williams, established stars. Williams, who turned 24 shortly after the World Series, was poised to join them in that category after his strong second half in 1989. There were still question marks surrounding their pitching, but the off-season signing of free agent Kevin Bass provided additional offense in the outfield while veteran catcher Gary Carter, who also signed as a free agent in the off-season, added depth behind the plate. Dan Quisenberry, a onetime elite closer for the Kansas City Royals, who was winding down his career coming off of a couple of decent seasons with the Royals and Cardinals, was another off-season pickup.

The team that had represented the NL in the 1989 World Series appeared, at first glance, well prepared to defend the pennant. By adding Kevin Bass, a speedy outfielder who hit .300/.357/.435 in an injury-shortened 1989 season with the Astros, the Giants looked to have made themselves better in right field, while adding depth in the bull pen and on the bench as well. These modest improvements made some sense, but they also did not take into account one of the more frustrating realities that pennant-winning teams face when they seek to repeat. Teams that win pennants are always very good, but they are also almost always very lucky. This was clearly true of the 1989 Giants. Kevin Mitchell, Will Clark, Brett Butler, and Robby Thompson were all very good players, but they all were healthy and had standout years, and in the case of Clark and Mitchell, career years, in 1989.

The best pitcher on the 1989 team, Rick Reuschel, was coming off of two good years, but at 40 years old there were no guarantees that he would continue to perform at a high level. Reuschel pitched 208 innings with an ERA+ of 115 in 1989. When that season started, only 24 times in baseball history had a pitcher who was 40 or older thrown more than 200 innings with an ERA+ of 110 or better. Even now, the total is only 35, but that includes three seasons by Roger Clemens, who had some additional factors keeping him "youthful" from 2003 to 2005. It turned out that after 1989, Reuschel was essentially finished as a pitcher and threw fewer than 100 more innings before he retired in 1991.

As the 1990 season approached, there was a different feeling around the Giants, even though 1989 had been, in many respects, such a great season for them. They won their first pennant in 27 years, Kevin Mitchell and Will Clark finished first and second in the NL MVP balloting, and the team drew more than two million fans for the first time in a history that dated back to the late nineteenth century in New York. Despite all that, the period from October 14, when the World Series began, through November 7, saw a series of blows—a humiliating World Series sweep, an earthquake, and a close loss at the polls—that cast a pall over a successful season and over the team's future as well. Corey Busch summarized the feeling around the Giants as the year began: "The earthquake, being swept . . . its salt in the wound to have that championship flag flying from a ballpark you can see from your ballpark. . . . There's no question that impacted the fan base, it impacted the players and it impacted the organization. It was a one, two, three punch."[1] The "three" to which Busch referred was the defeat of Proposition P.

Giants fans looking at the team going into 1990 knew the club had a strong nucleus and would likely be contenders again, but there was increasing uncertainty about where the team would be playing in the future. Those with a sense of history recalled that the New York Giants had moved to San Francisco only three years after winning the 1954 pennant and World Series. Like those pennant-winning Giants in 1954, the 1989 team played in a ballpark that, more or less everybody agreed, was not going to be the long-term home for the team. The Giants attendance in 1989 set a franchise record but was still only the 12th highest of the 26 big-league teams. If the Giants could not break into the top third for team attendance in a year in which they won the pennant, it was apparent that something needed to change.

For these reasons, despite the presence of many good young players, spring training in 1990 felt like the beginning of the end of an era. Something had to give, but it was not clear what. Bob Lurie had accelerated his search for a ballpark somewhere down the peninsula, while other cities who wanted a big-league team began eyeing the Giants. There was a fair amount of uncertainty about where the Giants would play in the future, but it was finally understood that the Giants would be leaving San Francisco, and probably relatively soon.

A *San Jose Mercury News* editorial from January 19, 1990, summarized this:

> Bay Area baseball fans can take heart from this week's formal beginning of the process that could keep the Giants in the area.
>
> In their first public meeting, Giants owner Bob Lurie said all the right things to the Santa Clara City Council, and the council responded positively. Lurie said that he wants to move the Giants to Santa Clara.
>
> The specter of yet another San Francisco deal, which has plagued South Bay plans to lure the Giants has apparently vanished at last.
>
> Lurie did say he's keeping his options open for other sites, but those are sites outside the Bay Area. And the Bay Area, he emphasized, is where he wants his team.[2]

Moving the team to Santa Clara county might have been an attractive idea for Bob Lurie and for Giants fan living in and around that part of the region, but many San Franciscans felt differently. Art Agnos reflected the views of many San Franciscans at the time when he told me that moving the team to Santa Clara "would have been the same as moving them to Tampa."[3] Despite Agnos's views and hopes, there were no new proposals coming out of San Francisco—no new ballot initiatives, proposed sites, or anything else. Moreover, Lurie believed that the team's future was in Santa Clara, so he continued to move forward with plans for a new stadium there. Accordingly, as the Giants prepared for the 1990 season, the team brass began to explore the Santa Clara option in earnest.

Thus, the Giants' 1990 season began with both high expectations on the field and a lot of questions about their future. By the time Opening Day arrived, it was clear that moving to Santa Clara was a real possibility, but also that if that didn't work out the team would relocate to another city. These questions may or may not have had an impact on the Giants' play, but for the first quarter or so of the season, the defending NL champs were dreadful.

The nadir of the season was Memorial Day, when the Giants lost to the Cubs, the team they had beaten in the previous year's NLCS, by a score of 5–1. At that point in the season, Brett Butler's on-base percentage was only .324. Robby Thompson, hitting .217/.263/.335, and Will Clark, hitting

.264/.311/.462, were both struggling as well. Kevin Mitchell was hitting an excellent .316/.387/.606, but even that was not quite as good as his magical 1989 season. Kevin Bass, who had been the Giants' major off-season acquisition, was not producing much either as the speedy outfielder's on-base percentage was only .301. Bass hurt his knee a few days earlier and would not return to the lineup until early September. More devastatingly for the Giants, Rick Reuschel, the ace of the 1989 squad, had lost the previous day to the Pirates, bringing his record to 2–6 and raising his ERA to 4.50. Like Bass, Big Daddy was also battling injuries and would be out until September.

The loss to Chicago was the Giants 28th of the season against only 17 wins. Their .378 winning percentage was the worst in baseball and put them in last place, 14½ games behind the division-leading Cincinnati Reds. It was not yet June and the Giants had effectively played themselves out of contention. In those days before the wild card teams rarely came back from that far behind. While the Giants may have lost the division before the kids got out of school, they were way too good to play .378 baseball for long.

The next day, they beat the Cubs 6–2 behind Don Robinson's strong pitching and began to turn their season around. From May 29 through the end of the year, the Giants were a solid 68–49, for a winning percentage of just over .581 The first-place Reds, from May 28 through the end of the season, won 62 and lost 60, but that was enough to hold off the Giants, who finished in third place, six games behind the Reds.

Several players also turned their season around beginning in June. Brett Butler finished with an on-base percentage of .397 and 51 stolen bases, making him, once again, one of the game's elite leadoff hitters. Will Clark did not repeat his great 1989 season but ended up hitting a very respectable .295/.357/.448. Kevin Mitchell solidified his standing as one of the baseball's best power hitters as his 35 home runs contributed to a strong .290/360/.544 season. Gary Carter exceeded the team's expectations, forming a very good catching platoon with Terry Kennedy and excellent right-handed bat off of the bench.

On balance, the Giants offense was about as good in 1990 when they scored 719 runs, the fourth best in the National League, as it was in 1989 when their 699 runs was a close second in the NL. The problem was the pitching. In 1989, the team allowed 600 runs, the third fewest of any NL team. In 1990, that ballooned to 710 runs, ninth best in a 12-team league. No starting pitcher had even 15 wins, or an ERA below 3.70. Steve Bedrosian was no longer able to close games, finishing the season at 9–9 with only 17 saves and an ERA of 4.20. By late in the season, Jeff Brantley had taken over as closer and had an excellent season, saving 19 games and finishing with a 1.53 ERA.

By midseason, the major Giants story was not occurring at Candlestick Park, but in Santa Clara County where the Giants were preparing for another ballot initiative. This one called for a 1 percent utility tax to help pay for a new home for the Giants. If the initiative passed, the Giants would begin construction and move to Santa Clara around 1995. Voters in Santa Clara county would vote on the utility tax called, Proposition H, while the voters of San Jose would also vote on a separate related measure for approval of the ballpark. That ballot measure was Proposition G. Passage of both bills was needed for Santa Clara and the Giants to move ahead with the proposed new ballpark. The proposed site of the ballpark was only about 35 miles south of Candlestick Park but would be well outside of San Francisco's city limits.

This initiative was different than the previous two because many fans, even from a baseball angle, were not sure whether they wanted it to pass or fail. For fans from San Mateo and Santa Clara counties, as well as other areas south of the city, the decision was easy. If the initiative passed, they would get to keep their Giants, but in a ballpark that would be better than Candlestick and closer to home. For fans based in the city and Marin County, the question was more complicated. If the initiative passed it meant that the Giants would be leaving San Francisco for somewhere in Santa Clara. In those pre–Silicon Valley days, Santa Clara County offered little to San Franciscans other than suburbs, a few nice hiking spots, and Stanford University. Real San Franciscans knew in our hearts that we would not get to the new ballpark very frequently. For us, the answer to Hal David and Burt Bacharach's musical query was "No, we don't know the way to San Jose." For fans from Marin, the journey to Santa Clara County would have been even more arduous.[4] However, if the initiative failed, it would be very likely that the Giants would end up a lot further away than Santa Clara.

The initiatives would be vying for space on a very crowded ballot in California. The highest profile race was to elect a new governor to replace George Deukmejian who was completing his second term. The Republican candidate, and eventual winner, was Pete Wilson. The Democratic nominee was Dianne Feinstein three years removed from finishing her tenure as San Francisco's mayor. Additionally, the entire House of Representatives, the entire state assembly and half the state senate, several local offices, a few other county initiatives, and 45 statewide propositions were on the ballot. Unlike the San Francisco election a year earlier, this time the ballpark initiative was not one of the most important choices facing voters.

The campaign pitted the ballpark against a slight tax increase. However, Santa Clara county voters, just like those voters a few miles north, remained

suspicious that there would be more costs associated with the proposed ballpark. Just as the 1989 election in San Francisco was framed by the earthquake a
few weeks before Election Day, the 1990 election occurred in a specific context
as well. That context was the beginning of what became a steep economic
downturn, one that would eventually contribute to Bill Clinton's victory over
George H. W. Bush in the presidential election of 1992. In that context, the
voters of Santa Clara were not inclined to support any tax increases, even
modest ones, or to make baseball a top priority.

The vote was very close, but for the third time in four years, Bay Area voters
rejected a ballpark. It was beginning to feel like a local ritual, like the Bay to
Breakers run or the gatherings every April 18 to commemorate the earthquake
of 1906. Countywide, the vote was 50.5 percent against and 49.5 percent for
the utility tax to fund the ballpark. In San Jose, the vote wasn't quite as close;
the separate proposition there failed with 51.1 percent against and 48.9 percent
for. The difference between failure and passage of both these initiatives was a
total of 6,702 votes. In 1989 in San Francisco, the ballpark initiative failed by
only 2,054 voters. Thus, the Giants had lost three elections in two years by a
total of fewer than 10,000 votes and were continuing to recognize that time
was running out for them in the Bay Area.

Writing in *The Sporting News* a few weeks after the election, Mark Newman captured the dilemma facing Lurie and the Giants: "For the third year
in a row [sic], Bay Area voters rejected a ballot proposal that would have led
to funding for a new stadium in the area. . . . Lurie hoped the 'Santa Clara
Giants' would be playing in a new stadium 35 miles south of their current
home, Candlestick Park, by the 1995 season. Instead, Lurie continues to be
stuck at the 'Stick, baseball's most unpleasant ball park, and owns one of the
major leagues' longest losing streak." Newman also provided his odds on
where the Giants would be playing in the mid-1990s. He got it right in that
he said the most likely outcome, at odds of two to one, was Candlestick, but
Sacramento, Denver, and Florida were all listed in his top five.[5]

THE NEW MAYOR

The 1991 election was unusual for that time because there were no ballpark-
related initiatives anywhere in the Bay Area. However, in San Francisco, Art
Agnos was running for reelection. Agnos had campaigned in 1987 by pro-
moting a progressive vision of San Francisco and a break with the Feinstein
administration which had come to be heavily influenced by downtown and

real estate interests. However, much of Agnos's time in office was framed by a major earthquake, an economic downturn, and the specter of losing the city's baseball team.

The late 1980s and early 1990s had been a tough time for San Francisco. Many voters blamed Mayor Agnos for the rise in homelessness and the downturn in the economy while never quite warming to the mayor's style. Art Agnos is a man of considerable personal charm, but some voters and journalists found him prickly and defensive. He had also made his share of political enemies due to his combative style. One of those enemies was Jack Davis, who had been indicted as part of the Ballpark Five following the 1989 election.

Because of Agnos's perceived vulnerabilities, he drew four strong opponents in the nonpartisan election. Two, Richard Hongisto and Angela Alioto, were on the left, while two, Tom Hsieh and Frank Jordan, were more conservative. No candidate won enough votes in the first round in November, so a runoff between the top two finishers, Agnos and Jordan, was held on December 10, 1991.

Jordan had been appointed Chief of Police by Dianne Feinstein in 1986 but resigned in 1990 to run against Agnos. Jordan had worked his way up the police hierarchy over several decades. One of his earliest assignments was helping provide security to Tony Kubek and Bobby Richardson after the Yankees won the 1962 World Series in San Francisco. When we met, Jordan, a lifelong San Francisco baseball fan, recounted doing that assignment professionally, but with no joy.[6]

Unlike Agnos, but like both Feinstein and Moscone, Jordan had been born and raised in San Francisco and graduated from Sacred Heart High School, a Catholic school that generations of blue-collar San Franciscans had attended. After joining the police force, Jordan worked his way through college and earned his degree from the University of San Francisco. Jordan was a product of the white, working-class San Francisco that had constituted a majority in the city and wielded a great deal of political power for the first eight decades of the twentieth century. By 1991, white, working-class San Francisco was all but disappearing, but Jordan had been able to put together a coalition of socially conservative, working-class San Franciscans, wealthier business and real estate interests, and voters who didn't like Agnos and were concerned about issues like homelessness and crime.

Jordan's senior political advisor was noted Agnos critic Jack Davis. Davis wanted to defeat Agnos and saw Jordan as the candidate with the best chance of doing that. Jordan was, in the context of San Francisco, a conservative. As a former police chief with strong ties to the city's business and real estate communities, Jordan was considerably to the right of Agnos. However, he was not quite an angry urban backlash candidate like, for example, Rudolph Giuliani, who had been narrowly defeated two years earlier and would be narrowly elected two years later in New York. In the early 1990s, Jordan was essentially a Clinton Democrat, which in San Francisco put him on the conservative side of the political spectrum.

The runoff was close, but Jordan won 52 percent to 48 percent. Jordan would become the fourth mayor in a row for whom the possibility of the Giants leaving would be something that required his attention, but he was the first since Moscone to take office when the Giants seemed to have at least one foot out the door. Jordan was a Giants fan, but he also knew that if the team left it could define his time in office. "I saw [potentially losing the Giants] as a very negative thing, but also as a San Francisco baseball fan, all my life . . . I don't want to be the person that loses a franchise, a major league franchise, like this and be tattooed with that the rest of my life."[7]

THE LAST YEARS OF LURIE

Following the disappointing 1990 season when the Giants regressed from their great 1989 success, the Giants did very little to improve the team, presumably because they still believed the core of the team was strong. Brett Butler was a free agent again and signed with the rival Dodgers on the December 14. Butler's free agency resulted from a settlement between MLB and the MLBPA following the revelation of collusion around free agency in the 1980s. The decision made Butler a free agent again, despite having time remaining on his contract with the Giants. That was a blow to Giants fans, but Butler had already been replaced because the Giants, anticipating Butler's departure, signed Willie McGee earlier in December. McGee was two years younger than Butler, and like the departing Giants leadoff hitter, McGee got on base a lot, stole a lot of bases, fielded his position well, and had limited power. He was the NL MVP in 1985, but his skills had diminished somewhat since then. Nonetheless, his .373 on-base percentage and 31 stolen bases in 40 tries made him a highly valuable player in 1990.

Steve Bedrosian was clearly declining in 1990, so the Giants needed to address the bull pen. They did this in two days in December 1990, signing Dave Righetti on December 4 and trading Bedrosian to the Twins the next day for second-tier prospects Jimmy Williams and Johnny Ard. Neither Ard nor Williams ever played a game in the big leagues for the Giants or anybody else. The four moves the Giants made over a four-day period seemed like a net gain for the team, but they constituted all the major player moves they made that off-season.

Dave Righetti is known to Giants fans today mostly because he served as the team's pitching coach from 2000 to 2017. He was the pitching coach for the Giants' three World Series–winning teams and is regarded as one of the best pitching coaches in baseball history. In December 1990, Righetti was a decade away from coaching and was coming off of a seven-year run with the Yankees as one of the best closers in the game. His 223 saves in that period were second only to Jeff Reardon's 224. His 12.6 WAR was fourth among all relievers, behind Hall of Famer Lee Smith, John Franco, and Tom Henke for those years. WAR is less useful for evaluating relief pitchers than other players, so the 1.9 WAR separating Righetti and Smith suggested all four pitchers had been almost equally valuable during the period in question.

Despite Righetti's impressive numbers coming out of the bull pen, there was always a sense of what might have been about him. "Rags," as he was known throughout his playing and coaching career, began his career as the first-round draft pick of the Texas Rangers in 1977. Following the 1978 season, when he was considered one of the top pitching prospects in the game, Righetti was sent to the Yankees in a 10-player trade. The Rangers and Yankees each received five players, but for most Yankees fans the trade boiled down to sending popular relief pitcher, and 1977 Cy Young Award winner, Sparky Lyle to Texas for the highly touted Righetti, who had never pitched above AA ball and would turn 20 later that off-season.

The Yankees and their fans were rewarded within a few years when Rags went 8–4 with a 2.05 ERA and won AL Rookie of the Year in a strike-shortened 1981 season. After regressing slightly in 1982, when he fell to 11–10 with a 3.79 ERA and was briefly sent to the minors, the 24-year-old lefty had a strong comeback year in 1983, going 14–8 with a 3.43 ERA—and then something very strange happened to the pitcher who was poised to take his place among the top lefty starting pitchers in the game.

In the 1983–84 off-season, Yankees closer Goose Gossage, a future Hall of Famer who was still highly effective, left the Yankees to sign with the Padres as a free agent. Yankees owner George Steinbrenner felt humiliated losing the Goose to the lowly Padres, who were no longer so lowly and would win the 1984 NL pennant with the help of two former Yankees stars, Gossage and Graig Nettles. The Yankees, seeking to minimize the loss of Gossage, made

Righetti their new closer. Between 1981 and 1983, Righetti started 79 games and relieved in only four. After being moved to the Yankees bull pen, he would not start another big-league game until 1992. Righetti proved himself to be an elite reliever, but he would have been more valuable, better known, and made more money if the Yankees had kept him in the starting rotation. It is also possible the Yankees, who missed the playoffs by two games in 1985 and 3½ games in 1988, might have made it back to the postseason sooner if they had left Rags in their rotation.

Adding two veterans, Righetti and McGee, who were still almost at the top of their games, to a team that won 85 games the year before, should have been enough to propel the Giants back into contention. Returning players Clark, Thompson, Williams, and Mitchell still constituted a strong nucleus, but there were holes, particularly in the starting rotation. Even the 1989 pennant winning team had relied heavily on the 40-year-old arm of Rick Reuschel, but Reuschel was more or less finished by 1991 and only pitched 10²/₃ innings that year. The bulk of the team's games were started by pitchers like Bud Black, Trevor Wilson, John Burkett, Paul McLellan, Bryan Hickerson, and Mike Remlinger, who were either forgettable or a few years removed, in one direction or another, from their best years.

The offense turned out to be no better than passable in 1991. The core of Clark (.301/.359/.536), Mitchell (.256/.338/.515), Thompson (.262/.352/.447), and Williams (.268/.310/.499) all had good years. McGee's .357 on-base percentage and 17 stolen bases were adequate in the leadoff spot, but the Giants got no production from catcher or shortstop, while Bass continued to underwhelm in right field. On balance, the Giants offense, which scored the seventh most runs in a 12-team league, was not good. However, the bigger problem was pitching, as a mediocre bull pen, even with the addition of Righetti, could not make up for the poor starting rotation. Despite playing in a pitcher's park, the Giants gave up the third most runs in the NL. The Giants ended up going 75–87, finishing in fourth place, 19 games behind the division-winning Atlanta Braves. The team's poor play on the field, combined with their uncertainty about where they would be playing in the future, brought back memories of the first years Lurie owned the team.

Following the 1991 season, the Giants made only one significant move, but it was a major one. Kevin Mitchell, who had been one of the best hitters in the National League since coming to the Giants midway through the 1987 season, was sent to Seattle for three pitchers, Dave Burba, Michael Jackson, and Bill Swift. Mitchell was coming off a strong season in 1991, but injuries had limited him to 113 games. Additionally, Mitchell had never gotten along with Giants president Al Rosen, so that likely accelerated his departure.

By trading Mitchell, the Giants definitively broke up the team that had won two division titles in the late 1980s. However, the emergence of Williams, who turned 26 following the 1991 season and had hit more than 30 home runs in his first two full big-league seasons, meant that Mitchell was expendable. The trade turned out to make even more sense because while Mitchell continued to play and hit well in the big leagues through 1998, injuries limited him to fewer than 100 games every year for the remainder of his career.

The major reason for the trade was that the Giants desperately needed pitching and thought the three pitchers they acquired could help. None of the three were as well known or as valuable as Mitchell at the time of the trade, but the Giants had to do something. Dusty Baker, who was a coach on the 1992 Giants squad and would take over as manager in 1993, described his feelings, which were shared by many fans, when one of his most successful mentees was traded away: "I didn't know what we were getting. I didn't know Burba. I didn't know Mike Jackson. I didn't know Billy Swift. I didn't know if it was a good trade or not. It ended up being a great trade. We had an instant pitching staff."[8]

Michael Jackson had three solid years as a setup man for the Giants before going to the Reds as a free agent. Burba was less productive but provided some depth to the pitching staff during his four years with the Giants. The key to the trade was Swift. At the time of the trade, Swift was 30 years old, had a 30–40 record, 24 saves, and a 4.04 ERA but in 1990 and 1991 was moved to the bull pen and pitched well in a relief role. In his last year managing the Giants, Roger Craig converted Swift back to being to a starter and he briefly became one of the best in the National League, winning 31 games with a 2.51 ERA over the 1992 and 1993 seasons. The Mitchell trade was not received well in San Francisco at the time it was made, but Baker was right, Rosen's last big trade turned out to be a pretty good one.

The other major news during the 1991–92 off-season was that the Giants, despite having had two initiatives rejected by voters in Santa Clara county, were close to an agreement to move to San Jose. In January, Richard C. Paddock of the *Los Angeles Times* reported: "The San Francisco Giants, who long ago lost their heart for windy Candlestick Park, found their way to San Jose Wednesday and announced a deal that could let them begin playing there by 1996. San Jose, seeking to move out of the shadow of San Francisco, agreed to put up $155 million to help finance construction of an open-air stadium seating 48,000."[9]

Amazingly, the Giants, just months after suffering another electoral defeat, had managed to find a home in the Bay Area. However, the move would be seen as a defeat for Mayor Jordan and was not a good solution for many San Franciscans. To add further insult to the always ample pride of San Franciscans, the team's name would change to the San Jose Giants, but most San Franciscans reluctantly conceded that was better than the Tampa Giants. Perhaps because he was writing for a Los Angeles newspaper and wasn't following Bay Area politics, Braddock's next line had an almost breezy tone to what should have been a warning. "The agreement between the city and the Giants must be ratified by the voters of San Jose—probably in June—and city leaders are optimistic of gaining approval."[10]

The June election meant that the Giants would know their fate by the all-star break. If the initiative passed, the Giants could begin plans to move to San Jose. Lurie had made it clear that if the proposition failed, he would move quickly to try to sell the team. Given the lack of interest demonstrated by wealthy San Franciscans, this meant that at the very least Lurie was open to letting the new owners move the Giants away from the Bay Area.

The 1992 season was a transitional one for the team both on and off the field. With Mitchell gone, the Giants had to look more to the future, but as the season began the Giants and many of their fans had to confront the grim reality that this was likely their last year in San Francisco. On the field, the recognition that the team had turned the page on the late 1980s became an even more glaring problem because the Giants farm system that had produced Clark, Thompson, and Williams in the mid-1980s was not about to deliver meaningful assistance.

The only exception was Royce Clayton, who the Giants drafted out of high school in the first round of the 1988 draft. In his first few years in the minor leagues, Clayton had shown himself to be a slick-fielding shortstop who could steal bases and get on base enough to be a valuable player. Clayton struggled a bit in a late 1991 season call up, hitting two singles and one double while drawing one walk in 27 trips to the plate, but that did not concern the Giants.

On Opening Day, Clayton was the Giants starting shortstop, joining Clark, Thompson, and Williams. That quartet was poised to become one of the best infields in the NL as they were all standouts defensively, and other than Clayton, could all hit. They were also all first-round draft picks. Clayton was sent down in mid-June because he wasn't hitting, but he was called up in late August and remained the Giants' starting shortstop through 1995.

The emergence of Clayton as a big-league-caliber shortstop, if not quite a star, and of Swift as an effective starting pitcher, were bright spots in an otherwise dismal season. For the first time since the dreadful 1983 to 1985 period, the Giants finished under .500 for a second consecutive year. They also finished in fifth place for the second year in a row, but in 1992 they won even fewer games, 72, and finished even further back, 26 games behind the division-winning Braves.

Overall, the season felt much more like an ending than a beginning. This was in part because of the Kevin Mitchell trade, but in a much larger sense it was because many believed 1992 would be the Giants last year at Candlestick and in San Francisco. The season coincided almost entirely with the accelerated efforts by Bob Lurie to sell the club. The first major news about the future of the team was that the June election wasn't even as close as similar initiatives had been in 1989 in San Francisco and 1990 in Santa Clara County. The initiative failed with only 45.5 percent of voters supporting it. That defeat at the polls, the fourth in almost five years, meant that the Giants would be looking for another home, but not in the Bay Area.

Throughout the season, the question of the Giants future home overshadowed anything that happened on the field. In the early part of the season, despite the announcement about the team moving to San Jose, Giants fans turned their eyes to H. Irving Grousbeck, who had made his fortune in cable television. Grousbeck was exploring buying the team from Lurie and keeping them in San Francisco, or at least the Bay Area, but the season was not even a week old when Grousbeck ended talks with Lurie and the city of San Francisco. On April 10, 1992 the *New York Times* reported "The effort to keep the Giants in San Francisco suffered a significant setback today when H. Irving Grousbeck, considered a potential major investor in an attempt to purchase the team, said he was no longer interested. Unless a committed group of investors steps forward quickly, the only step that remains is for National and American league owners to approve the sale of the club to a group in Florida." Grousbeck had stopped the negotiations because he believed he would lose money as the owner of the team and told the *Times,* "We weren't out to make a lot of money, but to avoid losing it."[11]

Another potential investor was George Shinn, the owner of the Charlotte Hornets basketball team. Shinn was greeted with cheers when he attended a Giants game in August as part of a visit to San Francisco to discuss buying the team and keeping them in the city. However, Shinn never made an offer and seemed to be mostly talk. Frank Jordan recalled how Shinn "flew in here in his private jet and talked to me and talked to some of the people we were trying to put together at that time. . . . His feeling was that . . . he wanted to be the managing guy and the principal partner." At that time, Jordan was trying to put a San Francisco–based group together that Shinn would have joined, but the wealthy San Franciscans Jordan was courting were not going to turn control over the team to Shinn."[12]

By early August, the future of the Giants was becoming clearer. They would be moving to Tampa at the end of the season as Lurie, exasperated with the inability, or unwillingness, of the people and governments of the greater Bay Area to find a home for the Giants, had agreed to sell the team to an ownership team led by Vince Naimoli for $115 million. Lurie was well liked around baseball and generally viewed as one of the more levelheaded owners during the years when people like Charlie Finley, George Steinbrenner, and Ted Turner were redefining what it meant to own a baseball team. For this reason, particularly outside of the Bay Area, the coverage of Lurie was relatively sympathetic to the longtime Giants owner while maintaining that the move was all but certain.

Ross Newhan from the *Los Angeles Times,* wrote:

Owner Robert Lurie of the San Francisco Giants, frustrated over the repeated failure of Bay Area voters to approve financing of a new stadium, said Friday he has agreed to sell the team to a Tampa Bay syndicate that will move it to the Suncoast Dome in St. Petersburg, Fla., for the 1993 season. Lurie refused to go beyond a statement in which he confirmed that a memorandum of agreement had been reached during a meeting in San Francisco on Thursday and that he would not receive any other bids for the team while the offer goes through the process of approval.[13]

Jerome Holtzman, writing the following day, was more direct in his support for Lurie. Holtzman was one of the best-known and respected baseball writers of his generation, so his words were both influential and reflected the views of many around baseball:

If it were somebody else I might be skeptical and inclined to think he was playing the angles, but Bob Lurie I believe. If Lurie says he has a signed preliminary agreement to sell the San Francisco Giants and, when sold, the Giants will be moved to St. Petersburg, Fla., that's all there is to it. Lurie doesn't play games. He isn't trying to hold the city of San Francisco hostage. It has been the other way around. Lurie has been the hostage. Anybody else, anyone with less civic spirit that Lurie would have said goodbye to the mayor and local pols years ago.[14]

Holtzman's views were not at all the consensus in San Francisco. Many
fans were sad, but also angry, that the Giants were leaving. Their anger was
sometimes targeted at Lurie but was frequently more unfocused. Jenkins view
that Tampa, Florida "might as well be St. Petersburg Russia. I mean what the
fuck. . . . It was beyond appalling. I didn't believe it because it was preposterous. Not only that they would leave but that they would go to Florida. I
didn't acknowledge it. I didn't let it sink in,"[15] was shared by many fans in
San Francisco who wanted the Giants to stay but were also just sick of these
questions and problems that had surrounded the Giants since the mid-1970s.

Herb Caen, the venerable columnist who kibitzed about politics, sports,
society, and culture in San Francisco six days a week in the *San Francisco
Chronicle* for roughly half a century, also came to Lurie's defense. Writing
on Monday following the weekend when the news of the Giants departure
became public, Caen wrote,

actually, it was not a nice weekend. Every time I turned on one of the talk-
shows, people were berating Mr. Lurie, some of them in four-letter words
that should've been bleeped. This is not right, folks. Even multi-millionaires
can't go on losing millions a year. For one thing, it makes them look like bad
businessmen. When considering the impending tragedy, we have to start at
the bottom line, which is simply that a major league ball club in this town
is a lousy investment.[16]

Caen's assessment that a big-league team in San Francisco was "a lousy
investment" reflected what, by the early 1990s, had become conventional
wisdom in San Francisco. This was partially because of the obvious reason
that Candlestick Park was a terrible stadium. By 1992, the Giants had been
playing in Candlestick for more than 30 years and during that time had tried
everything from the Crazy Crab to Willie Mays and had never consistently
drawn decent attendance. This put the Giants into the hole in which many
bad teams find themselves. Bad teams often have less revenue and, therefore,
cannot improve their team by signing top free agents, keep their own stars
from leaving via free agency, or compete in the international market, which
was becoming increasingly important in the early 1990s. The failure of the
city to help the Giants get a new ballpark was further evidence that running
a baseball team in San Francisco was bad business.

This was all suggested in Caen's comments, but there was more to what the
longtime columnist meant than just that. By the early 1990s, San Francisco

had experienced a quarter century of fairly radical social change that remade the city. San Francisco had been at the epicenter of the 1960s counterculture and during the next decade, the LGBT equality movement, followed by the AIDS plague beginning in the late 1970s. During this period, San Francisco had evolved into a city characterized by a strong progressive political tradition, a hard-earned commitment to tolerance, tremendous ethnic diversity, and a relatively weak economy that was hit hard by the recession of the early 1990s. In that environment, a baseball team, even one as good as the Giants were from 1986 to 1990, would find it difficult to succeed.

The Giants were still San Francisco's team, but the constant struggle to find a new ballpark had introduced tension into the relationship between the team and the city. With the exception of a few years, almost the entire period when Bob Lurie owned the team was dogged by discussions of whether the Giants would stay in San Francisco, attempts to build a new ballpark, and rumors they would be leaving. For fans, this was a consistent and unpleasant distraction. As these distractions continued into the early 1990s, many fans began to hedge their commitment to a team that was on their way out, and that by 1991 and 1992, was no longer particularly good. By 1991, the Giants' attendance was 21st out of 26 teams; in 1992, they fell to 22nd.

The early 1990s were also a crucial time in Bob Lurie's tenure as the Giants' owner. Lurie's reputation as the man who played such a critical role in keeping the Giants from leaving in early 1976, when they almost left for Toronto, was fading after 15 years of mostly mediocre teams and continued speculation about whether the Giants would be able to stay in San Francisco. A new generation of Giants fans increasingly saw him as the owner who was selling the team to Florida so he could maximize his investment, or even less kindly, as the rich man who was shaking down the city for a new ballpark and threatening to move if he didn't get his way. This dichotomy still exists in San Francisco today, as those who were paying attention to baseball in the mid-1970s still see Lurie primarily as the man who saved the Giants for San Francisco, while younger fans see him as the man whose greed almost caused the Giants to leave town for Florida.

While it is true that by the early 1990s Lurie was exasperated with the failure of voters and governments in the greater Bay Area to approve a stadium that would require very limited public funding, he was not motivated entirely by greed. Nor was it clear he had other viable options. Lurie explained his decision to sell the team in 1992 by saying, "I kinda thought, too many things were happening. We're not gonna get a new stadium. Stay at Candlestick for conceivably ever is not appealing . . . so had the offer from Florida. . . . I made it very clear the only goal I had was to keep the club in San Francisco."[17] Corey Busch expanded Lurie's comments adding, "when the deal was made with Tampa, the team had been on the market for several months and there was nothing from San Francisco. . . . Bob made it clear he was done and nobody from San Francisco [made an offer]."[18]

As the 1992 season wound down, so did Bob Lurie's 17-year ownership of the Giants. The game had changed dramatically during that period. Lurie had weathered the advent of free agency, a major player's strike in 1981, massive increases in player salaries, and an influx of money into the game. The offer Lurie was likely to take from the Tampa ownership team was for almost 15 times the $8 million Lurie and Bud Herseth paid for the team in 1976. Most teams had increased in value at a similar rate during the that period.

The period when Lurie owned the team was marked by the strike in 1981, but labor relations were frequently an issue during these years. In addition to the 1981 strike, there were threats of strikes and lockouts in 1976, 1985, and 1990. The early years of free agency were also difficult ones as players and owners sought to restructure their relationship. Owners did not take to free agency easily. Only a few years after the strike of 1981, it was revealed that from 1985 to 1987, owners had colluded to keep free agent salaries down.

The Collective Bargaining Agreement (CBA) that governed labor relations in baseball was due to expire at the end of 1993. Given the state of baseball at the time, particularly the increased concern that small market teams, such as the Kansas City Royals and Milwaukee Brewers, whose owner Bud Selig became acting commissioner in 1992, were not able to compete with wealthier teams like the Yankees, many around baseball believed a strike was likely. This created further incentive for Lurie to sell the team, as a strike could damage the value of his team or force him to stay in the game longer than he desired. Corey Busch explained, "When Bob decided to put the club up for sale in '92, baseball was already anticipating a really difficult labor situation coming up, and there were those who thought it could actually occur in '93. . . . He needed to sell it before there was a work stoppage. . . . It might have hastened Bob's decision. . . . By that point Bob had decided he'd done he best he could."[19]

On September 27, the fifth-place Giants began the day 23½ games behind the NL West–leading Atlanta Braves with only seven games remaining in the season. Nonetheless, 45,630 fans jammed Candlestick Park for what many believed was the last home game for the San Francisco Giants. Larry Carter, pitching in the fifth game of what would be a six-game career, gave up two runs in the top of the first and one more in the top of the sixth. Four Giants relievers held the Reds scoreless the rest of the game. A sacrifice fly by Cory Snyder in the seventh cut the Reds lead to 3–1. The Giants got another run back in the bottom of the ninth when Rob Dibble unleashed a wild pitch with two outs. Then, with the tying run on third and the winning run on second, Darren Lewis, a light-hitting but speedy outfielder, lined out to Reds center fielder Dave Martinez and it seemed that the Giants had played their last game in San Francisco.

As the fans filed out of Candlestick Park following that 3–2 defeat, many mourned the end of an era and the loss of their team. The San Francisco Giants still had six more games on the schedule, but those games were to be played in Atlanta and Cincinnati. The sale of the team to the Tampa group was all but final and last-minute efforts by George Shinn led nowhere. By the end of the 1992 season, the consensus that the Giants would never make money playing at Candlestick was strong; and the sting of four electoral defeats made it clear that no Bay Area community was interested in hosting a big-league team.

Scott Ostler, writing in the next day's *Chronicle,* bemoaned the lack of fanfare around the Giants last game ever in San Francisco, but explained it away by saying, "I guess the problem was if you bring out the big nostalgia package it's a concession, an admission that the Giants are gone. Just go about the normal business and hope those St. Petersburg gnats will buzz away." Ostler then elaborated that this created an atmosphere in which "the entire stadium seemed caught up in a state of mass denial." Ostler described how the groundskeeping crew was greeted with boos when after the game they dug up the pitcher's mound, but then quoted one of the groundskeepers as saying, "we do this after every game before a football game." Ostler's closing words in the column captured the feelings of many fans who knew they had just lost their team: "The guys with picks and shovels loaded Stu Miller's mound into little trucks and drove away. Wonder if St. Pete wants to buy a real big league mound."[20]

Bruce Jenkins's column following the last Giants home game in San Francisco was not quite as sentimental as Ostler's. Instead, Jenkins turned his vitriol toward Lurie and Corey Busch, referring to his sunglasses as his "Benedict Arnold Protectos, a dandy little item [that] blocks out Bob Lurie or Corey Busch should they pass into view." Jenkins also described the game as a "perfect day for the lunacy of the Giants' situation to finally sink in. What a wonderful opportunity to ridicule Bob Lurie's business deal—you know, the one that enriched his worth from $400 million to $518 million or whatever the hell it is." Jenkins then reminded voters of the good years and good teams when the Giants first got to San Francisco, while defending Candlestick, arguing that "all this team needs is some spark of inspiration, to say nothing of intimidation, and the glory days would be back—right here at Candlestick."[21] Jenkins's views, particularly about Lurie, were reasonably widespread among Giants fans by late 1992.

The Giants' 35-year sojourn in San Francisco had come to an end. They would soon join the Braves and Athletics as franchises that called three different cities home during the course of the twentieth century. Over the course of those 35 years, the Giants won three division titles and two pennants but failed to win a World Series. Willie Mays, Willie McCovey, Orlando Cepeda, Gaylord Perry, Juan Marichal, Bobby Bonds, John Montefusco, Vida Blue, Jack Clark, Will Clark, and Kevin Mitchell had brought fans some great and exciting moments, but there had also been years in the mid-1970s, and again in the mid-1980s, when the franchise had been in bad shape, losing far more often than they won while struggling to attract fans and generate much excitement or revenue. Yet, even during those thin years, the Giants were beloved by many and had, after a fashion, become part of the city and would be missed.

DÉJÀ VU IN 1992

There is an uncanny similarity between the events of late 1992 and those of early 1976 that framed the beginning and end of the Bob Lurie era. In both cases a relatively new mayor was faced with the possibility of losing the Giants during his first year in office. While for Moscone, the urgency began during his first days in office, Mayor Frank Jordan had taken office in January 1992 and spent much of his first year on the job trying to find a way to keep the Giants in town. Jordan, like Moscone, had to negotiate with the baseball powers for more time, and like Moscone played a major part in the search to find an ownership group that would keep the team in San Francisco. In 1976, only one person stepped forward right away to keep the Giants in town, but for much of 1992, nobody stepped forward who seemed committed to buying the Giants and keeping them in San Francisco. Bob Lurie, who had been the one person to step forward in 1976, was still at the center of the story in 1992.

Unlike in 1976, baseball had a new commissioner. Bud Selig took over from Fay Vincent and was still acting commissioner in late 1992. Selig was immediately confronted with the question of the Giants' fate. This time, San Francisco would have an ally in the commissioner's office. Selig had known Lurie since he bought the Giants in 1976. The two were friendly. In a 2020, interview Selig told me that "Bob Lurie and I were very very close friends."²² Nonetheless, Selig was not initially inclined to support Lurie's effort to sell the team to the Tampa group: "When I took over as acting commissioner, this was the first thing that confronted me and I understand that Bob had tried so hard and I think had been treated not well in certain circumstances, but I know that he wanted to sell the team and move the team, and I understood that, but by the same token I had to make a judgment on behalf of baseball as to what to do with this great franchise. And history has proven that we did the right thing," adding "it was a difficult situation, but I really felt that in baseball's best interest we were better off having a team in San Francisco than Tampa." Selig's view on the question meant that if a group capable of buying the Giants and keeping them in San Francisco finally emerged, they would not face the same time pressure as Bob Lurie and George Moscone did in 1976.²³

When the season ended, the move to Tampa was widely understood to be finalized. Lurie made it clear he was going to sell the team, and for months no individual or group of people had made a legitimate offer to buy the team and keep them in San Francisco. Despite this, many people worked to find a way for the Giants to remain in San Francisco. One of these people was a native San Franciscan who had worked for the Giants in the early 1980s before moving to the East Coast to attend business school. In 1992, Larry Baer was working for Westinghouse Broadcasting, but the lifelong Giants fan feared that his team was going to leave his hometown. Baer recalled, "the team was very close to leaving. There was a purchase agreement. In fairness to Bob Lurie, I don't think he saw evidence that the team could stay here. . . . It was dire and Bob really didn't have a lot of options."²⁴

By mid-October, as the Braves and Blue Jays prepared to play each other in the World Series, the dynamic was beginning to change again. For the second time in fewer than 20 years, a new mayor's efforts to keep the Giants in San Francisco was beginning to bear fruit. Baer and others had been working to put an ownership team together, and a week or so after Shinn's proposal finally collapsed, they had something to show for it. The leader of the new ownership group was a member of the Giants' board, as Lurie had been in 1975, who was also the chairman of Safeway, the huge supermarket chain. Peter Magowan was 50 years old in 1992 and had been a Giants fan for most of his life going back to when both he and the Giants were in New York. Joining Magowan and Baer were local civic and business leaders, such as Walter Shorenstein and Don Fisher. This was a group that had the money and San Francisco connections to give fans one last hope that their team would not leave. Unfortunately, they were about $15 million short of what the Tampa group was offering Lurie.

Lurie, who bought the team for a total of about $8 million, could have simply sold the team for $100 million, the amount that was being offered. Despite the handsome profit Lurie would have made even if he sold the team for the lower price, after losing money for so many years, being rejected by Bay Area voters, and now being vilified in the press as the greedy real estate mogul who was trying to take the team away from San Francisco, Lurie was not predisposed to sell the team at a discount, but he also wanted to find a way to keep the team in San Francisco.

The two sides eventually arrived at a solution where Lurie would lend the ownership group $15 million. Within a month the end of the 1992 baseball season and of the Blue Jays winning their first World Series, and thus finally bringing a championship to the city to which the Giants almost moved in 1976, the Magowan-led ownership group succeeded. Although it took until January 1993 for the deal to be approved by the National League and finalized, it was clear by November that the Giants would remain in San Francisco.

THE GIANTS AND THE CHANGING SAN FRANCISCO

During the 17 years Bob Lurie owned the Giants, San Francisco experienced the murder of a mayor and of a civil rights hero, the massacre of hundreds of former residents in a jungle encampment in Guyana, becoming the epicenter of the AIDS plague, and the city' biggest earthquake in 83 years. During that time, the Giants were often a bad team—in 1976, 1977, and 1983 to 1985—struggling to win ball games, draw fans, and stay relevant in San Francisco. They also had some good years—1978, 1982, and 1986 to 1990—when they won more games than they lost, drew fans, and occasionally reignited the hearts and imaginations of San Franciscans.

Throughout all these years, the Giants' future in San Francisco was never certain. By the late 1970s, around the time Lurie bought the team, it was already clear that Candlestick Park was a problem. Additionally, for much of this time, there was a broadly held belief that the Bay Area was not a big enough market for two teams. Accordingly, for most of the time from 1976 to 1992, rumors that the team was moving to Denver or Florida, going down the

Peninsula, splitting their home games between San Francisco and Oakland, or in one fashion or another leaving the city, never really went away. To be a Giants fan during these years meant seeing off-season media coverage of the team and local baseball talk split between what the Giants were going to do to improve and whether they would find a way to remain in the city. For this reason, Bob Lurie's biggest accomplishment as team owner was simply to keep the Giants in San Francisco. This may not seem so impressive now, but it was far from being a given at the time.

Today, the Giants are recognized as one of baseball's finest franchises, winning more World Series championships in the twenty-first century than any team other than the Boston Red Sox. In that context, it is easy to look at the Lurie years, which produced only one pennant and only two trips to the postseason in 17 seasons, as the nadir of the franchise's existence, but that would be an overstatement—one that misses an important aspect of what happened.

Larry Baer summarized how the Giants successes of the twenty-first century, both on and off the field, have their roots in the Bob Lurie era, and even earlier:

> Would Barry Bonds have been on the team if his father Bobby Bonds didn't play for the Giants in the '60s and Willie Mays, his godfather? I don't know, but I'd say probably not. Would we have laid the groundwork for the new ballpark in the year 2000 if we didn't have four ballpark initiatives that didn't pass, probably not. If we didn't have the rich history of Mays, McCovey, Marichal, Cepeda in the '60s, Will Clark, Matt Williams, Jeffrey Leonard in the '70s '80s . . . Jack Clark, Willie Montanez, Mike Ivie, Ed Halicki. . . . It cements people to the franchise.[25]

Busch was even less equivocal about the legacy of Bob Lurie on the Giants of this century: "The measure of a successful owner is did you leave the franchise better off than it was when you got it and there's no question that Bob and his organization did that for the Giants and teed it up for the next generation."[26]

Between the end of 1985 and the beginning of 1986, something else happened. Lurie brought in three men. One, Al Rosen, was a longtime baseball acquaintance and friend who Lurie had wanted to lead the organization for a while. Another, Roger Craig, was the man Rosen wanted to lead the team on the field. The third, Will Clark, was the young man around whom the Giants' front office and scouting department wanted to build the team's future. Those three men, all extremely competitive, and all very good at what they did, changed the team.

Clark's commitment to winning, clutch hitting, and leadership on the field changed the feel, and results, beginning with his opening-day home run off of Nolan Ryan in 1986. Craig made the team view Candlestick, with its wind, whirlwinds of peanut shells, and often freezing temperatures as an advantage, albeit a frequently unpleasant one. Rosen, for his part, was committed to constantly improving the team and never missing an opportunity for the team to make it to the postseason.

These three men led the Giants to success in 1987 to 1989 that had not been achieved in at least a generation, but they did something else as well. They changed the way the team competed and was perceived. The Giants have had bad years since 1986. The early 1990s, the late and initial post–Barry Bonds years, and more recently the hangover from the championship teams of 2010 to 2014 have been rough, but the Giants have never been a laughingstock the way that they were in the years immediately preceding the arrival of these three men.

When Magowan and Baer bought the team and ensured the team's future in San Francisco, they did so with one huge unanswered question. Baer and Magowan, in addition to being wealthy men, were dedicated Giants fans and San Franciscans, so their intentions regarding the future of the Giants were unquestionable. However, no amount of passion for the Giants was going to be enough as long as they continued to play in Candlestick Park. Everybody around the Giants, MLB, and San Francisco understood that, but as the group concretized their offer in late 1992, they still had no real plan for how to solve that problem. Baer explained, "we had to have a plan [for a new ballpark] in place and we had no time nor the expertise at the time to do the plan, so it was a trust me. It was 'we will figure it out.'"[27]

The plan in 1992–93 was vague. The new owners had a sense that the ballpark was likely going to end up where Agnos and Lurie had wanted to build it in 1989 and that there would have to be a fair amount of private funding, but they had nothing more specific than that. Gradually the specifics became clear. In the spring of 1996, yet another initiative, this time it was called Proposition B, was placed on the San Francisco ballot. By 1996, Frank Jordan was no longer mayor, having lost to Willie Brown in 1995.

Brown had served in the State Assembly since 1965 and had been speaker of that body since December 1980. Unlike Jordan, who defeated Agnos in 1991 running as an anti–City Hall outsider, Brown was a deeply political man. He understood how politics worked, laws were passed, and coalitions were assembled, and he had decades worth of experience, relationships, and favors to call on. Like Moscone, Feinstein, Agnos, and Jordan before him, Willie Brown wanted to keep the Giants in San Francisco. The mid-1990s were shaping up to be just the time to do it. The economy was strong. A new mayor had support across the political spectrum and the ownership team had the resources and vision to make it happen. Proposition B was different than Propositions W and P in two respects. First, it specified that the ballpark would be privately funded. Second, it passed—by a margin of roughly two to one.

The timing of that successful initiative could not have been better, as its passage largely coincided with economic growth in San Francisco that became part of the first dot com bubble that grew into the tech economy of San Francisco today. Thus, by the late 1990s, there was enough private money in San Francisco to largely fund the new ballpark. Only 20 years earlier, Bob Lurie could not find investors to come up with $4 million to keep the Giants in San Francisco. The new ballpark, then known as Pacific Bell Park, was ready by Opening Day 2000 and rapidly became known as one of the very best in all of baseball.

When they moved into the new ballpark, which is now known as Oracle Park, the Giants began a new chapter in their team's history. For the first time since they left the Polo Grounds, which was located in the northeast corner of Manhattan but was easily accessible by subway from midtown, the Giants had a home that was integrated into, and close to, the center of the city they called home. Because of the consistently high attendance at Oracle Park, the Giants were once again one of the wealthier teams in the game and able to sign top free agents like Johnny Cueto, Mark Melancon, and Jeff Samardzija. Not all of these deals worked out for the Giants, but money was not the issue. More importantly, when the team's farm system began to produce good players like Buster Posey, Brandon Crawford, Matt Cain, and Tim Lincecum, the Giants did not fear losing them to free agency. The exceptions were Pablo Sandoval, who left for reasons other than money following the 2014 season, and Madison Bumgarner, who had been slowing down for a few years and signed with the Arizona Diamondbacks during the 2019–20 off-season.

That success was hard won, not just by the ownership group led by Peter Magowan, who finally succeeded in getting a stadium approved, or Mayor Willie Brown, who helped get the approval and was in office while the stadium was constructed. Other mayors, like Frank Jordan, Art Agnos, and Dianne Feinstein played a major role too. One of Brown's predecessors stands out relative to the others in what amounted to a quarter-century struggle to keep the Giants in San Francisco. George Moscone and Willie Brown were good friends who got to know each other while students at Hastings, a law school in San Francisco that is part of the University of California system. Brown and Moscone bonded because they worked their way through Hastings as janitors and remained friends until Moscone's death. Brown was one of the last people to see Moscone alive on that terrible day in November 1978. Two guys who pushed brooms together in the mid-1950s ended up, almost two decades apart, making it possible for the Giants to remain in San Francisco.

Today, Moscone, despite being a groundbreaking progressive mayor, is too frequently, particularly outside of San Francisco, remembered as the straight politician who was killed alongside Harvey Milk, but Giants fans owe Moscone much more than that. Unlike Moscone, Bob Lurie lived well into old age and remained a baseball fan, Giants fan, and loyal San Franciscan into his 10th decade. Lurie was initially embraced, then rejected, and ultimately almost forgotten, but Giants fans should recognize the work he did not only to keep the Giants in San Francisco, but to modernize a franchise that by the mid-1970s was barely recognizable as belonging in the major leagues.

Among Giants fans today, memories of the years from 1976 to 1992 have faded. For many, they have consolidated into a decade and half stretch of mediocrity or perhaps one blurry recollection of a cold and windy night at Candlestick Park where Johnnie LeMaster, or maybe it was Rennie Stennett, or maybe Brad Wellman, struck out to end the game and Ed Halicki, Jeff Robinson, or maybe Rich Gale pitched well enough to win but didn't get enough offense and where a solo home run by Jack Clark or maybe it was Chili Davis or maybe Darrell Evans, occurred late in the game and wasn't enough. Even the good years seem less memorable as time goes by. From one perspective, the three months in first place in 1978, snuffing the Dodgers playoff hopes a day or so after they had done the same to the Giants in 1982, coming within one game of the World Series in 1987, or even finally making it to the World Series two years later, have lost some of their luster given the three exciting, dramatic, and fun World Series–winning teams from 2010 to 2014.

That history seems like a long time ago, while as Busch told me, "the Giants of today have cemented themselves as the number one sports franchise in the Bay Area."[28] However, the 17 years when Lurie owned the team were special ones for fans. It took a while, but once Lurie, Busch, Rosen, and Craig figured it out, the Giants were able to field good teams while embracing a character and personality that reflected the quirky, evolving, and extraordinary city they called home. And, most importantly, beginning in the 1970s, Lurie, Herseth, Moscone, Busch, and in later years, many others, including mayors and team executives made it possible for that home to be San Francisco.

NOTES

INTRODUCTION

1. All baseball statistics, box scores, game details, attendance figures, and team data are, unless otherwise specified, from baseballreference.com.

1. BIG-LEAGUE BASEBALL COMES TO TORONTO

1. Neil MacCarl, "Giants Agree to Sale, Toronto Warms up for Baseball," and "$1 for Bleacher Seats," *Toronto Star,* Jan. 10, 1976, 1.

2. Ken MacGray, "Baseball Stadium Deal Born at Football Game," *Toronto Star,* Jan. 10, 1976, 1.

3. "Candlestick Park," Ballparks of Baseball, https://www.ballparksofbaseball.com/ballparks/candlestick-park/

4. These three numbers represent a player's batting average, on-base percentage, and slugging percentage and provide a good quick sense of a player's performance at the plate. They are referred to as "slash lines."

5. Bruce Jenkins, interview with author, Jan. 15, 2020. The *San Francisco Examiner* was the afternoon newspaper in San Francisco.

6. Corey Busch, interview with author, Mar. 12–13, 2019.

7. Busch, interview with author, Mar. 12–13, 2019.

8. Information on Benson's background from a press release from the Office of Governor Ronald Reagan, March 3, 1974, Ronald Reagan: Gubernatorial Papers, 1966–1974: Press Unit, Ronald Reagan Presidential Library, Digital Library Collection, https://www.reaganlibrary.gov/sites/default/files/digitallibrary/gubernatorial/pressunit/p15/40-840-7408623-p15-009-2017.pdf.

9. "Giants Stay—For a Day at Least," *San Francisco Chronicle,* Feb. 4, 1976. Ellipses in original.

10. The Washington Senators had been one of the original American League franchises at the dawn of the twentieth century. However, they moved to Minnesota and became the Twins in 1961. That same year, Washington was awarded an AL expansion

team, also called the Senators. That team, under Short's leadership, moved to Texas and became the Rangers in 1972. Washington was then without a big-league team until 2005, when the Expos moved Montreal and became the Nationals.

11. Neil MacCarl, "San Francisco Judge Holds up Giants' Move," *Toronto Star,* Feb. 4, 1976, c1.

12. Milt Dunnell, "Stoneham Starves while Benson Balks," *Toronto Star,* Feb. 4, 1976, c1.

13. "NL Owners' 'Ultimatum': Lurie Must Be 'Boss,'" *San Francisco Chronicle,* Feb. 26, 1976, 45.

14. Wells Twombly, "Short Long on Desire for Harmony," *San Francisco Examiner & Chronicle,* Feb. 29, 1976, sec. C, 2.

15. Art Rosenbaum, "Murcer Wants the Answer," *San Francisco Chronicle,* Feb. 2, 1976, 44.

16. Chris Speier, interview with author, Mar. 13, 2019.

17. Bob Lurie, interview with author, Mar. 12–13, 2019.

18. Lurie, interview with author, Mar. 12–13, 2019.

19. Jenkins, interview with author, Jan. 15, 2020.

20. Lurie, interview with author, Mar. 12–13, 2019.

21. Busch, interview with author, Mar. 12–13, 2019.

22. Lurie, interview with author, Mar. 12–13, 2019.

23. Bob Stevens, "Beef King Saves Lurie, Giants," *San Francisco Chronicle,* Mar. 3, 1976, 51. For many years the business and sports section of the *Chronicle* were printed on green paper. The sports section was therefore known as the Sporting Green. This was due to a sexist idea from the midcentury that the man of the house could easily grab the sports and business section, topics in which women would have no interest, on his way to work. Similarly, for many years, the entertainment section of the Sunday paper was printed on pink paper and known as the Pink Section.

24. "What They Are Saying," *New York Times,* Feb. 15, 1976, S3. Thomson was indeed alive and well in 1976. He was 52 years old and still had many years ahead of him of signing memorabilia and discussing his famous home run. Thomson died in 2010 at the age of 86.

25. Jenkins, interview with author, Jan. 15, 2020.

26. Lurie, interview with author, Mar. 12–13, 2019.

27. Glenn Schwarz, "Giants Discover Their First Spring Nugget," *San Francisco Examiner,* Mar. 25, 1976, 55.

28. During his slightly less than three years in office, Moscone, due to his very progressive politics, particularly around tolerance and diversity issues, was a divisive political figure. However, old-time San Franciscans remember the role he had in saving the Giants. I have an old friend who lived through the Moscone era as an adolescent and still lives in San Francisco. Whenever the former mayor's name comes up, they say, "don't forget, he's the guy who kept the Giants in San Francisco."

29. "Strike Threatens Giants Opener," *San Francisco Chronicle,* Apr. 6, 1976, 45.

30. Bob Hurte, "John Montefusco," SABR Biography Project, https://sabr.org/bioproj/person/5e3343be.

31. Speier, interview with author, Mar. 13, 2019.

32. Jenkins, interview with author, Jan. 15, 2020.

33. Lurie, interview with author, Mar. 12–13, 2019.

34. Bob Stevens, "Montefusco: $60,000?," *San Francisco Chronicle,* Mar. 12, 1976, 49–51.

35. Eric Golanty, "Andy Messersmith," SABR Biography Project, https://sabr.org/bioproj/person/caef6d23.

36. Lurie, interview with author, Mar. 12–13, 2019.

37. WAR, or Wins Above Replacement, is a formula-based statistic that seeks to capture the overall value of a player. It is not perfect, but it is probably the best and easiest statistic of this kind. A single season WAR of five or more is very good, eight or more represents an MVP season, and three to five is a solid to good Major League player. Players can also have negative WAR if they play poorly. There are different formulas for calculating WAR. I use baseballreference.com WAR data.

38. Bill James, *The New Bill James Historical Baseball Abstract* (New York: Free Press, 2001), 546–47.

39. Lurie, interview with author, Mar. 12–13, 2019.

2. BOB LURIE'S TEAM AND BOB LURIE'S CHALLENGES

1. Will Clark, interview with author, Mar. 26, 2019.

2. Corey Busch, interview with author, Nov. 6, 2019.

3. Kevin Mitchell, interview with author, Mar. 16, 2019.

4. Chris Speier, interview with author, Mar. 13, 2019.

5. Dusty Baker, interview with author, Nov. 6, 2019. Baker had moved to Sacramento from Southern California as a teenager and had family in Northern California.

6. Bud Selig, interview with author, Feb. 4, 2020.

7. Speier, interview with author, Mar. 13, 2019.

8. Mike Murphy, interview with author, Apr. 25, 2019.

9. "1970–1979 Ballpark Attendance," Ballparks of Baseball, https://www.ballparksofbaseball.com/1970-1979-mlb-attendance/.

10. ESPN, MLB Attendance Report, 2019.

11. Another pitcher, lefty Dave McNally of the Baltimore Orioles, had also played without a contract in 1975 and joined Messersmith in the challenge to the reserve clause, but he retired following the 1975 season.

12. Betty Cuniberti, "Giants Set Sight on Fingers, Rudi, Tenace," *San Francisco Chronicle,* Nov. 5, 1976, B1.

13. Cuniberti, "Giants Set Sight on Fingers, Rudi, Tenace," B1.

14. Bob Lurie, interview with author, Mar. 12–13, 2019.

15. Lurie, interview with author, Mar. 12–13, 2019.

16. Busch, interview with author, Nov. 6, 2019.

17. Ron Bergman, "Garvey Says Giants in Running," *Oakland Tribune,* Nov. 19, 1982, F1.

18. Bergman, "Garvey says Giants in Running," F1.

19. Corey Busch and Bob Lurie, interview with author, Mar. 12–13, 2019.

20. "Giants Retract Offer to Carew," *New York Times,* Jan. 16, 1979, 45.

21. Lurie, interview with author, Mar. 12–13, 2019.

22. Tom Schott and Nick Peters, *The Giants Encyclopedia* (Champaign, IL: Sports Publishing, 2003), 140.

23. https://www.baseball-reference.com/leagues/MLB/misc.shtml

24. Michael J. Haupert, "The Economic History of Major League Baseball," EH.Net Encyclopedia, ed. Robert Whaples, Dec. 3, 2007, http://eh.net/encyclopedia/the-economic-history-of-major-league-baseball/.

25. Jonah Keri, *Up, Up, & Away: The Kid, the Hawk, Rock, Vladi, Pedro, Le Grand Orange, Youppi!, the Crazy Business of Baseball, & the Ill-Fated but Unforgettable Montreal Expos* (Toronto: Random House, 2014), 144.

26. Keri, *Up, Up, & Away,* 851.

3. CULTS, ASSASSINATIONS, AND BOB LURIE'S FIRST GOOD TEAM

1. Bruce Jenkins, interview with author, Jan. 15, 2020.

2. Vida Blue, interview with author, June 25, 2019.

3. Bob Lurie, interview with author, Mar. 12–13, 2019.

4. Blue, interview with author, June 25, 2019.

5. Pat Gallagher, "The Lurie Years: Selected Memories from Our Time with the San Francisco Giants, 1976–1992" (unpublished manuscript, 2018), 49–50.

6. Larry Baer, interview with author, Oct. 31, 2019.

7. Blue, interview with author, June 25, 2019. McCovey died in October 2018, thus Blue's mention of the loss of McCovey.

8. Gallagher, "The Lurie Years," 49.

9. Blue, interview with author, June 25, 2019.

10. OPS stand for on-base plus slugging. It is calculated by adding a player's on-base percentage and slugging percentage and provides a quick idea of a player's offensive production.

11. Corey Busch, interview with author, Nov. 4, 2019.

12. Bill James, *The Bill James Baseball Abstract* (New York: Ballantine, 1982), 134. Parentheses in original.

13. Bob Stevens, "Ivie, 27, Says He's Retiring," *San Francisco Chronicle,* June 26, 1980, 67.

14. Glenn Dickey, "Bristol Set to 'Dump' Ivie," *San Francisco Chronicle,* Oct. 17, 1980, 75

15. Chris Speier, interview with author, Mar. 13, 2019.

16. Because it costs the team an out, being caught stealing, on balance, does more harm to a team than the marginal gain from moving up a base helps. Therefore, a base stealer needs to be safe roughly two thirds of the time to help the team.

17. Jenkins, interview with author, Jan. 15, 2020.

18. Mike Murphy, interview with author, Apr. 25, 2019.

19. Busch, interview with author, Nov. 4, 2019.

20. For a more detailed examination of the 1978 Giants, as well as of that year more broadly in San Francisco, see Lincoln Mitchell, *San Francisco Year Zero: Political Upheaval Punk Rock and a Third-Place Baseball Team* (New Brunswick: Rutgers Univ. Press, 2019).

21. "Population of the 100 Largest Urban Places: 1980," US Bureau of the Census, https://www.census.gov/population/www/documentation/twps0027/tab21.txt.

22. Busch, interview with author, Nov. 4, 2019.

23. "San Francisco Giants News," Press Release, May 13, 1981.

24. "Giants Issue Study on Candlestick Park," San Francisco Giants Press Release, Mar. 29, 1982.

25. Lurie, interview with author, Mar. 12–13, 2019.

4. LABOR PROBLEMS

1. Marvin Miller, *A Whole Different Ball Game: The Sport and Business of Baseball* (New York: Carol Publishing Group, 1991), 9.

2. "History," Major League Baseball Players Association, http://www.mlbplayers .com/ViewArticle.dbml?DB_OEM_ID=34000&ATCLID=211157501.

3. Corey Busch, interview with author, Mar. 12–13, 2019.

4. Bob Lurie, interview with author, Mar. 12–13, 2019.

5. "Free Agent Compensation," Baseball Reference, https://www.baseball-reference .com/bullpen/Free_agent_compensation_draft. Baseball Reference provided useful background for this section.

6. Following the 2004 season, the Expos left Montreal for Washington and changed their name to the Nationals. Robinson managed the team from 2002 to 2006.

7. OPS+ is OPS normalized over year and ballpark. An OPS+ of 100 is league average; over 130 is an all-star-caliber season; over 150 for a career is usually well above Hall of Fame level.

8. Interview with Bob and Connie Lurie, Mar. 12–13, 2019.

9. Corey Busch, email exchange with author, Feb. 28, 2020.

10. Vida Blue, interview with author, June 25, 2019.

11. Dusty Baker, interview with author, Nov. 6, 2019.

12. Baker, interview with author, Nov. 6, 2019.

13. Duane Kuiper, interview with author, June 24, 2019.

14. Gary Lavelle, interview with author, June 9, 2019.

15. Minton was well liked by Giants fans during his years in San Francisco. The "Moooon" sound was a sign of affection that usually greeted the pitcher as he came into a game. I cannot recall the exact date, but on one of these occasions, longtime Giants radio announcer Hank Greenwald told listeners "the fans are mooning Minton."

16. Baker, interview with author, Nov. 6, 2019. The "general" to whom Baker was referring was Reggie Smith.

17. Larry Baer, interview with author, Oct. 31, 2019. Capitals approximate the change in Baer's tone.

5. THE WORST GIANTS TEAMS EVER

1. Duane Kuiper, interview with author, June 24, 2019.

2. Mike Krukow, interview with author, June 24, 2019.

3. Gary Lavelle, interview with author, June 19, 2019.

4. Vida Blue, interview with author, June 25, 2019.

5. Blue, interview with author, June 25, 2019.

6. Kuiper, interview with author, June 24, 2019.

7. Krukow, interview with author, June 24, 2019.

8. Bruce Jenkins, interview with author, Jan. 15, 2020.

9. Larry Baer, interview with author, Oct. 31, 2019.

10. Baer, interview with author, Oct. 31, 2019.

11. Baer, interview with author, Oct. 31, 2019. The *New Yorker* illustration to which Baer referred was the map of the United States as seen by a provincial New Yorker. Baer was suggesting San Franciscans have that same provincialism but place San Francisco at the center.

12. Pat Gallagher, interview with author, June 18, 2019.

13. Gallagher, interview with author, June 18, 2019.

14. Bob Lurie, interview with author, Mar. 12–13, 2019.

15. Baer, interview with author, Oct. 31, 2019.

16. Lurie, interview with author, Mar. 12–13, 2019.

17. Ralph Berger, "Al Rosen," SABR biography project, https://sabr.org/bioproj/person/40d66568.

18. Berger, "Al Rosen." Koufax also was a proud Jew who did not tolerate anti-Semitic comments from opponents. Oddly, there were fewer cases of this during Koufax's career. Apparently, the courage of the bigot melts when confronted with the possibility of a well-placed Koufax fastball. Sullivan had an interesting relationship with Jews as well. In 1933, he argued in the *New York Daily News* that Jews were naturally good at basketball, hypothesizing that "perhaps this is because the Jew is a natural gambler. Perhaps it is because he devotes himself to a problem more closely than others will." See Richard E. Lapchick, "Psuedo-Scientific Prattle about Athletes," *New York Times,* Apr. 29, 1989, 15.

19. Will Clark, interview with author, Apr. 26, 2019.

20. Dave Dravecky, interview with author, Apr. 29, 2019.

21. Jenkins, interview with author, Jan. 15, 2020.

22. Lurie, interview with author, Mar. 12–13, 2019.

23. Kevin Mitchell, interview with author, Mar. 16, 2019. Throughout our discussion of Rosen, Mitchell focused on issues between white and African American people in baseball. At no point did Mitchell mention, allude, or speak in coded language about Rosen being Jewish. As a Jew with a non-Jewish last name, I often hear things that are not meant for me and have a decent ear for coded anti-Semitism. Nothing of that sort came from Mitchell when discussing Rosen or any other topic during the several hours we spent together.

24. Dusty Baker, interview with author, Nov. 6, 2019.

25. Baker, interview with author, Nov. 6, 2019. Baker's father was a well-known baseball coach in Riverside, California. Among the players he helped develop were Bobby Bonds and several other big leaguers.

26. Mitchell, interview with author, Mar. 16, 2019.

27. Mitchell, interview with author, Mar. 16, 2019.

28. "Population of the largest media markets in the U.S. as of 2017," Statista, https://www.statista.com/statistics/183600/population-of-metropolitan-areas-in-the-us/.

29. "Historical Population of American Cities by Decade," http://www.city-data.com/forum/city-vs-city/1786915-historical-population-metropolitan-areas-decade.html.

30. Lurie, interview with author, Mar. 12–13, 2019.

31. Corey Busch, interview with author, Nov. 4, 2019.

32. C. W. Nevius, "Feinstein OKs Giants Plan—Oakland Mayor Angry," *San Francisco Chronicle,* Oct. 3, 1985, 1

33. C. W. Nevius, "Cautious Denver Is Hoping for Giants, Even Temporarily," *San Francisco Chronicle,* Oct. 11, 1985, Sports 1, 5.

34. David Bush, "Giants to Play at Candlestick," *San Francisco Chronicle,* Jan. 30, 1986, 1.

6. TWO ROOKIES AND A RETURN TO THE POSTSEASON

1. Robby Thompson, interview with author, July 3, 2019.
2. Bob Lurie, interview with author, Mar. 12–13, 2019.
3. Thompson, interview with author, July 3, 2019.
4. Will Clark, interview with author, Apr. 26, 2019.
5. Mike Krukow, interview with author, June 24, 2019.
6. Clark, interview with author, Apr. 26, 2019.
7. Vida Blue, interview with author, June 25, 2019.
8. Krukow, interview with author, June 24, 2019.
9. Bruce Jenkins, interview with author Jan. 15, 2020.
10. Corey Busch, interview with author, Feb. 28, 2020.
11. Thompson, interview with author, July 3, 2019.
12. Dave Dravecky, interview with author, June 29, 2019.
13. Chris Speier, interview with author, Mar. 13, 2019.
14. This use of the bull pen to get the advantage on key matchups in a pivotal inning is one of the most exciting components of baseball strategy. Notably, the three batter rule that MLB had hoped to introduce in 2020 as an effort to speed up the game, and that required pitchers to face at least three batters, would preclude this.
15. Krukow, interview with author, June 24, 2019.
16. Kevin Mitchell, interview with author, Mar. 16, 2019.
17. Clark, interview with author, Apr. 26, 2019.
18. Mitchell, interview with author, Mar. 16, 2019.
19. Speier, interview with author, Mar. 13, 2019.
20. Dravecky, interview with author, June 29, 2019.
21. Dravecky, interview with author, June 29, 2019.
22. Dravecky, interview with author, June 29, 2019.
23. Krukow, interview with author, June 24, 2019.
24. Corey Busch, interview with author, Nov. 6, 2019.
25. Jenkins, interview with author Jan. 15, 2020. "Krukow's game" refers to the complete game victory Krukow pitched in Game Four in San Francisco that tied the series at two games and set up the Giants' win in Game Five.
26. Atlee Hammaker, interview with author, July 24, 2019.
27. Busch, interview with author, Nov. 6, 2019.
28. Bob Lurie and Corey Busch, interview with author, Mar. 12–13, 2019.
29. Art Agnos, interview with author, June 19, 2019. The west and northwest parts of San Francisco were, and are, home to more conservative, in the context of San Francisco, voters.
30. Dianne Feinstein, written response to questions from author, June 24, 2019.
31. Agnos, interview with author, June 19, 2019.
32. Busch, interview with author, Nov. 6, 2019.
33. Feinstein, written response, June 24, 2019.
34. Marshall Kilduff, "New Ballpark on Ballot," *San Francisco Chronicle,* Aug. 6, 1987, 18.
35. Historical Voter Turnout," San Francisco Board of Elections, https://sfelections.sfgov.org/historical-voter-turnout.
36. Jay Patterson, *San Francisco Voter Information Pamphlet,* 1987, 109–11
37. Patterson, *San Francisco Voter Information Pamphlet,* 112

38. Patterson, *San Francisco Voter Information Pamphlet,* 114–17

39. Patterson, *San Francisco Voter Information Pamphlet,* 117. Bold in original. Brackets mine.

40. "San Francisco Mayor," Our Campaigns, https://www.ourcampaigns.com/Race Detail.html?RaceID=129474propo.

41. Thompson, interview with author, July 3, 2019.

42. Clark, interview with author, Apr. 26, 2019.

43. Mitchell, interview with author, Mar. 16, 2019.

44. Dravecky, interview with author, June 29, 2019.

45. Peter Ueberroth, interview with author, Mar. 14, 2019.

7. THE YEAR EVERYTHING WENT RIGHT AND WRONG FOR THE GIANTS

1. Kevin Mitchell, interview with author, Mar. 14, 2019.

2. Mitchell, interview with author, Mar. 14, 2019.

3. Dave Dravecky, interview with author, June 29, 2019.

4. Dravecky, interview with author, June 29, 2019.

5. Dravecky, interview with author, June 29, 2019.

6. Bruce Jenkins, interview with author, Jan. 15, 2020.

7. Atlee Hammaker, interview with author, July 24, 2019.

8. Robby Thompson, interview with author, July 3, 2019.

9. Will Clark, interview with author, Apr. 26, 2019.

10. Dusty Baker, interview with author, Nov. 6, 2019.

11. Mitchell, interview with author, Mar. 14, 2019.

12. Thompson, interview with author, July 3, 2019.

13. Clark, interview with author, Apr. 26, 2019.

14. Clark, interview with author, Apr. 26, 2019.

15. Clark, interview with author, Apr. 26, 2019.

16. Thompson, interview with author, July 3, 2019.

17. Clark, interview with author, Apr. 26, 2019.

18. Jenkins, interview with author, Jan. 15, 2020.

19. Clark, interview with author, Apr. 26, 2019. Clark fell behind in the count 1–2, not 0–2.

20. Clark, interview with author, Apr. 26, 2019.

21. Jenkins, interview with author, Jan. 15, 2020.

22. Corey Busch and Bob Lurie, interview with author, Mar. 12–13, 2019.

23. Thompson, interview with author, July 3, 2019.

24. Dravecky, interview with author, June 29, 2019.

25. Hammaker, interview with author, July 24, 2019.

26. Bob Lurie, interview with author, Mar. 12–13, 2019.

27. Chris Speier, interview with author, Mar. 13, 2019.

28. Thompson, interview with author, July 3, 2019.

29. Jenkins, interview with author, Jan. 15, 2020.

30. Mike Murphy, interview with author, Apr. 25, 2019.

31. Mitchell, interview with author, Mar. 14, 2019.

32. Corey Busch, interview with author, Nov. 4, 2019.

33. Bruce Jenkins, "The Teams—A's Win Matchups, but It's Not Played on Paper," *San Francisco Chronicle,* Oct. 13, 1989, C8.

34. Mike Krukow, interview with author, June 24, 2019.

35. Clark, interview with author, Apr. 26, 2019.

36. Thompson, interview with author, July 3, 2019.

37. Mitchell, interview with author, Mar. 14, 2019.

38. Dravecky, interview with author, June 29, 2019.

39. Hammaker, interview with author, July 24, 2019.

40. Krukow, interview with author, June 24, 2019.

41. Chris Speier, interview with author, Mar. 13, 2019.

42. Jenkins, interview with author, Jan. 15, 2020.

43. Baker, interview with author, Nov. 6, 2019.

44. Bob Lurie, interview with author, Mar. 12–13, 2019.

45. Art Agnos, interview with author, June 19, 2019.

46. Richard Ben Cramer, *Joe DiMaggio: The Hero's Life* (New York: Simon and Schuster, 2000), 431–32.

47. Cramer, *Joe DiMaggio,* 431–32

48. In 2013, work on the new Oakland Bay Bridge was completed. The new bridge looks a little different but covers the same area of San Francisco Bay.

49. Herb Caen, "The Way It Goes," *San Francisco Chronicle,* Nov. 16, 1989, B1.

50. Hammaker, interview with author, July 24, 2019.

51. Clark, interview with author, Apr. 26, 2019.

52. Krukow, interview with author, June 24, 2019.

53. Mitchell, interview with author, Mar. 14, 2019.

54. Agnos, interview with author, June 19, 2019.

55. Duane Kuiper, interview with author June 24, 2019.

56. Jenkins, interview with author, Jan. 15, 2020.

57. Lurie, interview with author, Mar. 12–13, 2019.

58. Agnos, interview with author, June 19, 2019.

59. Clark, interview with author, Apr. 26, 2019.

60. In 2007, the Rockies had an even worse World Series as they were swept by the Red Sox while being outscored 29–10.

61. Jenkins, interview with author, Jan. 15, 2020.

62. Frank Jordan, interview with author, Apr. 25, 2019.

63. Busch, interview with author, Nov. 4, 2019.

64. Germaine Q. Wong, "San Francisco Voter Information Pamphlet," Office of the Registrar of Voters, 1989.

65. Kathy Bodovitz, "It Looks Like a Tight Race—S.F. Voters Back Ballpark, 46% to 40%," *San Francisco Chronicle,* Sept. 5, 1989, 1.

66. Busch, interview with author, Nov. 4, 2019.

67. Busch, interview with author, Nov. 4, 2019.

68. Busch, interview with author, Nov. 4, 2019.

69. Busch, interview with author, Nov. 4, 2019.

70. Agnos, interview with author, June 19, 2019.

71. Agnos, interview with author, June 19, 2019.

72. Agnos, interview with author, June 19, 2019.

73. Bud Selig, interview with author, Feb. 4, 2020

74. Lurie, interview with author, Mar. 12–13, 2019.

8. TAMPA BOUND

1. Corey Busch, interview with author, Nov. 4, 2019.

2. "In the Ballpark, at last," *San Jose Mercury News,* Jan. 19, 1990.

3. Art Agnos, interview with author, June 19, 2019.

4. San Jose is the biggest city in Santa Clara County, so for many San Franciscans, the cities of Santa Clara and San Jose, as well as Santa Clara County, are essentially one and the same.

5. Mark Newman, "Three Strikes in San Francisco: Will Lurie Ship Out Giants After Latest Voter Rejection," *The Sporting News,* Nov. 19, 1990, 48.

6. Frank Jordan, interview with author, Apr. 25, 2019.

7. Jordan, interview with author, Apr. 25, 2019.

8. Dusty Baker, interview with author, Nov. 6, 2019.

9. Richard C. Paddock, "A Giant Decision: Team Is Moving to San Jose in '96: Baseball," *Los Angeles Times,* Jan. 16, 1992.

10. Paddock, "A Giant Decision."

11. Michael Martinez, "Baseball: Potential Investor Pulls out on Giants," *New York Times,* Apr. 12, 1992, B11.

12. Jordan, interview with author, Apr. 25, 2019.

13. Ross Newhan, "SF Giants Owner Agrees to Sell to Tampa Bay Group," *Los Angeles Times,* Aug. 8, 1992.

14. Jerome Holtzman, "You Can Book Giants' Cross-Country Move," *Chicago Tribune,* Aug. 9, 1992.

15. Bruce Jenkins, interview with author, Jan. 15, 2020.

16. Herb Caen, "Memos on Monday," *San Francisco Chronicle,* Aug. 10, 1992, B1.

17. Bob Lurie, interview with author, Mar. 12–13, 2019.

18. Corey Busch, interview with author, Mar. 12–13, 2019.

19. Busch, interview with author, Mar. 12–13, 2019.

20. Scott Ostler, "The Mourning Officially Has Begun," *San Francisco Chronicle,* Sept. 28, 1992, C1, C9. Stu Miller was a Giants reliever who allegedly was blown off the pitcher's mound by a gust of wind in the 1961 All-Star Game.

21. Bruce Jenkins, "Mixed-Up Emotions Dominate at the 'Stick," *San Francisco Chronicle,* Sept. 28, 1992, C3.

22. Bud Selig, interview with author, Feb. 4, 2020.

23. Selig, interview with author, Feb. 4, 2020.

24. Larry Baer, interview with author, Oct. 31, 2019.

25. Baer, interview with author, Oct. 31, 2019.

26. Busch, interview with author, Mar. 12–13, 2019.

27. Baer, interview with author, Oct. 31, 2019.

28. Busch, interview with author, Mar. 12–13, 2019.

INDEX